COOPERATION AND COMPETITION
IN THE GLOBAL ECONOMY

COOPERATION AND COMPETITION IN THE GLOBAL ECONOMY
Issues and Strategies

Edited by
ANTONIO FURINO

BALLINGER PUBLISHING COMPANY
Cambridge, Massachusetts
A Subsidiary of Harper & Row, Publishers, Inc.

International Standard Book Number: 0-88730-307-2

Library of Congress Catalog Card Number: 88-11973

Printed in the United States of America

LIBRARY OF CONGRESS
Library of Congress Cataloging-in-Publication Data

Cooperation and competition in the global economy: issues and
strategies / edited by Antonio Furino.
 p. ca.
 Includes bibliographies and index.
 ISBN 0-88730-307-2
 1. United States—Commercial policy. 2. United States—Foreign economic relations. 3. Competition, International. 4. International cooperation. I. Furino, Antonio.
HF 1455.C75   1988   88-11973
337.73—dc19   CIP

CONTENTS

LIST OF FIGURES

LIST OF TABLES

FOREWORD

The single dominant characteristic of our times is change. We live in a period in which change occurs in massive scale and at an extremely rapid pace. Yet, it has a quality of permanence about it because it is creating new institutions.

Change, of course, takes many forms. Industrial change has been chronicled so often as to become a cliche. A major implication of that change is whether or not we will have enough jobs and whether the adjustments in the salary structure will support the middle class, on which we have traditionally built our politics and foreign policy. The impact on education is immense. We are struggling to transform an educational system from one that teaches the three R's of reading, writing, and arithmetic, to one that prepares people for the challenges of the three C's: the ability to calculate, compute, and communicate in the new language of high technology. As industries and workplaces are requiring unprecedented levels of technological literacy, the chasm between those who are technologically literate and those who are technologically illiterate continues to grow, and the pressure on our institutions to correct it is mounting.

Another dimension of change sweeping across the landscape of our country involves the demographics of America. In 1990, for the first time, there will be more Americans over sixty-five years of age than there will be teenagers. The important questions are related not only to the financing of health care but to how we will be able to obtain sufficient tax revenue to support education and research in a society less preoccupied with the future. Other demographic changes of relevance are the impact of women in the workplace and the critical role of minorities, particularly in the central cities.

Another dimension of change is the major focus of this book. It has to do with a new global reality deeply linking the United States to the economic fortunes of the rest of the world.

In these times of evolution, several themes emerge as important. One of them is the notion of targeting, of strategic planning. It is a concept familiar to business leaders, but too often ignored by those responsible for the affairs of nations, states, and cities. There will be cities and nations unable or unwilling to change that will suffer from higher unemployment, internal hostility, and political instability. Others will prosper. Those will be the ones recognizing that in a global context everyone may play a winning role if, through cooperation, the intrinsic strengths of all nations are wisely utilized.

A second theme is the recognition that we must not only be economically competitive, but we must find ways to include all Americans in our efforts. We have as much of an obligation to remain competitive in the international markets as we do to provide income for all people, offer them social mobility, and integrate newer arrivals into the American society. A professor from Northwestern University, William Ouchi, makes, in his book *The M-Form Society*, powerful observations on this notion of inclusiveness. He argues that American society has become so adversarial, so litigious, that the result is stalemate, a gridlock. With the breakdown of traditional authoritarian roles—a characteristic of our times—very few individuals any longer exist who alone can make things happen. There are no more political bosses or business barons to single-handedly shape social institutions. But there are many individuals who, alone, can keep things from happening, through litigation and countless other methods of blockage. The winning style of leadership is, then, how to bring people together, how to search in the darkness created by walls of obstruction for a sliver of daylight from which to energize consensus.

Finally, success will be won by those who can translate thoughts into action. It has always been a proclivity for action that has set this country apart from the rest of the world. In this context, the insights offered by the authors of this volume are of great significance. The dialogue they promote should be encouraged and followed by appropriate and timely policies. We learn from this book that the jobs of most workers, the success of many businesses, and, ultimately, the quality of life of most citizens greatly depends on the U.S. performance in international trade and on domestic savings and investment. We learn that competitiveness is the combined result of all those national qualities and policies that help people and companies perform at more effective levels. Then, we conclude, competitiveness is a healthy national and international objective, enhancing comparative strengths of firms and nations alike for a better life. Let us act upon these findings.

—Henry G. Cisneros

PREFACE AND ACKNOWLEDGMENTS

Most of the chapters of this book were presented as papers at the 1986 Conference on Industrial Science and Technological Innovation sponsored by the National Science Foundation (NSF) Directorate for Scientific, Technological, and International Affairs. Many of the papers were subsequently revised and extended. Chapters 1, 2, 7, 19, and the appendix are original contributions to this volume.

NSF's foresight in encouraging the early discussion of a now popular topic is gratefully acknowledged. Besides the director of NSF, Mr. Erich Bloch—who personally contributed to both the conference and this book—I wish to express my gratitutde to Mr. Richard J. Green, Assistant Director for Scientific, Technological, and International Affairs, to Dr. Donald Senich, the head of NSF's Division of Industrial Science and Technological Innovation, and to the NSF program managers, Mr. Robert O. Lauer and Mr. Thomas M. Ryan. Their commitment to the project made possible the gathering of an extraordinary group of people that inspired not only this volume, but other important initiatives addressing issues of competitiveness and cooperation.

The mayor of San Antonio, the Honorable Henry G. Cisneros, personally contributed to the proceedings. Also, his charisma attracted and energized speakers and participants in a manner difficult to attain by just good planning. He has my admiration and deepest gratitude.

I am grateful to the hosts of the conference, Dr. John P. Howe, III, President of The University of Texas Health Science Center at San Antonio, and Dr. James W. Wagener, President of The University of Texas at San Antonio, for their total support of that event and this book. Also, a very special thank you goes to those on the faculty and staff of both institutions who were generous with their time and useful suggestions.

Dr. George Kozmetsky, Director, and Dr. Raymond Smilor, Executive Director of The Univesity of Texas at Austin IC^2 Institute, besides their contribution to the meetings, played a key role in making this volume possible; their comments, their encouragement, and IC^2 support in transcribing the proceedings are gratefully acknowledged.

Finally, I would like to express my gratitude to General Robert F. McDermott, President and Chairman of the Board of United Services Automobile Association (USAA); to Mr. Mike Waterman, Chairman of the Board of The Waterman Group, Inc.; to Mr. Charles M. Wender; to Mr. Martin Goland, President of Southwest Research Institute; to Dr. Duncan Wimpress, President of the Southwest Foundation for Biomedical Research; to Dr. Gerry E. Cooke, President of Texas Research and Technology Foundation; and to Dr. Kenneth W. Daly, then Director of the Department of Economic and Employment Development of the City of San Antonio. Individually, and through their associates and institutions, they greatly contributed to the quality of the discussion recorded here.

Relevant to one of the two main themes of this book is the impeccable cooperative effort that, at the time of the conference, allowed us to reach, through teleconferencing, audiences at remote sites. Approximately 150 conference participants were linked interactively through all three teleconferencing approaches (video, audio, and computer-assisted) with groups in Sweden, Mexico, Washington, D.C., Florida, and California. Besides the value of experimenting with these emerging technologies, the successful accomplishment of the linkages proved that large groups of people scattered around the globe can effectively discuss, in real time, urgent issues of common interest. The expanded dialogue gave a special quality to the meeting and is reflected in the writings of this book.

The teleconferencing experiment would not have been possible without generous donations of technicians' time, funds, services, and equipment by two major industrial sponsors: USAA, and American Telephone and

Telegraph (AT&T). The complex organization of activities at the remote sites was successfully accomplished nationally by NSF in cooperation with specialists from the University of Texas Health Science Center, the University of Texas at San Antonio, and KENS-TV Channel 5, and abroad, by the Swedish National Board of Technical Development and the Mexican National Council for Science and Technology. I am grateful to all in those organizations who worked relentlessly with me to demonstrate, against the odds of time constraints and lack of precedents, how the people of the twenty-first century may directly communicate, in a manner not before possible, to address effectively problems of great urgency and complexity.

Part 1 of the book introduces the framework of a pragmatic approach to a national policy on competitiveness. Part 2 brings comparative and historical perspectives to the competitiveness and cooperation issues. Part 3 and the appendix review the present understanding of the competitiveness problem and explore public and private strategies that could assist in solving it. Part 4 offers the view on competition seen by those directly facing the challenge of the market contest. Part 5 describes institutions and activities that have indirect but strategic impact on national and global cooperation and competition. Part 6 provides examples of national and foreign viewpoints on cooperative and competitive policies. Part 7 reviews the challenges of inducing the adjustments in private- and public-sector policies that may bring global prosperity.

—Antonio Furino

INTRODUCTION
The Issues

1 OVERVIEW

Antonio Furino

Fundamental changes in the world economy have brought new challenges to the American people. Persistent losses by U.S. industry of national and international market shares are expected to produce painful declines in the standard of living of our citizens and trigger a chain reaction of destabilizing events throughout the globe. The ability of this country to compete and cooperate with other nations has become a major national security problem and a central factor in ensuring balanced economic growth on our planet.

This book explores the nature of the challenges and offers insights on how to manage global competition. What one discovers is that the learning curve for survival in the world economy begins with redefining national interest in the broader context of global competition, understanding the evolutionary forces at play, seeing cooperation and competition as complementary rather than mutually exclusive objectives, and viewing success in international markets as the mechanism to improve not only the world quality of life, but our own.

The facts are well known: the last time the United States logged a surplus in its merchandise trade balance account was 1975; from a trade deficit of approximately $40 billion per year with current account surpluses and creditor nation status in the early 1980s, America was reporting, in 1986, a record trade deficit of $169 billion and a current account deficit of about $130 billion per year, and has captured the top position

3

of largest debtor nation in the world; the trade deficit is dangerously changing from mostly an oil deficit to a manufacturing and agricultural deficit (the heart of U.S. export strength); in 1986 America was passed by West Germany as the world's leading exporter and won the second place over Japan by a narrow margin (10.3 percent of world export for the United States versus 10 percent for Japan) (U.S. Congress 1987: 2, 3; Guenther 1986:1–7).

In 1983 and 1984, the shock from the trade deficit, according to the International Trade Commission (ITC), caused a loss of nearly 20 percent of potential gross national product (GNP), in real values. The secondary tremors of the economic quake, according to the National Association of Manufacturers (NAM), prevented our plants from creating two million jobs during that same period. The structural changes in the deficit crippled the growth of high-wage industrial jobs and relegated positive changes in employment for the decade to the lower wage service sector. While the dollar value of U.S. imports increased almost 40 percent between 1980 and 1985, world trade had the lowest growth in thirty years (U.S. Congress 1987:2, 3; Guenther 1986:1–7). According to a report by the General Agreement on Tariffs and Trade (GATT) (1987:21): "World trading manufacturers, traditionally the fastest growing of the three main product categories, increased by a mere 3% in volume in 1986, down from 5.5% in 1985. Leaving aside the recession years 1958, 1975, and 1982, this was the poorest performance in three decades."

These shocks and secondary waves may require adjustments of such magnitude that experienced observers of international commerce are voicing concern over the possibility of a recession in the global economy. The stage is set by divergent objectives among the United States, trade surplus countries such as Japan, and the developing economies. The flaw is that unless trade deficits are reduced to manageable sizes, the United States may adopt, contrary to its traditions, a policy of trade interference that would produce trade surpluses. On the other end, countries like Japan are likely to continue their expansion of government spending, and developing economies, pressed by increasing indebtedness, may induce reductions in domestic demand to augment exports. Unfolding from this scenario is a drama of vicious recessionary interactions between "demand-generating efforts" and "demand-reduction requirements" (Okita 1987).

There are no easy answers to the challenges of global competition and cooperation. But some unique contributions to understanding the problem and the decisions we face are made individually and collectively by the authors of this volume. The discussion is undertaken from conceptual, historical, economic, managerial, and public policy viewpoints. All these dimensions must be explored to address the complexity of the problem with a composite of manageable tasks likely to harness the synergy existing among the forces that produce a competitive edge.

The following brief descriptions of the seven sections of this book, in spite of best intentions, are imperfect indicators of the substance of each chapter and merely reflect this author's understanding and interpretation of their significance to the general topic.

PART I: INTRODUCTION

The introductory chapter by Professor **Laura Tyson** proposes a departure from conceptual frameworks grounded in traditional economic theory and ideologically based, but often ineffective, economic policies. Instead, she offers the elements of a pragmatic approach to an urgently needed national competitiveness policy.

The mobility of capital and technology leave competitiveness increasingly dependent on the quality of labor and on national policies. Therefore, Tyson argues, traditional assumptions of perfect competition, free trade, and unchanged technology cannot guide policy reliably. Also, reducing the problem to a mere exchange-rate issue ignores the negative effect of the drop in the value of the dollar on real wages and incomes and, therefore, on the standard of living of American citizens. The approach of enlightened empiricism invoked by Tyson, freed from ideological dogma, may include specific and different aggregate, sectoral, and industry policies, depending on their effect on national competitiveness and welfare. Part of the approach is the inclusion of ''cooperativeness'' as a strategy complementing competitive strategies and enhancing the vision of benefits accruing to all trading partners from a growing international economic system fostered by coordinated rather than conflicting national policies.

The need for a different national economic agenda is the inevitable consequence of changes in the world economy. Some of the changes, such as volatile exchange rates and oscillating capital flows, have been policy-induced and are temporary. Others, such as technological development, are more autonomous and permanent. Among them, five trends observed and described by Tyson have such dramatic impact on national and international competitive postures that responding to them, either by action or by default, is inevitable and ultimately determines the share of global product that each country is capable of claiming.

Damaging contradictions may emerge within national economies. While the mobility of technology and capital makes international trade a condition for economic growth and makes traditional comparative advantages irrelevant, short-term national and special-sector interests, by preventing policymakers from thinking globally and cooperatively, may reduce economic exchanges between nations. As for the United States, its trade and current account deficits have become not only larger, but more worrisome since, lately, they include the traditionally surplus sectors of high-tech products and productive services. This is, however, just one symptom of the low competitiveness malaise. Other indicators are more revealing of the nature of the illness. Among them, Tyson cites declines in real wages, slow growth in productivity, loss of technological leadership, and loss of market shares by manufacturers, with negative spillovers into the service sector. The evidence casts doubts on this country's capability to sustain competitiveness, even after enjoying short-term advantages due to technological innovations or transitional economic forces. A revealing observation by Tyson is that the dollar appreciation after 1982, resulting from a combination of U.S. economic recovery, deregulation, and tax policy, masked and aggravated the erosion of competitiveness and poor trade performance of the country.

Given the recent unrefutable evidence of the impact of government policies on competitiveness, and knowing about its related welfare creation, a compelling case can be made for a national effort directed at creating or enhancing advantage in global markets. The effectiveness of the approach rests on the adequacy of the policy mix relative to the complementarity of the factors influencing competitiveness. At the macro level, policies must be examined for their effect on savings, capital formation, general and specialized education, investments in physical- and human-capital innovation, entrepreneurship, and long-term liberalization of trade barriers. It is not the ideological base of the policies that should matter, but their interaction toward competitive advantage. Even protectionism, explains Tyson, may at times, and in the short run, be justified to improve national welfare for industries with exceptionally high returns or large spillover effects on the rest of the economy—for instance, Japanese policies favoring steel and shipbuilding in the 1950s and 1960s. Tyson's argument is that the traditional view that competition will eventually eliminate earnings differentials for labor and capital and that market prices are reliable indicators of social returns, does not explain contemporary economic events. Today's imperfections in product markets and distortions in capital markets may produce risks and uncertainties that discourage the timely flow of private capital to investments of great significance to the whole economy. Therefore, Japanese public support of semiconductor, computer, and telecommunication industries, and earlier, of steel and shipbuilding, is meant to activate a virtuous cycle linking the expansion of downstream businesses benefiting from national input production back to the expansion and higher economies of scale of the initially targeted, input-producing industries. Policy creates industry-specific advantage because world trade flows increasingly depend less on national differences in resource endowment and more on temporary advantages from technology-related economies of scale, product differentiation, and other non-price competition. The chapter ends describing five major areas for action toward a needed national competitiveness policy.

PART II: LEARNING FROM EXPERIENCE

Is Japanese success endemic or transferable? Professor **Ezra Vogel** ascribes it to the struggle of compensating for few natural resources and to high dependency on the rest of the world. Can similar results be attained in America?[1] After dispelling some cherished beliefs about U.S. economic supremacy and exposing the main reasons for the U.S. demise, Vogel identifies the strategic factors accounting for Japan's ascendance to the economic limelights. Central among them is that country's ability to manage change without producing serious disruptions in its socioeconomic fabric. This is evident in the transition to the automated factory and in the able handling by Japanese management of displaced workers. Also, coping successfully with change results from favorable long-term linkages between manufacturers and bankers, from reciprocally advantageous interactions between service industries and manufacturing, and from research and development activities fueled with increasing portions of Japanese national product and persistently focused on commercial applications. Finally, Professor Vogel underlines the importance of cooperation among people, businesses, and countries.

When Professor **Walt Rostow** asks the question, "Is the United States capable of making the adjustments necessary to meet our challenges?" the beam of his eyes sweeps history and the future. History is the insight of David Hume, the Scottish philosopher and historian who recognized, against the prevailing mercantilistic doctrine of the mid-eighteenth century, the potential bilateral advantages of trade between rich and poor countries. That insight is used by Rostow to pierce the reality of a twenty-first-century world destabilized by redistributions of political and economic influence reminiscent of those that, at the end of the nineteenth century, set in motion the disruption of two world wars.

Rostow ascribes these changes to a "Fourth Industrial Revolution," unique in its impact on our future. Basically, the new technological innovations have both greater scientific complexity and greater accessibility. The greater complexity requires scientists to have a central role not only in inventions, but in their applications. The greater accessibility—made possible by higher and increasing levels of general and scientific education throughout the world—accelerates diffusion and applicability of new technologies. The results are comparative advantages no longer bound by the geography of natural resources and the emergence of cooperation as the preferred strategy for individual and global survival.

During the Fourth Industrial Revolution, the American mission is clear. Diffusion of new technologies is fueled by the rate of gross investment and slows down during weak economic growth. In the world's political economy, slow growth and a weak competitive position undermine the U.S. stabilizing role on the world markets and compromise the debt positions and futures of developing nations. The scenario intimately links the economic status of this country not only with its own national security but with that of those nations that rely on the United States as a call of last resort. "Whom," Rostow asks, "could 'we' call for help?" The answer may lie in the wisdom of David Hume, who viewed the entrepreneurship of emerging eighteenth-century economies as an opportunity rather than as a threat to increasing commerce. The key, Hume and Rostow explain, is a proclivity for hard work coupled with the desire for cooperation and peaceful coexistence expected from civilized nations.

Productivity, adds Chancellor **Joseph Duffey**, is an attitude that places human-resource development and individual self-realization at the center of economic policy. It was true in the 1950s, at the height of the American economic success. It is compelling now when knowledge rather than capital is the main gear of economic development. That attitude is needed to create economic excellence in this new world where geographic boundaries have little economic importance, technology determines marketing advantage, and trading is essential to national welfare. Unfortunately, notes Duffey, the United States suffers in this new world from a lack of national consensus on the competitiveness issue and from an inadequate sense of urgency among legislators and businessmen about a national policy on competitiveness.

PART III: NATIONAL STRATEGIES

From his vantage point as the head of the National Science Foundation, Mr. **Erich Bloch** outlines a strategy to compete by maintaining the quality of U.S. research and technology. Such a national program is needed, Bloch explains, because U.S. technical manpower is insufficient and laboratories, equipment, and other research infrastructures are deteriorating; R&D share of GNP, relative to other nations and particularly for civilian R&D, is decreasing; changes in the nature of research are requiring more interdisciplinary input and the sharing of sophisticated and expensive equipment; shorter lags between basic research and applied technology combined with the growing military value of unclassified research are producing changes in research sponsorship and in the ways research is conducted and used; and finally, because of the impact of science and technology on national security and economic well-being.

Bloch's proposed strategy consists of seven broad actions aimed at enhancing simultaneously and harmoniously the funding, the research infrastructure, and the linkages of research organizations with government, industry, and the public. What transpires is the importance of greater coordination of programs, greater policy focus, and greater attention to *all* the components of excellence in science and technology. Delaying a comprehensive approach is the fact that competitiveness is not perceived yet as a compelling national challenge of the importance of nuclear power during World War II or space exploration at the time of the Apollo program. Progress has recently been made in some of the areas discussed by Bloch, but the problems remain unabated; Bloch's seven points continue to offer a valid framework for organizing and evaluating a national research strategy.

Technological and scientific advancements do not in themselves guarantee economic growth. A critical mass of economic and institutional forces must spring into action to realize the economic potential that investments in science and technology create. Professors **Peter Jones** and **David Teece** note that problems affecting technology transfer have, unfortunately, been documented more thoroughly than solutions. To improve this condition, they distill many years of work on competitiveness into a comprehensive set of research findings—from recent studies and personal interaction with business executives—and into a research agenda for the nation's business schools. Jones and Teece believe that colleges of business are in the best position to undertake the task of leading the way toward solutions to the competitiveness problem because they are close to industry—the essential driver of any implementation program—and because, by their very nature, they are interdisciplinary, a necessary quality for addressing complex issues of technological innovation, manufacturing, organizational behavior, finance, industrial relations, compensation, business history, institutions, and law.

The authors organize the discussion under the major institutional settings—such as the corporation, the industry, and state, local, and federal governments—within which decisions that affect U.S. competitiveness are made. The needed research is outlined in the chapter and discussed more extensively in the appendix to this volume. The research questions probe the internal (management, employees, physical facilities, operations), operating (suppliers, customers), and external (industry, competitors, governments) environments of the business enterprise. What emerges are not only guidelines for the systematic investigation of pressing problems, but an unprecedented, well-organized, and ready-to-use primer on business competitiveness that depicts the range, significance, and quality of decisions that must be made by public- and private-sector policymakers.

To understand competitiveness, Jones and Teece maintain, one must recognize the spillovers and interdependencies produced by competitive performance in the international economic system and, consequently, the inadequacy of standard measures of business activity and success to describe the richness of the competitiveness concept. They propose a hybrid definition encompassing comparative notions of relative economic growth, market shares, and international account balances; efficiency notions of a firm's potential and realized productivity;

and equity notions of real income and welfare. The conclusion is a strong case for a nationwide research and outreach program combining learning with programmatic action.

PART IV: INDUSTRY STRATEGIES

The section on industry strategies offers the view on competition seen by those who directly face the challenge of the market contest. The seven authors contributing to this section are either business executives or professional writers close to management.

Dr. **John Rouse**, former academician and university administrator and presently CEO of a research organization, sees the problem of competitiveness originating from inside U.S. companies. The flaws are shortsighted, quarterly-profit-oriented, investment choices and traditional product development strategies consisting of iterative processes and independently optimized steps. Solutions require fundamental changes in the corporate culture to allow all decisions associated with the product generation cycle to be evaluated in relation to competitive strategies. Rouse believes that a true manufacturing science supported by systematic studies and experiments is the answer to competitiveness. Yet, there is a major barrier to the development and implementation of scientific approaches to manufacturing, and that is the scarcity of trained management and technical personnel. Other obstacles originate from the fear of allowing, with automation, the decoupling of industrial growth from employment opportunities. Rouse argues that, through competitive advantage, truly successful automated manufacturing, by reducing the cost per unit of output, creates larger markets, the expansion of business enterprises, and ultimately, increases rather than decreases in employed labor.

Mr. **William Weber**'s personal experience in the market contest reinforces the view that improvements in manufacturing are essential to competitiveness. The Japanese advantage in manufacturing is made possible, reports Weber, by tax policies favoring business development and by a banking system that, satisfied with long-term growth objectives, provides industry with low-cost capital and therefore allows lower after-tax profits than those possible in the United States. Reinforcing this advantage are the well-known educational gap—which favors the Japanese population in both general and technical education—and the greater adaptability of Pacific Rim industry to incorporate new ideas into products.

Changes in the corporate culture and the integration of all phases of the manufacturing process into strategic planning are now possible. This is so because the quality and quantity of information on performance and cost improvements have made intelligent devices on the factory floor both possible and affordable. While government policy is needed to create the environment favorable to the creation of competitive advantage, Weber believes that the responsibility for realizing that advantage lies in the private sector and that success will depend on the determination with which business enterprises pursue the opportunities offered by the new global environment.

Of all the new technologies, the biotechnologies have generated the most debate on dangerous spillover effects while opening the largest vistas of commercial benefits and human progress. The field is still new, and outcomes are uncertain, but competition is fierce, and international cooperation on regulations and intellectual property laws is needed to unlock the promises of the modern cornucopia. Mr. **Douglas McCormick**'s review of the field offers a mixed picture of hopes, only a few serious efforts, and mostly unclear plans for maintaining the present U.S. advantage. While Japan has recently made biotechnology a national priority, central coordination and leadership for the emerging industry are not prevailing in the United States and Europe.

Cooperation is the inevitable outcome of an international hypercompetitive environment, conclude Mr. **Alfred Stein** and Mr. **Somshankar Das**. Their vantage point is that of top management in the semiconductor industry. Their experience has been shaped by rapid changes in product and process technologies, short product life cycles, and the systematic positioning of European and Japanese competitors in the U.S. market through acquisitions and other direct and indirect means. They argue that the expanding global market has increased the number of competitors and is forcing even the smaller companies to adopt an international perspective and international strategies. These include shopping worldwide for least-cost/high-productivity factors of production and using financial resources accumulated in one country to improve the firm's competitive posture in another.

What works in creating market advantage for smaller companies, suggest Stein and Das, is the development of customized, distinctive competencies for strategically significant buyers. On the other end, larger companies are likely to adopt a strategy linking low-cost manufacturing with trade barrier opportunities, gains from exchange-rate fluctuations, and appropriate combinations of purchased and manufactured product components.

Independently from the size of the business, a company may develop appropriate customer-vendor relationships, special R&D cooperatives, and even strategic partnerships with foreign competitors. These alliances are typically short-term, but can be very successful when, based on an understanding of cultural differences, they allow the best utilization of the richer human resource pool that the partnership makes available.

A topic implied but rarely addressed in discussions of technology transfer is technology marketing. Yet, it is part of the connective tissue between research and commercial ventures and a critical contributing factor in the support of R&D. In exploring tech marketing, Mr. **Edward McCreary** directs his attention to a vital and often ignored aspect of technological progress: the critical, and elusive, communication network between men and women of science and men and women of commerce.

His observations and preliminary conclusions are derived from an informal survey of top senior operations and tech-user managers in companies that develop and/or buy-and-apply technology. Simply put, decisions on technology utilization are not made by a single person but result from and are affected by the interaction within a decision group. Decision groups typically consist of tech-user specialists, operations managers, and top management. Different types of information about the same technology must reach the three levels of users to produce the convergence of wills necessary for adopting the technology or supporting its further development. This group dynamic based on education, personality, and partial knowledge bears a large and mostly unnoticed responsibility for the early adoption and commercial development of scientific ideas. McCreary's observation underlines the importance of adequate technical education for managers and marketeers, who must have a sufficient grasp of the nature of technology development and utilization. McCreary reports that such specialized knowledge is lacking not only in the United States but throughout the world.

PART V: SPECIAL-SECTOR STRATEGIES

The study of competitiveness includes many areas indirectly but strategically related to some of the main topics, such as scientific inquiry, entrepreneurship, and the commercialization of science. The chapters of this section review some of these additional dimensions of the central theme.

A former college of business dean as well as successful businessman and entrepreneur, and presently the creator and "energizer" of a university-based research institute, Professor **George Kozmetsky** sees technology venturing as the catalyst for activating the interaction of many institutions that are key to the creation of national competitive advantage. The phenomenon, Kozmetsky points out, is a recent one (since 1979) and reflects the change of public- and private-sector policies from a reactive to a proactive mode. In the new approach, the commercialization of technology occurs because of deliberate, risk-taking actions and strategies, not just because it is expected as an inevitable, almost autonomous, outcome of research.

Future activity in technology venturing will cluster around the five industries—automotive, fuel, information processing/computers/electronics, pharmaceuticals, and chemicals—with the largest R&D expenditures and, therefore, with the highest likelihood of spin-offs, leveraged buy-outs, and acquisitions and mergers.

Kozmetsky notes changes in traditional sources of venture capital, a larger role being played by the private sector in funding R&D, and new institutional developments resulting in successful cooperation between universities, industry, and local, state, and federal governments. These events are facilitating the emergence of new industries, entrepreneurial talent, and the type of flexible research and financial infrastructures needed for competing in international markets. The realization of the promises offered by these new developments rests on their effectiveness in promoting entrepreneurship while maintaining the integrity, the quality, and the depth of scientific investigation.

While technology venturing is needed to undergird the product evolution process, the creative force propelling the process is the entrepreneur. It all begins, explains Professor **Robert Hisrich**, at a point where knowledge—particularly new knowledge—interacts with a recognized social need. Entrepreneurs, coming usually from the ranks of researchers or marketers and having innate or acquired qualities of leadership and vision, perceive the opportunity for personal and social gains and provide the energy and perseverance needed to create a new business or perhaps a new industry. The process may occur within an existing firm—a case of intrapreneurship—or externally, in the economic environment—a case of entrepreneurship. Specific environmental conditions must prevail in each case. In describing the preconditions to innovation and commercialization within a business, Hisrich depicts a scenario different from the one prevailing in most U.S. companies and indirectly presents another explanation for the loss of economic preeminence in the world economy by American business. As for the external conditions facilitating the formation of new businesses, Hisrich notes that only a few programs, such as "incubation" centers or enterprise development centers, are in place, and that coordination among them as well as complementary national programs are needed and lacking.

While the private sector is increasing R&D expenditures but resists the flexibility in management and organizational structure vital to entrepreneurship and innovation, the public sector, traditionally known for spending most of the R&D monies but harvesting the least commercial results, is opening the gates to a new era of unprecedented interaction with industry. Dr. **E. J. Soderstrom**, Mr. **W. W. Carpenter**, and Dr. **H. Postma**, all members of the highly sophisticated and well-funded scientific network of federal laboratories, explain that at the root of dramatic changes in legislation and programs is the recognition of the bi-directional nature—an exchange for reciprocal benefits—of technology transfer. Scientists in the employment of governments must deal with the opportunity cost of using their time for scientific pursuits that bring psychic and carrier rewards versus that of using their time for patent disclosure routines and commercialization efforts, which are burdened with red tape and uncertainties and bring little personal recognition. Therefore, appropriate incentives toward technology transfer, in addition to enabling legislation, must be in place to trigger the interaction of government-employed scientists and managers with private-sector entrepreneurs and marketers. The authors report that following recent legislative action, a program aimed at facilitating technology transfer is being successfully implemented by one of the federal laboratories. The success of the program offers hopes of dramatic improvements in the utilization of government funded research. This is a development of particular significance during present federal research efforts, which are engaging large numbers of scientists at the cutting edge of knowledge to pursue military objectives. The questions raised by extensive utilization of science for national defense are both philosophical—Is the scope of basic research being narrowed and the value of the quest for knowledge compromised?—and pragmatic: Are we getting enough value for the tax dollars being spent? USAF Major General **Donald Cromer** addresses the pragmatic issues by first describing the Strategic Defense Initiative (SDI)—the most sophisticated among the defense programs, from a science and technology viewpoint —as well as the reasons for its implementation, and then by discussing the commercial applications likely to emerge from SDI research.

PART VI: FOREIGN STRATEGIES

In discussing global competition, attention should be given to all the players of the international game. Adequate coverage of foreign country issues and strategies is not in the scope of this volume. The two contributions that have been included are limited to the case of the developing countries but provide an example of the ambiguity of some of the issues when they are seen from different sides of the competitive arena.

Dr. **Kenneth McLennan** sets the stage by reviewing the progressive expansion of global markets during the past twenty years and showing that both industrialized and developing countries benefited, if somewhat disproportionately, from the expansion. The largest shares of the gain went to those newly industrialized countries with a high savings and investment rate, a rapidly growing manufacturing capacity, and the advantages of lower labor cost for some of the manufactures involving routine production processes. Benefits decreased or disappeared as the countries with the comparative advantage began to enjoy the results of rapid economic growth. McLennan states that among all the possible courses of action that can be undertaken to counteract loss of competitiveness, the only ones that will produce real gains—that is, gains in trade balances without reductions in real income—are those that induce increases in productivity, as in the case of massive investments in R&D and in human capital. Allocating resources to strategies that create productivity may require temporary sacrifices of all U.S. citizens and may not allow continuing expansions of defense spending but, observes McLennan, lack of productivity growth would result in large and permanent negative adjustment to U.S. real incomes and the loss of U.S. supremacy in world markets. The latter is the true first line of defense for U.S. national security.

American economic growth has great significance for the welfare of the developing and newly industrialized economies, since it represents a large portion of the world demand for their exports. On the other end, argues McLennan, the GATT and the international monetary systems should be reformed. In the former, special preferences in trade arrangements for some of the newly industrialized nations should be eliminated. For the latter, more equitable and realistic conditions under which countries can manage their exchange rates should be enacted.

The viewpoint of a lesser developed country is verbalized by Dr. **Herminio Blanco** of Mexico. The central issue is technology transfer. Developing economies plagued by a high national debt and a history of economic difficulties are unable to assemble sufficiently large investments in technology. Increasing protectionism worldwide, coupled with the faster pace of technological progress, is likely to produce a widening gap between industrialized and developing economies. These and other problems justify pessimism that technology transfer, particularly in production technology, would naturally occur at the pace needed by many developing economies to avoid bankruptcy. Also, technological progress, which is mostly funded by economically advanced countries—General Motors R&D expenditures, notes the author, are larger than the whole Mexican R&D budget—is biased toward labor-saving technologies that have dubious value in countries where this factor of production is abundant. In spite of the barriers against technology transfer, some of the newly industrialized economies have been able to compete effectively in selected world markets, and more success stories are in the making.

Cooperation among governments of industrialized and developing nations is the obvious yet elusive formula for a better life guided by the enlightened self-interest of neighbors in a shrinking world.

SECTION VII: EPILOGUE

Professor **Furino** and Professor **Kozmetsky**'s last chapter draws on the preceding ones to underline the magnitude and the scope of adjustments that must be made to cope with present and future changes.

A review of legislation presently being discussed in Congress to promote a more effective national trade policy reveals that, while the proposed laws address most of the issues discussed in this volume, they also generate much debate and are accused of being restrictive and therefore not conducive to the growth of the United States and the rest of the world.

As for the private sector, not only technological sophistication and sound economic reasoning are required, but attitudes and managerial styles must be transformed.

The conclusive note is one of hope that the emerging awareness of the competitiveness challenge in industry, Congress, and the media will induce the adjustments in private- and public-sector policies necessary to prevent the occurrence of a compelling jolt from a major economic catastrophe.

NOTE

1.   Vogel's *Comeback* (1985) is, in a sense, an answer to this very question also raised by Vogel's previous best-seller *Japan as Number One* (1979). Vogel's answer is in the affirmative and suggests that America can pursue competitiveness objectives similar to Japan's by taking advantage of its own unique resources and institutions.

REFERENCES

General Agreement on Tariffs and Trade (GATT). 1987. *International Trade in 1986 and Current Prospects*. Geneva: GATT (March).

Guenther, Gary L. 1986. "Industrial Competitiveness: Definitions, Measures, and Key Determinants." Unpublished report. Washington, D.C.: Congressional Research Service (February 3).

Okita, Saburo. 1987. "The Emerging Prospects for Development and the World Economy." Third Raul Predisch Lecture, Geneva, July 9.

U.S. Congress. Senate. Committee on Finance. *Omnibus Trade Act of 1987*. 100th Cong., 1st sess., 1987. S. Rept. 490.

Vogel, Ezra F. 1979. *Japan as Number One*. New York: Harper & Row.

———. 1985. *Comeback*. New York: Simon and Schuster.

2 MAKING POLICY FOR NATIONAL COMPETITIVENESS IN A CHANGING WORLD

Laura D'Andrea Tyson

The international competitiveness of the American economy has become a central and bipartisan national policy concern. The Commission on Industrial Competitiveness appointed by President Reagan unanimously concluded in its 1985 report that the United States faced a serious competitiveness problem requiring both public- and private-sector actions for its solution. The commission was not alone in reaching that conclusion, but its report, like others issued at the time, went largely unheeded. The huge trade deficits of recent years, however, have focused national attention on competitiveness. A congressional competitiveness caucus with bipartisan leadership was formed during the fall of 1986. The President's State of the Union message for 1987 focused on the need to restore American competitiveness and proposed several policy initiatives. Indeed, national competitiveness is emerging as a major rallying point for both parties in the 1988 presidential campaign.

The reason for concern is clear. America's capacity to provide for the well-being and security of its citizens is reduced if its producers cannot compete effectively in world markets. Certainly, the last few years' economic growth, albeit at a declining rate, has prolonged the economic recovery. Millions of jobs have been created, and inflation and interest rates have declined. But signs of real trouble are evident. The stock market crash of October 1987 reflects growing concern about the underlying strength of the economy. U.S. trade deficits in recent years have been colossal; indeed, the deficit in 1987 was the largest in U.S. history and the largest ever recorded by a single country. As a result of six years of mushrooming deficits, the United States has amassed a huge debt with foreign creditors and has become the largest and, ironically, the richest debtor nation in the world. The United States has financed current consumption, both private and public, by borrowing abroad rather than by balancing income and expenditures at home. In industry after industry—ranging from low-wage, labor-intensive apparel to high-wage, technology-intensive semiconductors—U.S. producers have lost world market share, scaled down domestic production or employment, and shifted operations abroad.

At an aggregate level, the nation's productivity—not simply how much we produce but, in a sense, how well we produce and how fast we are able to expand when we invest—has grown more slowly than the productivity of virtually all of its major trading partners for the last three decades. The jobs created during the recent recovery pay average wages that are substantially below the average wages of the jobs lost, and the average wage has fallen significantly below the levels realized in the early 1970s. At the same time, U.S. technological leadership in a variety of critical industries has all but disappeared. In some industries, U.S. producers have fallen behind in the development and implementation of vital technologies on which national security rests.

To understand the competitiveness problem and to begin to fashion public and private policy responses, it is critical to begin with a meaningful definition of competitiveness. To some, especially many economists, competitiveness is simply an exchange-rate issue. If the dollar falls far enough, the prices of U.S. goods will fall sufficiently relative to the prices of foreign goods to restore U.S. trade balance and rebuild U.S. shares in world markets. This view, while logically correct, misses a critical point. A protracted drop in the value of the dollar will undeniably reduce the trade deficit and restore U.S. competitiveness in world markets, but only at the expense of a drop in the relative real incomes and relative real wages of the domestic population. But it is precisely an underlying concern about future trends in the U.S. standard of living that motivates most of the policy discussions about competitiveness. In these discussions, competitiveness is implicitly or explicitly defined in a broader sense as the ability to compete effectively in world markets while simultaneously raising real incomes.[1] According to this definition, if the United States has to rely on currency depreciation rather than on productivity and technological performance to improve its position in world markets, then it most certainly has a competitiveness problem.

To develop meaningful policy measures to solve this problem, the factors that gave rise to it in the first place must be understood.

In a world of increasing mobility of capital and technology, the competitiveness of a nation depends increasingly on two factors that are not traded: the quality of its labor force and the quality of its economic policies. Good policies can enhance national competitiveness, while bad policies can seriously undermine it. Certainly, it would be hard to deny that U.S. policy choices resulting in relatively high U.S. interest rates, a soaring value of the dollar, a deteriorating educational system, and cutbacks in real federal funding for nondefense R&D have weakened the competitiveness of the U.S. economy in recent years. It would be equally difficult to deny that Japanese policy choices promoting high savings and interest rates, supporting a national educational system of recognized excellence, and encouraging cooperative R&D activities in commercial areas have strengthened the competitiveness of the Japanese economy in recent years.

The case rests on the idea that national competitiveness at both the aggregate and sectoral levels can be created by government policy. From this analytical perspective, debates about free trade versus protectionism are outmoded. The meaningful policy questions are: How do government policies create national competitiveness? Which policies are most effective at the aggregate or sectoral level? Under what circumstances will a particular set of policies to create advantage be welfare-improving?

Correct answers to these questions require an approach of enlightened empiricism rather than one of ideological dogma. In the complex technological and international environment in which national economies function, there are no simple policy prescriptions. Economic theories based on assumptions of perfect competition, free trade, and unchanging technology are not a reliable guide to policymaking. Policies must be shaped to the particulars of the industry and the country in question. What is good policy for the U.S. apparel or textile industry may not be good policy for the U.S. semiconductor industry, and what is good policy in the United States may not be good policy in Japan. Empirical evidence must replace theoretical, often ideological, arguments as a guide to policy formation if the goal of policy is to strengthen national competitiveness in the long run.

Finally, it is important to note that the definition of competitiveness used here does not imply that national competitiveness is a zero-sum game. Competitiveness focuses on the ability of a nation to compete with other nations in international markets. Because of this focus, discussions about competitiveness are often nationalistic in tone, concentrating on issues of relative national economic welfare rather than aggregate economic welfare, independent of how it is distributed among nations. But policies to enhance the competitiveness of one nation need not necessarily work to the detriment of other nations. For example, policies to accelerate productivity growth and quicken the pace of technological innovation and diffusion in one nation can work to the benefit of its trading partners by providing cheaper, higher quality, more technologically advanced products. At an aggregate level, such national policies add to world welfare over time by making more productive use of the world's stock of technological knowledge. How individual nations share in the benefits over time depends largely on *cooperative* rather than *competitive* efforts among nations to shape rules for the international economic system, coordinate macroeconomic policies to support growing international markets, and bolster development prospects in less developed countries.

CHANGES IN THE WORLD ECONOMIC ENVIRONMENT

The last fifteen years have witnessed dramatic changes in the world economy, with profound consequences for individual nations. Some of these changes—such as technological developments in production, transportation, and communications and their integrating effects on product and capital markets—are permanent and are not directly tied to the policy choices of any nation or group of nations. Others, such as unprecedented volatility in exchange rates and related changes in the magnitude and direction of global capital flows, can be traced to policies of individual nations or groups of nations; because of its dominant economic and political power, the policies of the United States have been of particular importance. Although there have been many permanent and policy-induced changes, five stand out: dramatic changes in the terms of trade between commodities and manufactured goods; major changes in world credit market conditions, including dramatic swings in real interest rates; a major increase in global capital flows, and major shifts in the direction of such flows; a dramatic increase in the volatility of exchange rates and in the influence of capital-market forces on exchange-rate determination; the rise of the developmental states and the growth of protectionist pressures in world trade; and the growing mobility of capital, information, and technology across national borders made possible by revolutions in transportation, communications, and production technologies.

Led by oil prices, overall commodity prices rose sharply relative to manufactured goods prices in the early to mid 1970s. By 1977, however, the collapse of non-oil commodity prices had already begun, joined after 1980 by the gradual and then spectacular collapse of oil prices. According to Drucker (1986), by 1986 raw material prices were at their lowest level in recorded history in relation to the prices of manufactured goods and services—in general, as low as the levels realized in the Great Depression and even lower for some commodities. No one who looks carefully at the experience of the last twenty years can ignore the pivotal role of oil prices in international economic developments and in the economic performance of individual nations. Oil price increases encouraged a reallocation of resources to energy development, resulted in major changes in the profitability of different industries, producers, and countries, fueled the inflationary surge of the 1970s, generated stagflationary conditions in the developed economies, and produced the oil surpluses that financed the ill-fated growth of commercial bank lending to developing countries.

The second surge of oil prices in 1978–79 triggered the imposition of contractionary demand policies throughout the developed world. These policies caused the deepest and most prolonged recession in world growth and trade since the Great Depression. The heads of state of most of the developed economies lost power to new leaders as part of this general policy shift. In the United States and in several European countries, a new era of economic conservatism dawned in which the struggle against inflation was accorded priority over the traditional liberal goals of full employment and greater distributional equity.

The switch to anti-inflationary monetary policies in the developed market economies, along with the decline in the surpluses of the oil-exporting countries, pushed real interest rates up sharply. Borrowing decisions that had seemed prudent given high inflation, low interest rates, and high oil prices, suddenly became disastrous. In the United States, the consequences of such decisions showed up in a record number of bankruptcies, bank failures, and bailouts, and in growing economic difficulties in regions dependent on oil, agriculture, and other natural resources.

Higher real interest rates and weak demand in developed-country markets together fostered growing debt repayment difficulties throughout the developing world. For oil-rich countries, like Mexico, Nigeria, and Venezuela, the fall in oil prices added an extra blow. Whereas during the 1970–1980 period total net real financial flows to the developing countries grew by 9.1 percent a year, they fell by nearly 10 percent between 1980 and 1984 (World Bank 1985). Confronted with the need to finance a net transfer to their creditors, most indebted developing countries were forced into austerity, and even then many found themselves unable to service their debt.

Meanwhile, as the developing countries of the world found themselves increasingly starved of capital, one of the richest countries in the world began to attract huge capital inflows. The result was a dramatic shift in the direction of international capital flows, along with continued growth in their size. Although capital flight from indebted developing countries played some role in the flow of capital to the United States, much more significant was the rise in relative real interest rates and other real rates of return in the United States. The elimination or liberalization of capital controls in the developed economies, extending even to Japan by 1982–83, along with advances in telecommunications and innovations in banking, provided the institutional framework within which investors could move huge amounts of funds across national borders to chase higher returns. The resulting capital flows dwarfed trade flows by comparison. By 1985, the annual value of transactions on the London Eurodollar market reached $15 trillion, at least twenty-five times the value of world trade (Drucker 1986). Capital mobility, as expected, created strong links among interest rates around the world. Thus the upward thrust of interest rates in the United States between 1981 and 1983 exerted upward pressure on interest rates in Europe and Japan, and the ensuing decline in U.S. interest rates permitted similar declines in foreign interest rates.

A third area of change in the world economy—and one that is clearly related to greater capital mobility—is the behavior of exchange rates. Short-term volatility of exchange rates, both in real and in nominal terms, has been one of the most striking features of the flexible exchange-rate system. Volatility reflects the growing influence of capital-market conditions on exchange-rate determination. Existing empirical evidence suggests that short-run volatility poses no threat to the international trading system because futures markets allow importers and exporters to hedge the risks of such volatility. What does pose a severe threat are long-term misalignments of exchange rates from purchasing-power parity levels caused by capital-market conditions. With flexible exchange rates, the frequency of real exchange-rate cycles has increased, as has the frequency with which the real economic costs of misalignment have been incurred (Krugman 1985).

The dramatic real appreciation of the dollar vis-a-vis the European and Japanese currencies between 1980 and mid-1985 is a stunning example of such misalignment. There is widespread agreement that the dollar was "overvalued" relative to underlying competitive conditions in U.S. and foreign markets for at least six years. There is also widespread agreement that this overvaluation resulted from the bidding up of the dollar's value on world capital markets. The strength and longevity of the dollar's real appreciation had profound, economic effects, both in the U.S. economy and around the world. Jobs lost, factories shut down, production located abroad, and trade patterns changed in response to the higher dollar, all imposed substantial adjustment costs on the United States. Recently, in response to the dollar's dramatic decline after 1985, other nations, especially Japan, have been faced with similar adjustment costs. The rising value of the yen has resulted in reduced profits, layoffs, firm closures, and reduced growth in the Japanese manufacturing sector.

A fourth area of change in the world economy is the rise of non-tariff barriers to trade and the strengthening of protectionist pressures on the international trading system. Non-tariff barriers to trade have taken a variety of forms, including overt import quotas, "voluntary" export restraints, orderly marketing arrangements, discretionary licensing, and state trading. Developed countries, including the United States, have increasingly resorted to such barriers to protect domestic producers threatened by either worldwide excess capacity—as in steel, shipbuilding, and some agricultural products—or by import competition from lower cost producers, often from the developing countries. Although often hailed as temporary, many non-tariff barriers become permanent; so the share of world trade covered by them has increased. For example, in the United States the percentage of manufactured goods protected by non-tariff restrictions increased from 20 percent in 1980 to 35 percent in 1983.

The growing importance of non-tariff trade barriers has also resulted from the growing share of world trade accounted for by the rapidly developing states of East Asia, particularly Japan, Korea, and Taiwan. A critical feature of these states is the conscious use of a variety of domestic tax, credit, regulatory, and spending policies to promote exports and limit domestic market access to foreign producers. Austerity programs have strengthened similar policies in indebted developing countries in other parts of the world.

The fifth and arguably most fundamental set of changes in the world economy stems from underlying changes in production and communications technologies. The new technologies permit not only the increasing integration of world capital markets, but also much greater decentralization of production and distribution facilities across national boundaries. Jobs that previously had to be located close to one another can now be widely scattered throughout the world. Thus the new technologies have hastened the automation of labor-intensive jobs within the developed countries and the migration of many low-wage, low-skill jobs from these countries to the developing world.

In the new technological environment, the production location decisions of large multinational companies, which account for a large share of world trade flows, are increasingly driven by considerations of labor costs and government policies in different countries. With physical capital and the technology embodied in it more mobile across national boundaries, national competitiveness in world markets depends increasingly on the price, productivity, and skills of labor and on government policies that affect the relative attractiveness of locating production facilities in a particular country. In this new global environment, the scope for potential conflicts between the profit objectives of multinational companies and the production, employment, and trade objectives of national governments has become even greater than it was in the past.

The greater international mobility of capital and technology requires a rethinking of the forces underlying national trading patterns. In a world where labor is the only immobile factor of production, standard theories of comparative advantage may not be relevant. In a world where the newest process or product technology diffuse rapidly across national borders, often as a result of the global production strategies of multinational firms, the standard product-cycle theory of trade must also be reexamined. In such a world, the ability of an innovator to capture the returns to a new product or process depends not simply on being the first to market but on remaining competitive in international markets as the innovation diffuses to other producers and locations throughout the world. At a national level, the implications of these trends are clear: maintaining or strengthening a competitive advantage based on technological innovation will be an insufficient foundation for continued growth in national income and for maintaining an external trade balance. Without a "complementary" competitive advantage in related manufacturing capabilities (Teece 1986), innovating countries stand to lose a large share of the commercial returns to their research efforts to other countries with superior manufacturing performance.

The changes in international economic and technological conditions discussed here pose challenges and opportunities for individual nations. How each nation responds to these changing circumstances will determine its wealth and power in the international economy. For the United States, nothing less is at stake than its relative standard of living and its continued support for the open international trading system that it helped to create. There are disturbing signs that the United States has not fared well in the changing world economy in recent years.

THE CHANGING POSITION OF THE UNITED STATES IN THE WORLD ECONOMY

During the last several years, the United States has become more vulnerable to international economic conditions as openness in both its trading and financial relationships with the rest of the world has increased. At the same time, the U.S. trade deficit has hit unprecedented levels. And, between 1981 and 1985, the United States squandered assets accumulated over a half-century and became the world's largest debtor nation, the richest economy ever to enjoy such a distinction.

The dramatic deterioration in the U.S. external position was the consequence of both short-term and long-term factors. The short-term factors were rooted in macroeconomic conditions in the United States and the rest of the world. Fiscal stimulus from tax cuts and increases in government spending fueled a Keynesian demand expansion that propelled the U.S. recovery beginning in 1983. The expansion in U.S. spending predictably spilled over into growth in U.S. imports. At the same time, continued stagnant or recessionary conditions throughout Europe and Japan restrained demand for U.S. exports. The restraint was even greater in several developing countries, including Brazil, Mexico, Argentina, and Chile, where debt repayment difficulties required major cutbacks in imports, a large fraction of which came from the United States. The largest debtor developing countries, including Korea, also mounted major export drives to the United States—one of their main export markets—in order to earn the foreign exchange required to service their debt.

Domestic monetary and fiscal policies were also a major impetus behind the dollar's appreciation, which most economists believe to be the single most important factor behind the deterioration in the trade deficit. Growing fiscal deficits forced the federal government to become a major borrower on U.S. credit markets, while monetary policy followed a restrictive or cautiously expansionary course that kept credit market conditions tight and limited the availability of funds. Tight supply conditions on domestic credit markets, combined with growing credit demand fueled by the federal deficit, drove real interest rates up, and higher real interest rates acted as a magnet for foreign capital. Deregulation, changes in tax policy, and the strong U.S. recovery after 1982 also made U.S. financial instruments more attractive to foreigners. Foreign demand for U.S. debt and equity investments was the principal force behind the appreciation of the dollar.

Until late 1985, the effects of the U.S. macro imbalance on the dollar exchange rate and the trade deficit were either not understood or widely disregarded by the Reagan administration and most members of Congress. To paraphrase Nixon's famous quote on the lira, the architects of U.S. fiscal policy acted as if they did not "give a damn about the value of the dollar." Yet the dollar appreciation, hailed by some as a sign of the strength of the U.S. economy, weakened the already precarious competitive position of U.S. producers in world markets.

The dollar's appreciation aggravated a longer term erosion in U.S. competitiveness, reflecting both decades of relatively low U.S. productivity growth compared to productivity growth abroad and the disappearance of the U.S. technological lead in a number of industries.[2] As a result of these longer term trends, the U.S. trade position would have deteriorated during the 1980–86 period unless the dollar had declined steadily.[3] In other words, if trade performance rather than capital-market conditions had driven exchange rates during this period, the dollar would have fallen, not risen as it did. From this perspective, the dollar appreciation superimposed a short-term competitiveness problem on a more disturbing longer term problem. Unfortunately, the short-term problem masked the longer term one for many observers, leading to the erroneous perception that but for temporary exchange-rate misalignment, the U.S. economy was competitively healthy.

The long-term erosion of U.S. competitiveness does not show up in any single indicator; rather, it is suggested by several different indicators. Certainly, the massive deteriorations in the U.S. trade and current account positions after 1981 are signs of declining U.S. competitiveness. By 1986, even the traditional U.S. trade surplus in high-technology products had given way to a trade deficit. U.S. shares of world markets for most manufactured goods, including many high-technology goods, continued the decline that first began in the late 1960s and early 1970s.

Significantly for those who argue that these declines reflect a shift in the U.S. competitive position toward service exports, the U.S. share of world exports of productive services, as opposed to service flows representing net earnings on overseas investment, also began to decline in the 1970s (Leontief and Duchin 1985). In 1985, the value of U.S. service exports—excluding earnings on U.S. direct foreign investments abroad and military hardware exports (which appear as service exports in U.S. statistics)—was $55 billion, while the total value of imported goods and services was approximately $463 billion. In the same year, the United States imported $58 billion of services, running a deficit in important industries like tourism and insurance and an overall deficit in civilian service trade (Commerce Department 1986). As these numbers suggest, earnings from civilian services cannot conceivably be expanded enough, for the foreseeable future, to pay for the volume of manufactured products the United States now imports.

Although huge trade and current account deficits are the most widely cited indicators of U.S. competitiveness difficulties, they do not tell the whole story, and taken in isolation they can be misleading. In particular, according to the definition of competitiveness presented earlier, an improvement in the trade balance as a result of a steady decline in the dollar's value or a cut in money wages would not mean an improvement in the nation's underlying competitive position, since it would occur at the expense of real wages.

Real wages in the United States grew steadily and rapidly from the end of World War II through 1973. Thereafter, they began to decline, erratically but persistently. Today, real wages are lower than the peak level attained in 1973 and are on a par with levels realized in the second half of the 1960s. In other words, real wages have stagnated over approximately twenty years. The decline in real wages has occurred throughout the economy, from manufacturing to retail trade and other services. In manufacturing, the real weekly wage (measured in 1985 prices) fell by about 4.3 percent between 1973 and 1985; the comparable fall in the real hourly wage in manufacturing was 3.9 percent. Overall, real average hourly earnings in all non-agricultural establishments fell by 5 percent between 1973 and 1985. The decline in real wages shows up in a similar decline in real family incomes during the same period, regardless of differences among families in the number of income-earners per family or differences in the race and age of family members. Overall, the median real family income declined by about 5 percent between 1973 and 1985, while the proportion of American families with incomes below $20,000 increased from 30.6 percent to 34.0 percent (Economic Policy Institute 1986).

Perhaps the most telling evidence of a long-term competitiveness problem is the comparatively slow pace of productivity growth in the U.S. economy. After the early 1970s, productivity growth declined sharply through most sectors of the American economy.[4] Although productivity growth rates also declined in most other industrial countries at the time, U.S. productivity growth continued to lag behind that of its major industrial trading partners. For the period 1960–85, U.S. productivity growth, measured as the growth in real gross domestic product (GDP) per employed person, was the lowest among the advanced industrial countries by a substantial margin. As a result of twenty-five years of relatively poor productivity growth, the substantial advantage in productivity levels enjoyed by U.S. producers had narrowed dramatically by 1985. In several sectors, such as steel, autos, machine tools, and semiconductors, productivity levels in several competitor countries now equal or exceed U.S. levels. The erosion in the relative U.S. position has been concentrated in manufacturing and has been particularly dramatic vis-a-vis Germany and Japan.

The economic recovery that began in 1983 caused productivity growth to pick up, as is usually the case in a cyclical upturn. But the pace of productivity growth has been disappointing. For the first several quarters of the recovery, productivity growth in the non-farm business sector closely matched that of previous U.S. postwar expansions, thus raising hopes that the long productivity slowdown since the early 1970s would be reversed. Productivity growth began to lag past recovery rates, however, and stagnated in 1985. The 1.6 percent rate of increase in productivity from late 1982 through September 1986 is the smallest of any U.S. postwar expansion (Federal Reserve Bank of Cleveland 1987).

In manufacturing, productivity growth during the expansion has performed better than the average of past expansions and better than any recent expansion since 1961. Productivity in manufacturing has risen at an average annual rate of 4.3 percent since the trough of the recession in 1982, although it showed signs of a deceleration of growth in 1986 (Federal Reserve Bank of Cleveland 1987). This level of productivity growth suggests that the slowdown in manufacturing productivity growth since the early 1970s may have been reversed, at least temporarily. Indeed, between 1979 and 1985, U.S. manufacturing productivity grew at approximately the same rate as it grew between 1960 and 1973. Nonetheless, even during the 1979–85 period, U.S. manufacturing productivity growth remained slower than that enjoyed by most of our trading competitors, most notably Japan.

Technological innovation and diffusion are major factors affecting national competitiveness. Evidence reported by the President's Commission on Industrial Competitiveness, and more recently by the Council on Competitiveness, documents a weakening in U.S. technological capabilities. Perhaps the most dramatic evidence of continued erosion in U.S. technological leadership comes from the recent study by the Defense Science Board (1987) of the semiconductor industry. Just ten short years ago, the U.S. technological lead in semiconductors and other microelectronics was unchallenged. Now the Japanese have achieved leadership in several critical areas, and in others they are fast gaining on the U.S. position. Reflecting the domestic industry's competitive difficulties, the U.S. share of the worldwide merchant market declined steadily from nearly 60 percent in 1975 to below 45 percent in 1986, and the U.S. share of the captive and merchant market declined from 67 percent to 50 percent in the same period. The decline in the U.S. share was mirrored by the increasing share of Japanese producers, from 25 percent of the captive and merchant market in 1975 to 39 percent by 1986.

The long-term deterioration in U.S. competitiveness shows up most dramatically in manufactured goods. The losses in U.S. world market share have been largest for manufactured products, and they account for the lion's share of the trade deficit. Partly as a result of declining exports and growing import penetration, manufacturing employment fell sharply after 1979.[5] Between July 1981, the last cyclical peak in the economy, and July 1986, jobs in manufacturing declined by 1.2 million. During the same period, the economy generated 8.6 million jobs, reflecting a gain of 9.5 million new jobs in services. Because manufacturing jobs pay wages that on average are substantially higher than the wages of service jobs, the average weekly wage of jobs lost—$444—was substantially higher than the average weekly wage of jobs gained—$272 (Council on Competitiveness 1987).

To some observers, the decline in the competitiveness of the U.S. manufacturing sector is not cause for alarm, because it reflects a "market-driven" transition to an "information-based" services economy and a growing comparative advantage in services. As noted earlier, one problem with this argument is that the U.S. competitive position in world export markets for many services has declined. A second and more fundamental problem is that many services are what Cohen and Zysman (1987) call "tightly linked" to manufacturing activities, in the sense that competitive difficulties in these activities are likely to cause competitive difficulties in related engineering and design services, software design, business consulting services, and repair and maintenance services.[6] Similarly, the erosion of the U.S. competitive position in capital-goods industries, such as construction equipment and robotics, is likely to spill over into an erosion in related construction, engineering, and architectural services.

Where linkages between services and products are tight, services are often specialized for particular products or even for particular suppliers, and these services together with the products they support or use are best thought of as an interrelated system rather than as separate commodities. This is especially true for many high-technology products and their specialized support services. Under these circumstances, close, frequent communication between producers of output and specialized services is common; such communication involves more than just the exchange of price information and often includes a substantial element of risk on both sides that results in long-term contractual relationships. For tightly linked services, it is hard to imagine how a competitive erosion in product lines in world markets would not spill over into an erosion in related services.

CREATING ADVANTAGE AND POLICY FOR NATIONAL COMPETITIVENESS

Despite supply-side rhetoric, U.S. policy choices during the Reagan years have failed to address the long-run decline in U.S. competitiveness.[7] Investment rates, while rising from cyclically depressed levels in 1981–82, remain low compared to our major competitors, and the U.S. saving rate, already low by international standards, fell to record lows in

1984–86. Civilian research and development, although increasing in some areas of the economy, remains a smaller fraction of GNP than in Japan or Germany, and the most rapid peacetime military buildup in history has drawn scientific and engineering talent into military projects with limited commercial applications for the foreseeable future (Stowsky 1986). The quality of the U.S. labor force continues to suffer from long-term difficulties in the educational system, as reflected in higher dropout rates, lower literacy rates, and poorer math and science training than in the other advanced industrial countries.

Recent concern over U.S. trade performance has stimulated interest in the need for a policy package to restore national competitiveness. Both the Reagan administration and Congress are working on competitiveness initiatives. One might be tempted to discount many of the proposed measures as disguises for protectionism and to question whether any of them will improve national economic welfare over the long run. But a hasty conclusion that policies to improve national competitiveness are neither necessary nor desirable would be a mistake. There is a growing body of analytical and empirical research suggesting that government policies can help create or destroy competitive advantage in international trade, with significant long-term effects on national welfare.

At the macro level, it is clear that government policies can affect national competitive advantage over time by influencing the quantity and quality of labor, capital, and technology.[8] A competitive advantage in capital-intensive or technology-intensive industries is not an immutable fact of nature, but the result of a host of interrelated, economywide policies that affect the incentives to save, invest, acquire human capital, and innovate and diffuse technology. This point, although basic, is often overlooked by those who view the gradual erosion in the U.S. competitive position in such industries, or the gradual strengthening of Japan and the East Asian nations in the same industries, as the result of some natural catch-up process. Both the extent and the pace of the catch-up were significantly influenced by policy choices in all of the countries involved.[9]

The notion of creating advantage at the micro or industrial level is both more interesting and more controversial. This notion rests on the observation that a large and growing part of world trade consists of exchanges that do not reflect national differences in resource endowments, even those resources whose quantity and quality are influenced by government policy. Instead, such trade reflects apparently arbitrary or temporary advantage resulting from static or dynamic economies of scale, shifting positions in technological leadership, or product differentiation and other forms of "imperfect" non-price competition.[10] For trade in these products it seems obvious that national policies can have an enduring effect on trade flows and national welfare.

Recent developments in international trade theory have demonstrated that under certain conditions, national policies to promote or protect domestic producers in international competition can improve national welfare. There are essentially two different kinds of conditions that give rise to results of this kind. First, industries that are imperfectly competitive, most often as a result of static or dynamic economies of scale, earn supernormal returns (rents) in the sense that resources employed by them earn higher returns than those available in the rest of the economy.[11] Under these conditions, national welfare may be improved by government policy to win a larger market share for domestic producers in world markets and hence a larger share of world profits for the domestic population. A second set of conditions that provide a justification for welfare-improving policy draws on standard notions of externality, or spillover effects. Simply put, certain industries may be more important than others because they generate benefits for the rest of the economy, and government policy to promote or protect them can improve welfare by fostering these spillover effects. Under either set of conditions, the industries involved are defined as "strategic," either because resources employed by them earn higher returns than they would earn elsewhere or because they generate special benefits for the rest of the economy (Krugman 1986).[12]

The real analytical and policy debate is over how widespread and important such strategic activities are. If one believes that competition rapidly eliminates large intersectoral differences in the earnings of equivalent qualities of labor or capital and that market prices are good indicators of social return, then there are few strategic activities that can benefit from market-promoting policies. If instead, one believes that there are persistent and large deviations in factor returns between different sectors and that prices are not often good indicators of social return because of spillover effects between individual sectors and the rest of the economy, then the scope for beneficial market-promoting policies can be quite broad.

An examination of Japanese industrial policy suggests that the latter perspective motivated policy in that country. For example, in the 1950s and 1960s steel and shipbuilding were promoted because they were believed to provide substantial spillover benefits in the form of infrastructure for other industries. Proponents of this view argue that Japanese success in other industries, such as autos and machine tools, was based in part on the access to cheaper, higher quality steel and on cheaper access to imported raw materials. From this perspective, an evaluation of the wisdom of targeting steel and shipbuilding in the earlier phase of development requires an assessment of spillover effects of this type on other sectors at a later phase of development.

The spillover effects provided by the steel and shipbuilding industries are "pecuniary" in the sense that they are reflected in lower input prices to their downstream users. Because pecuniary externalities are reflected in market prices, economists often argue that there is no need for government policy—markets left to themselves will provide the optimal amount of investment and production. This condition holds, however, only as long as there are no "imperfections" in product markets and no "distortions" in capital markets, reflecting difficulties in raising significant amounts of private capital to finance large, irreversible, non-marginal projects whose returns are ex ante unknowable, given the existing economic structure, and recoverable only over the long run. Once these real world conditions are recognized as facts of economic life, the Japanese rationale for targeting critical input industries appears more compelling.

Take, for example, the case of the Japanese steel industry in the 1950s. Because steel was an important intermediate input produced with economies of scale, policies to promote rapid expansion of high-quality domestic steel resulted in lower prices and reduced costs for steel-using industries. This encouraged the expansion of these industries, which in turn fed back into further expansion of the steel industry and still lower costs. This virtuous interdependence between the steel industry and downstream users gave rise to a true externality—private increasing returns in the steel industry resulting in social increasing returns in the downstream user industries. Krugman (1987) has recently coined the phrase "linkage externality" to apply to this type of spillover effect resulting from increasing returns in the production of inputs and their effects on the costs of downstream producers. Such a notion underlies arguments in favor of policies to promote infrastructure in the usual sense of transportation and communications networks.

In the Japanese case, infrastructure was and continues to be more broadly defined to encompass industries whose outputs are not geographically restricted, as national transportation and communications networks are, but are tradable. For such products, the standard economic presumption is that there is no need for a national industry policy: domestic users of freely tradable inputs will benefit from linkage externalities in the world markets for these inputs. Thus Japan did not need to promote its own steel industry as long as user industries in Japan could obtain steel from foreign suppliers, whose costs and prices would fall as the demand from these industries expanded. Since the world steel industry in the 1950s and 1960s could hardly be called competitive, and since restrictive state policies on domestic steel production throughout the world hindered the free flow of steel products across national frontiers, the Japanese targeting of its domestic steel industry cannot be dismissed as a policy mistake on theoretical grounds alone. Instead, detailed empirical work is required of a kind that is very difficult to do, and that neither the skeptics nor the believers in the wisdom of Japanese industrial policy have tried to do. Thus the question about the wisdom of Japan's market-promoting industrial policy in this industry remains open. Correct answers depend not on theoretical assertions but on the market realities of the time.

In recent years, Japanese market-promoting policies have concentrated on high-technology sectors, such as semiconductors, computers, and telecommunications. The Japanese view these industries, like steel and shipbuilding in the past, as providing infrastructure on which the future competitive success of a variety of sectors depends. A policy of promoting R&D, investment, and growth in these new "infrastructural" activities is viewed as generating beneficial effects throughout the economy. As the arguments above make clear, these industries certainly satisfy some of the conditions required for a linkage-externality argument for market-promoting policies. Seen from a narrow perspective, they provide inputs for production throughout a broad spectrum of the economy, and they enjoy both dynamic and static increasing returns. Indeed, increasing returns have been nothing short of spectacular in semiconductor production in the last decade, with spillover effects or increasing returns in related computer and telecommunications equipment. Private increasing returns in this complex of industries, in turn, are the basis for social increasing returns throughout the economy, as the standard linkage-externality argument suggests.

Even if one discounts the linkage externalities of these high-technology industries, standard externality arguments about the returns to R&D and innovation provide a traditional case for market-promoting policies. Economists generally focus externality arguments of this variety on the issue of appropriability.[13] As long as the returns to in-novation and R&D are appropriable, there is no divergence between private returns and social returns and hence no rationale for policy intervention. In the context of discussions about national industrial policy and high-tech industries, the issue of appropriability can be better understood by examining different kinds of knowledge generated by R&D and innovation. Three kinds of knowledge, all of which are pres-ent in the high-tech electronics industries, can be distinguished: knowl-edge, such as production process knowledge reflected in firm-specific learning curves, that can be internalized within a firm; knowledge, such as knowledge of product design, that can be reverse-engineered and, once generated, is available internationally; and knowledge that spreads beyond the firm but not very easily beyond national or sometimes even regional boundaries (Krugman 1987). This third kind of knowledge seems to be the reason behind the development of geographically con-centrated "high-technology centers," where information is embodied in people and transmitted through social and academic networks rather than mediated through the price system.

The economic literature on innovation and diffusion has focused on the second kind of knowledge—knowledge that is only partly ap-propriable by the innovating firm. For such knowledge, the evidence suggests overwhelmingly that social returns to R&D and innovation are significantly greater than the private returns, and this is the most widely accepted rationale among economists for government support for R&D. The argument is particularly powerful for basic R&D, which by its nature is likely to generate knowledge whose benefits extend widely beyond the innovating firm.

Discussions of the spillover effects of R&D did not usually address the issue of the geographical concentration or dispersion of knowledge. Recently, however, both because of the apparent tendency of high-technology firms to cluster together in distinct communities and because of concern about the extent and pace at which technological knowledge diffuses across national boundaries, the issue has received considerable attention. Of particular interest to the questions of how policy creates national advantage in trade is the idea that government support for R&D and innovation helps to create a national pool of in-novative talent. The history of technological change in a variety of industries and nations indicates that technological change both supports and is supported by the creation of an ability to innovate embodied in a pool of specialized knowledge and a specialized labor force. By its nature, this ability is not easily contained within firms or sectors but is much more easily contained within national boundaries. A nation that promotes R&D and investment in its high-tech industries is encouraging the development of a highly skilled pool of innovative talent, which in the long run, given the mobility of goods, technology, and capital across national borders, may be the single most important factor on which national competitive advantage rests.

A general lesson suggested by this line of analysis is that there is no natural pace of innovation and diffusion in an industry or in a nation. Because of the uncertainty and risk surrounding these activities and the limits on appropriability of the returns involved, performance depends critically on a variety of institutional factors, including government policies, firm and market structure, the links between business and higher education, and the availability of different kinds of finance.[14] These are the background factors that are traditionally overlooked in much economic analysis, but to overlook them at the level of policy formation is to overlook the possibility that political and institutional reform can have a powerful effect on competitive success in research-intensive activities.

Finally, if high-technology industries are strategic because of their linkage and knowledge externalities, they are also strategic in the sense that they are characterized by imperfect competition. By any common measure of market structure, most segments of the semiconductor, computer, and telecommunications equipment industries are best characterized as dynamic oligopolies.[15] A variety of characteristics—including significant learning-curve economies and the advantages they yield to early entrants, product heterogeneity based on changing technological positions and changing product standards, the importance of marketing-distribution channels to market penetration, and implicit or explicit preferential or protectionist treatment for domestic producers in many national environments, most notably the Japanese—cause these industries to diverge sharply from the competitive model.

From the point of view of U.S. firms and U.S. policymakers, the concentrated nature of these industries, the vertical linkages among them, and the government's role in coordinating joint activities among them in Japan are cause for particular concern.[16] The Japanese computer industry consists of three large firms (Fujitsu, NEC, and Hitachi) that are also three of Japan's four largest semiconductor producers. These same firms control more than two-thirds of all telecommunications equipment production in Japan and dominate domestic and global markets in many consumer electronics items. They are also tightly linked to the largest Japanese producers of semiconductor capital equipment (Ferguson 1985). Given this market structure, it is reasonable to conclude that even in the absence of promotional policy measures, U.S. firms as sellers would face significant barriers to market entry in Japan, and that U.S. firms as buyers would be unable to purchase frontier technology inputs from Japanese producers to compete with the same producers in downstream, higher value-added product markets. Both conclusions are consistent with the case study results of the Berkeley Roundtable on the International Economy (BRIE) on U.S.–Japanese competition in semiconductors and telecommunications.[17] This study also reveals an important role for promotional-protectionist policies—ranging from those favoring the consumer-electronics industry in the 1960s to those aimed at the semiconductor and computer industries in the 1970s and 1980s—in creating the competitive advantage of Japanese firms in both Japanese and world markets.[18]

The constellation of arguments indicating the "strategic" nature of high-technology industries provides a powerful prima facie case in support of market-promoting policies of the Japanese variety. The evidence suggesting that the competitive strength of Japanese producers in these industries has been bolstered by these policies to the disadvantage of U.S. producers indicates that this case should be treated seriously in U.S. policy discussions of whether and how the United States should respond. It is not enough to argue glibly that closure of the Japanese market to U.S. firms simply worsens consumer welfare in Japan, or that Japanese promotional policies simply lower prices to U.S. consumers, with a net welfare gain for us. These policy prescriptions apply only in a static, perfectly competitive world without adjustment costs and without externalities, a world which does not fit the high-technology industries. As both the new trade theory and the case study evidence documented by BRIE and other research groups indicate, the correct policy prescription is much less certain—it all depends on many factors, including the nature and size of the market externalities and imperfections involved and the kinds of policy measures considered. It is time that these issues rather than the traditional theory or ideology of perfectly competitive markets inform U.S. policy.

CONCLUSIONS

The U.S. economy is confronting a crisis in its international competitive position. The staggering trade deficits of the last several years and the foreign borrowing that has financed them cannot be sustained over the long run. At some point during the next few years, the U.S. trade position will have to adjust dramatically, with profound consequences for the level and composition of production and employment at home and abroad. Both domestic and foreign policymakers will have to grapple with ways to improve U.S. export performance and to reduce U.S. import dependence. Macroeconomic policy choices will play a critical role in these adjustments, as they did in the spectacular erosion in the U.S. trade deficit after 1982. Given the magnitude of the adjustment required and the underlying, longer term weaknesses in U.S. productivity performance, however, reliance on macroeconomic policy alone will prove risky. Reliance on exchange-rate corrections, with or without a deceleration in U.S. growth rates compared to growth rates abroad, runs the risk of higher inflation rates and recessionary conditions—or more likely a combination of both—in the United States and in the rest of the world.

The adjustment process can be made easier by policies that improve the underlying competitiveness of U.S. producers. Higher productivity growth, better quality products, and innovations in product and process technology, like exchange-rate adjustments and a recession in domestic demand, can improve the U.S. trade imbalance, but with a far lower cost in relative living standards and in foregone output and consumption in the United States. What is needed to make the required adjustment of the U.S. trade position less costly is the development of a national competitiveness policy. Such a policy would represent the true realization of the supply-side objectives of the late 1970s, rather than the distortion of such objectives as a result of the "supply-side" fiscal policies of the last six years.

A national competitiveness policy would have many parts linked by a common objective of strengthening the competitive position of U.S. producers in world markets over the long run. Among the most important parts would be policies to promote R&D and the diffusion of new commercial technologies, policies to improve the quality and flexibility of the work force, policies to increase industrial investment, policies to augment export incentives, policies to open closed foreign markets, and policies to speed the transition of resources from declining firms, sectors, and regions to expanding ones. Although the precise form of the policies fashioned to realize these goals requires more study, a few fundamental conclusions are already apparent.

First, the process of strengthening the competitiveness of the U.S. economy is a long-term one. There are no quick fixes. Just as the erosion in the U.S. competitive position was a long-run phenomenon reflecting years of policy inattention and failure, any improvement from changes in policy will be realized only gradually. The danger is that policymakers frustrated by the apparent lack of success of prudent measures may adopt misguided policies of protection that may improve the trade balance quickly but will undermine real competitiveness in the long run.

Second, the unprecedented explosion of U.S. trade deficits and U.S. debt during the last several years makes policies to improve competitiveness even more critical to future living standards. During the next several years, the United States will gradually have to scale down its trade deficit, at some point generating a trade surplus to service outstanding debt. To the extent that the United States relies on a continued drop in the dollar's value, a continued slowdown or decline in real wages, protectionism, or recessionary conditions at home to achieve the required trade adjustment, the real incomes of U.S. citizens will suffer. In contrast, to the extent that the United States is able to improve its productivity and enhance its technological performance, it will be able to finance debt repayment not out of future consumption and income levels but out of additional output and income growth and an improved competitive position.

Third, the effects of policies to restore U.S. competitiveness over the long run can be undermined by misguided macroeconomic policies. During the 1980–1985 period, macroeconomic conditions were the major cause of the dollar's appreciation and its disastrous consequences on the competitive positions of U.S. producers. Such consequences are not easily or costlessly reversible, as the period of the dollar's decline since the end of 1985 demonstrates. Because many foreign suppliers expanded their capacity to satisfy the U.S. market, because many domestic suppliers offshored or subcontracted more of their production abroad, and because domestic consumers changed their tastes toward new, previously unknown and unavailable foreign goods, the protracted decline in the dollar has had a smaller effect on the competitiveness of U.S. producers than would have been the case under earlier supply-and-demand conditions.

The experience of the first half of the 1980s indicates that the restoration of macroeconomic balance in the U.S. economy is a necessary condition for an improvement in U.S. competitiveness over the long run. America can no longer afford another bout of the "American disease" of this period—that is, adopting macro policies that push national spending above national income, draw in foreign capital, drive up the dollar's value, and undermine the competitive health of U.S. producers.

Fourth, in addition to adopting its own agenda of competitiveness policies at home, the United States should take a more active leadership role in forging cooperative efforts to modify the international financial and trading regimes so that pressing, unresolved problems may be addressed. In the first half of the 1980s, as in the past but with potentially more disastrous consequences, U.S. policymakers exhibited "a serene irresponsibility" to the effects of U.S. policy on economic conditions in the rest of the world and on the viability of the international trading and financial system (Schmidt 1985). Instead of fashioning policies of greater international coordination and negotiation to cope with the costs and reap the potential benefits of growing economic interdependence, the United States under Reagan's leadership set out to reassert U.S. autonomy in economic as well as in military affairs, unmindful of the constraints posed by growing economic interdependence.

As a result of a vacuum in world economic leadership, serious problems have been left unresolved, threatening the existing system. Violations of existing rules of international trade have become more widespread. Existing rules have not been modified to fit the changing nature of trade in new "technology-wise" conditions. There has been much talk about rules for trade in agriculture and services and about rules for foreign direct investment, but little action. The debt crisis has been left to fester in the Third World, with deleterious consequences for development prospects and political stability. Recently, there has been some successful coordination of exchange-rate policy by the developed countries, but with no supporting coordination of macro policy. The prospects for continued successful coordination of exchange rates are uncertain.

Without coordinated efforts by the developed countries to confront such problems, competitiveness policies in the United States are likely to be viewed by others as part of a zero-sum-game strategy—a "beggar thy neighbor" approach to improve national economic welfare at the expense of one's trading partners. Such policies by themselves in no way guarantee a growing world economy that would allow for an improvement in the U.S. trade position without the destruction of employment and production in the many countries with which the United States currently runs a trade deficit.

Fifth, in designing a national competitiveness policy, questions about whether industry-specific measures should be adopted must be taken seriously. At the very least, new ideas about the strategic nature of certain economic activities suggest that there are no simple, off-the-cuff answers to such questions. Empirical evidence, specific to the industry in question and to the policy measures proposed, must replace simple theoretical or ideological arguments as a guide to policy formation. Even with this replacement, uncertainty about the correct policies will persist because of the market and technological uncertainties that are an endemic feature of high-technology industries. Because of these uncertainties, and because the potential national losses stemming from continued losses in the international competitive position of these industries are large, it might be better to err in the direction of introducing policies when they are not needed than in the direction of overlooking policies when they are.

NOTES

1. This definition is similar to the definition adopted in the 1985 Report of the President's Commission on Industrial Competitiveness (Cohen et al. 1985) and more recently by the Council on Competitiveness (1987).
2. For evidence on the long-term erosion in the U.S. competitive position, see Cohen et al. 1984 and the report by the Council on Competitiveness (1987).
3. A similar conclusion is reached in recent articles by Thurow and Tyson (1987) and Krugman and Baldwin (1987).
4. For evidence on the extent and causes of the decline in productivity growth, see Baumol and McLennan 1985.
5. For evidence on the effects of trade on U.S. manufacturing employment, see the essays in Tyson, Dickens, and Zysman (forthcoming).
6. According to a recent study by the Office of Technology Assessment (1986), about 25 percent of the U.S. GNP is made up of services that provide inputs to the U.S. manufacturing sector. This suggests that, taken together, manufacturing and services tightly linked to manufacturing still account for a little less than 50 percent of the U.S. GNP.
7. This section draws heavily on an earlier discussion by the author appearing in Lipsey and Dobson 1987.
8. For an extended discussion of the role of government policy in shaping competitive advantage at the macro level, see the works of Thurow (1986) and Scott (1985) and the President's Commission on Industrial Competitiveness (Cohen et al. 1984).

44   INTRODUCTION

9. For evidence on the role of Japanese policy in the competitive successes
    of Japanese producers in world markets, see the works by Johnson
    (1983), Yamamura (1982, 1986), Zysman et al. (1984), Borrus, Tyson,
    and Zysman (1986), Borrus, Millstein, and Zysman (1983), and Borrus
    et al. (1985).

10. In economic terminology, "static economies of scale" arise when an
    increase in inputs results in a more than proportionate increase in output,
    so that average cost per unit falls as output levels increase. "Dynamic
    economies of scale" arise when average cost per unit falls as the cumula-
    tive level of output increases.

11. In economic terminology, "rents" are defined as returns over and above
    the returns that resources would earn in a perfectly competitive market
    system in equilibrium.

12. In addition to the esays contained in Krugman 1986, there are several
    important contributions to the new trade theory literature, including
    Helpman and Krugman 1985, Brander and Spencer 1981 and 1985, and
    Dixit 1984.

13. "Appropriability" means the extent to which the innovator can earn
    or "appropriate" the returns resulting from his innovation. When returns
    are completely appropriable, they accrue to the innovator and hence
    are private returns. When returns are not completely appropriable, a
    portion of them do not accrue to the innovator, in which case private
    returns are less than the total or social returns resulting from the
    innovation.

14. For insightful discussions of the institutional factors that influence the
    pace of innovation and diffusion on different national settings, see
    Nelson 1982.

15. Some of the low-cost, labor-intensive product segments of these indus-
    tries, such as consumer premise telecommunications equipment or
    home computers, might be better understood as examples of monopolis-
    tic competition.

16. For an illuminating discussion of government coordination of Japanese
    semiconductor firms and their vertical structure, see Yamamura 1986,
    Borrus, Tyson, and Zysman 1986 and Borrus, Millstein, and Zysman
    1983.

17. In addition to the studies by BRIE researchers cited above, see the com-
    pelling evidence cited by Ferguson (1986).

18. Yamamura (1986) makes a convincing case that protectionist policies
    toward television producers in Japan had an important effect on the
    growing competitiveness of the Japanese semiconductor industry.
    Baldwin and Krugman (1986) use a simulation model to demonstrate
    that in the absence of protection of the Japanese market, Japanese pro-
    ducers of semiconductors would have been unable to compete against
    U.S. producers in world markets.

REFERENCES

Baldwin, Richard, and Paul Krugman. 1986. "Market Access and International Competition: A Simulation Study of 16K Random Access Memories." National Bureau of Economic Research, Working Paper No. 1936.

Baumol, William J., and Kenneth McLennan. 1985. "U.S. Productivity Performance and its Implications." In *Productivity Growth and U.S. Competitiveness*, edited by William J. Baumol and Kenneth McLennan. New York: Oxford University Press.

Borrus, Michael; James Millstein; and John Zysman. 1983. "*Responses to the Japanese Challenge in High Technology: Innovation, Maturity and U.S.-Japanese Competition in Microelectronics.*" BRIE University of California, Working Paper No. 6.

————; Tyson, Laura; and John Zysman. 1986. "Creating Advantage: How Government Policies Shape International Trade in the Semiconductor Industry." In *Strategic Trade Policy and the New International Economics*, edited by Paul Krugman. Cambridge, Mass.: MIT Press.

Brander, James, and Barbara Spencer. 1981. "Tariffs and the Extraction of Foreign Monopoly Rents under Potential Entry." *Canadian Journal of Economics* 14:371–389.

————. 1985. "Export Subsidies and International Market Share Rivalry." *Journal of International Economics* 18:83–100.

Cohen, Steve, and John Zysman. 1987. *Manufacturing Matters: The Myth of a Post-Industrial Economy.* New York: Basic Books.

————; David Teece; Laura D'Andrea Tyson; and John Zysman. 1984. "Competitiveness." In *Global Competition: The New Reality.* Working Paper of the President's Commission on Industrial Competitiveness, Volume III. Washington, D.C.

Council on Competitiveness. 1987. *America's Competitive Crisis: Confronting the New Reality.* Washington, D.C. (April).

Defense Science Board. 1987. *The Report of the Defense Science Board Task Force on Defense Semicontor Dependency.* Department of Defense (February).

Dixit, Avinash. 1984. "International Trade Policy for Oligopolistic Industries." *Economic Journal Conference Papers* 44:1–16.

Drucker, Peter. 1986. "The Changed World Economy." *Foreign Affairs* 64, no. 4 (Spring).

Economic Policy Institute. 1986. *Family Incomes in Trouble.* Washington, D.C. (October).

Federal Reserve Bank of Cleveland. 1987. *Economic Trends* (May).

Ferguson, Charles. 1985. "Strategic Technologies and Strategic Interactions: Economic Policy in the Face of High Technology Decline." Paper presented at the meetings of the American Political Science Association, Washington, D.C.

Helpman, Elhanen, and Paul Krugman. 1985. *Market Structure and Foreign Trade.* Cambridge, Mass.: MIT Press.

Krugman, Paul. 1985. "Comments on Obstfeld Paper," *Brookings Papers on Economic Activity*, No. 2.

———. 1986. "Introduction: New Thinking about Trade Policy. In *"Strategic Trade Policy and the New International Economics*, edited by Paul Krugman. Cambridge, Mass.: MIT Press.

———. 1987. "Strategic Sectors and International Competition." In *U.S. Trade Policies in a Changing World Economy*, edited by Robert M. Stern. Cambridge, Mass.: MIT Press.

———, and Robert Baldwin. 1987. "The Persistence of the U.S. Trade Deficit." *Brookings Papers on Economic Activity*, No. 1:1–56.

Johnson, Chalmers. 1983. *MITI and the Japanese Miracle.* Stanford, Calif.: Stanford University Press.

Leontief, Wassily, and Faye Duchin. 1985. *Automation, the Changing Pattern of U.S. Exports and Imports and their Implications for Employment.* New York: Institute for Economic Analysis.

Lipsey, Richard, and Wendy Dobson. 1987. *Shaping Comparative Advantage.* Ontario: Prentice-Hall Canada.

Nelson, Richard. 1982. *Government and Technical Progress: A Cross-Country Analysis.* New York: Pergamon Press.

Schmidt, Helmut. 1985. *A Grand Strategy for the West.* New Haven: Yale University Press.

Scott, Bruce R. 1985. "U.S. Competitiveness." In *U.S. Competitiveness in the World Economy*, edited by Bruce R. Scott and George C. Lodge. Boston: Harvard Business School Press.

Stowsky, Jay. 1986. "Beating Our Plowshares into Double-edged Swords: The Impact of Pentagon Policies on the Commercialization of Advanced Technologies." University of California, BRIE Working Paper No. 17.

Thurow, Lester. 1986. "A General Tendency Toward Inequality." In *American Economic Review, Papers and Proceedings* 76, no. 3 (May).

———, and Laura D'Andrea Tyson. 1987. "The Economic Black Hole." *Foreign Policy* no. 67 (Summer).

Teece, David J. 1986. "Profiting from Technological Innovation." *Research Policy*, 15, no. 6.

Tyson, Laura D'Andrea; William T. Dickens; and John Zysman. In *The Dynamics of Trade and Employment*, edited by Laura D'Andrea Tyson, William T. Dickens, and John Zysman. Cambridge, Mass.: Ballinger. Forthcoming.

United States Department of Commerce, International Trade Administration. 1986. *United States Trade: Performance in 1985 and Outlook*. Washington, D.C.: Government Printing Office.

World Bank. 1985. *World Development Report*, 1985. New York: Oxford University Press.

Yamamura, Kozo, ed. 1982. *Policy and Trade Issues of the Japanese Economy*. Seattle: University of Washington Press.

―――. 1986. "Caveat Emptor: The Industrial Policy of Japan." In *Strategic Trade Policy and the New International Economics*, edited by Paul Krugman. Cambridge, Mass.: MIT Press.

Zysman, John, and Laura Tyson. 1984. "The U.S. and Japanese Trade and Industrial Policies." University of California, BRIE Working Paper No. 2.

II LEARNING FROM EXPERIENCE

3 COMPETITION AND COOPERATION
Learning From Japan

Ezra F. Vogel

Many people who enjoy the American quality of life and realize how comfortable it is compared to others in the world, are under the illusion that it can be sheltered from disruptive or competing forces and preserved indefinitely. But, we have entered the age of international trade and commerce, where the know-how of industry, one time the exclusive ownership of Europe and North America, has spread to East Asia and, there, it has risen to greater and higher standards of productivity, efficiency, quality, and reliability.

A year ago, in early 1985, our president's Commission on Industrial Competitiveness, headed by John Young of Hewlett-Packard, delivered a report on the problems of the American competitive position in the world markets. It concluded that the United States is confronting a very serious erosion of its competitiveness, and that, since this condition affects the country's ability to meet its national goals, it must be addressed with haste. Yet, in Washington, the report has been basically shelved. Perhaps that happened because it is easier to focus on our wonderful achievements than face the erosion of our scientific superiority, worry about our manufacturing capacity and financial security, or cope with the realization that we must borrow heavily from other countries to sustain our standard of living.

Addressing the problems related to our declining competitiveness requires new thinking at odds with three cherished ideas. First, the powerful and attractive idea that one should leave things to the free market. This idea has served us well in the past.

After World War II, the United States enjoyed an unusual era of economic supremacy as a consequence of the destruction of the major industrial economies and the high concentration of scientists attracted by our free and open American society. These conditions, combined with our industrial ingenuity and know-how, allowed us to rule the world in science, technology, capital, and industrial productivity. We must recognize that this period, brought about by special historical events, has ended. Now, if we are going to maintain a competitive position in the world, we need to work and try harder.

Now, other countries have adopted competitive strategies that develop human resources, concentrate capital, and focus research where it has commercial impact. With these countries, where people work together deliberately to improve competitiveness, the "leave it to the market" approach loses out.

Another cherished idea is that appropriate and timely changes in the exchange rate will solve our problems. The idea is based on the belief that the dollar has been overvalued and, once it is brought back to its proper value, American competitiveness will be restored. Unfortunately, this idea overlooks the fact that industrial production requires a complex organization of business plans and relationships. Many years, sometimes decades, are needed to build the appropriate level of organization and cooperation, and those talents and organizational structures cannot be created in the United States just by changing the exchange rates. We must look at facts squarely. In 1971, the U.S. dollar bought 360 yen. In 1985, it bought about 240 to 260 yen.

While the yen appreciated about 50 percent over those fourteen years, the Japanese have become more rather than less competitive, and our trade balance has worsened rather than improved. Today our dollar buys about 170 yen. Some people estimate that it will soon buy 150 or 160 yen. The appreciation of the yen relative to the dollar is due to the fact that Japan has become more productive and more competitive. Therefore, to buy the same goods now that we were buying fifteen years ago, we must work harder. Or, to put it in another way, it takes about twice as much American labor and productive effort to buy what we used to import from Japan. The dollar exchange rate with the yen simply reflects an adjustment to the realities of competitiveness and cannot, alone, solve our problems.

A third notion that requires rethinking is the traditional view that economic power stems from a geopolitical base. That is, we believe that countries with abundant natural resources and large geographical areas are likely to prevail in the economic contest. While this notion is firmly rooted in historical evidence, it is no longer valid in today's world. The Middle Eastern countries have the greatest petroleum resources, and yet they do not have world power. The military power of the Soviet Union does not produce commensurate economic influence among the countries of the world. In Asia, for example, one sees very little Soviet influence, and the Soviet Union is considered a "has-been." Latin America, Eastern Europe, and Africa are increasingly looking to East Asia as the hub of new ideas, trained human resources, and economic power. Japan is about the size of Montana, yet through an appropriate development of human resources and technological know-how, it has become the great power of our times. In the information age, the United States can no longer rely on petroleum, other natural resources, a large geographical area, and the efficiency of its agriculture to maintain world supremacy. Its efforts must focus on the development and wise utilization of human resources and science and technology. This requires high levels of cooperation. Since the intellectual breadth to deal with the complex tasks of our times does not reside in any one individual, many people with varied and broad backgrounds must work together.

As a Japan specialist, I have followed that country since 1958. Also, I have tried to follow developments in Taiwan, South Korea, Hong Kong, Singapore, and mainland China. When I first went to Japan in 1958, the United States was so far ahead that the problem of future competition did not even occur to me. And I was just as wrong as those other observers who underestimated what was in store for us in East Asia.

I remember coming back to Japan in 1963, after an absence of three years, and observing the progress that had taken place in Tokyo during that time. One night around midnight, walking to my hotel, I noticed everywhere frantic construction activity. Japan was getting ready for the 1964 Olympics. The whole country was trying to change its image from a military power of World War II into a modern, peace-loving country in step with the times. They were building new subways, new hotels, new convention centers. Even six months before the Olympics were scheduled to begin, it was standard procedure to have three construction crews working around the clock. Where I used to live back in 1958, they had chopped down all the buildings on both sides of the old street, and even though it was not one of the major Tokyo thoroughfares, they were widening it for about seven miles. Back then, it was easy to dismiss this Japanese determination as no more than preparation for the prestigious Olympics. But the energy I saw in 1963 and 1964 did not die after the Olympics. It went on, and we continued to underestimate Japanese achievements.

I remember in the early fifties we were saying, "Well, the Japanese make junk goods but not high-quality products," and later, "Well, they can make little transistor radios, but not bigger items like television sets." When we had to recognize that they could make television sets, we believed that they would not know how to produce steel. And when they competed successfully with our steel industry or, later, in our auto market, we felt that high technology was out of their reach. Now, they have established themselves in the computer hardware field, but we choose to believe that they cannot do as well in the software market, or that they will fall behind in inventiveness and creativity. As a student of Japan, I can predict that those expecting the Japanese not to excel in software, in R&D, or in the service sector will be just as surprised as those earlier forecasters who thought that the Japanese could not compete in manufacturing.

Are these market successes the result of superior characteristics of the Japanese people? The people of any nation whose economy is doing well are likely to attribute their successes to inherent qualities entrenched in their country's history. When U.S. economic power was at its peak, we felt that our democracy and our past gave us an unbeatable edge over the rest of the world. Now, many Japanese believe that their hard work, better craftsmanship, discipline, and cooperation are innate characteristics dating far back into Japanese history. I, for one, do not believe that explains current Japanese success. Nor do I believe that Americans are inherently lazy, since the work ethic is not alien to the American tradition. What has happened in Japan is the result of a concentrated effort in catching up. That effort became particularly intense after World War II when the loss of its colonies left Japan practically without resources. A population growth from 30 million in the late 1860s to 90 million in the 1980s demanded that the country provide more food. As they became more dependent on the rest of the world for food and resources, Japanese became more determined to achieve world competitiveness so that they could import basic necessities. Japanese determination to achieve competitiveness shaped its institutions, organizations, and human resources.

Is Japanese success likely to continue? Not only will it continue, but it is likely to become greater in at least three areas. First is the manufacturing area. A new industrial transformation is now taking shape in the economically advanced countries of the world, one that results from the matching of electronic wizardry with the manufacturing process. After going to Japan every year for the past twenty years to observe all types of socioeconomic organizations, I can say that what is happening in that country fits the term "new industrial revolution." Within a period of fifteen to twenty years, I expect that most Japanese factories will be operating with very few industrial workers. Already, the Japanese are putting in place as many robots as the rest of the world combined; but more important than using robots, they are shaping their organizations to make them capable of promoting and maintaining technological progress. American engineers have observed that the Japanese are good not only at new product design but at implementing change all the way down to the production line. This is so because Japanese engineers are often stationed on the production line and from there generate continuous improvements in the manufacturing process.

Another reason why the Japanese are likely to continue their lead in new manufacturing processes is that they graduate about 50 percent more electrical engineers than we do in the United States and place a higher proportion of graduates in the manufacturing sector. In the United States most engineers are attracted to the high-tech and modern software service sectors, but not to basic manufacturing.

Japanese success in manufacturing is also the result of their ability to manage change. Since many of the industrial improvements in the West over the past 100 years have in Japan been made in the last twenty to thirty years, the Japanese managers now in charge have experienced several rounds of organizational and technological change. They have learned through their own experience how to pace layoffs and job reassignments, or how to structure the pay system so that, when new technology is introduced, people can switch jobs without fear of unemployment.

It may well be fifteen to twenty years before some of these new technologies have eliminated most of the work force, but in some of the more advanced factories in Japan, one can already see the change taking place. In the recently updated assembly lines, most of the work has been automated. One can push a few buttons to send materials from a warehouse to an unmanned vehicle, which transport them to the appropriate manufacturing process. Other buttons control the transfer of work in progress from one machine to another. More buttons determine how the work is to be machined or processed and, finally, sent to the shipping room, without ever being touched by human hands.

In a couple of factories I visited last summer, companies with roughly 1,000 workers had a ten-year plan to gradually introduce new technology. About 100 workers were removed from the assembly line each year, either because of attrition or reassignment to other positions in manufacturing, marketing, or sales. Over the ten-year period, most employees were going to be eliminated.

In ten to twenty years the work force in Japanese manufacturing will probably be 5 to 10 percent of the total labor force, or less. It is now about 30 percent. In the United States in the late nineteenth century, most of our people were employed in agriculture. Now, only 3 percent of the labor force is employed in that sector, but it produces enough food for the United States and a 30 percent surplus for the rest of the world. After the new industrial revolution, the Japanese may produce enough manufactured products for themselves and for much of the rest of the world, while employing very few workers in factories.

Another reason accounting for the Japanese manufacturing edge is the cost of capital. Simply, it costs the American entrepreneur several percentage points more to invest, and therefore, he or she must generate far higher profit margins. Japanese banks, which lend most of the money, have a longer term perspective than America's stock markets. Under these circumstances, Japanese business people are likely to make more investments in new technology and equipment than their American counterparts.

The service sector is the second area most likely to be affected by the Japanese advances. News about the preeminence of Japan in this sector is just beginning to appear in the business literature. Back in the 1970s, when the Japanese were doing well in heavy industry, strategists from their Ministry of International Trade and Industry (MITI) and from the private sector began discussing the performance of the Japanese economy ten, fifteen, and twenty years into the future. Naturally, they saw the opportunities emerging around the world in the service industry. Resources were targeted to exploit those opportunities, and we are now seeing the payoff of those early decisions. In the past five years, Japanese names have appeared in the worlds of fashion, entertainment, television, cosmetics, construction, consulting, insurance, advertising, and above all, in financial services. The Japanese companies in all these areas are becoming the largest in the world. Not only is Nomura the largest securities company in the world, but it owns about $10 billion more in assets than Merrill-Lynch, Shearson Lehman Brothers, and Solomon Brothers combined.

The six largest trading companies in the world are all Japanese. And in advertising, the largest company in the world is now Dentsu of Japan. A similar situation exists in banking. Of course, there are different ways to measure a firm's size, and this ranking may be challenged, depending on the type of measurement used, but the top ten banks in the world are Japanese. There is no doubt that the Japanese are creating in the service sector the same kind of strength they have gained in the manufacturing area. The same intensity, the same determination, and the same kind of cooperative effort and overall perspective they once used successfully to conquer the markets of manufactured goods, are being used to attain supremacy in the financial markets.

One bottleneck for the Japanese expansion in the service sector has been the absence of efficient typewriters. Because there are about 2,000 characters in the Japanese language, until recently huge typewriters with about 2,000 characters had to be used. It took a typist about six months to learn their operation. The machines were also terribly expensive and therefore not commonly used. With the advent of electronically assisted word processing, it is now possible to enter a syllable in one stroke of the key and produce written documents with speed and efficiency. This has caused a revolution in the Japanese office structure and terminated the inefficiency of their offices. The service sector will be taking advantage of this development to fuel its rapid expansion.

Another aspect of the Japanese strength that Westerners are underestimating is the strategic importance of the linkages between the manufacturing and service sectors. Rather than decreasing manufacturing activity because higher value-added is realized in the service sector, in Japan, the two sectors are linked, to enhance the strength of both. For instance, when a Japanese factory comes to the United States, it will use a Japanese construction company and Japanese banks. Therefore, the Japanese manufacturing advantage is creating the preconditions for domination in the service sector.

Research and development is the third area undergirding the continuing commercial success of Japan. It has been customary and comfortable to say: "Look at the Nobel Prizes, look at the number of research ideas, look at how much the Japanese have copied, look how many people are sent from Japan to study in the United States." These are true statements. During their catching-up period, the Japanese have looked to the West to borrow the products of R&D. In 1970 Japan spent about one percent of its gross national product (GNP) on R&D. In 1980 R&D expenditures had grown to 2 percent of the value of its national output. R&D was expected to become 3 percent of GNP in 1990. Recently, that forecast was changed to 3.5 percent, and extrapolating from present data, the Japanese are right on target. America has been spending approximately 2.7 to 2.8 percent of GNP on R&D.

Due to the fact that the U.S. economy is roughly twice as large as the Japanese economy, this country is still spending more on R&D in absolute totals. A very high proportion of our expenditures, however, is allocated to defense-related research, and while in the 1960s and 1970s military expenditures had tremendous spin-offs into commercial products, the highly specialized nature of the military technology presently being promoted is producing relatively fewer applications in the private sector.

What is happening now in R&D is similar to what took place in the 1950s in steel production. While the Japanese were building state-of-the-art steel plants, we had on hand a large stock of mature steel companies. We now have a large number of aging laboratories, while the Japanese are introducing state-of-the-art facilities to answer the new research questions of the late eighties and nineties. Also, it may be true that American venture companies may still precede their Japanese counterparts in many discoveries, but the limited availability of capital in this country is likely to delay the commercialization of the new technology. The Japanese will be able to buy those innovating companies and rapidly utilize the new ideas in the marketplace. So we must not take consolation from the simple fact that we have creative new companies, and we must find ways to hasten the use of that creativity.

In discussing competition, one should not ignore the importance of "cooperation," for issues are complex and require people in different sectors to work together. To deal effectively with the issues raised by Japanese competition, we must find new ways of cooperating within and outside the United States.

We need cooperation between Americans involved in product engineering and Americans involved in manufacturing. We need cooperation between production and marketing, and between management and workers.

We have made good progress—at the state and local levels more than at the national level—in cooperation between government and industry. Universities must join in, as they did in the nineteenth century, when agricultural colleges developed new solutions for agriculture. This time, we must have greater and closer linkages in the United States between government, industry, and universities.

In spite of the competition, we should not shy away from continued cooperation with Japan. In the past, many joint ventures of American and Japanese companies have not gone well. The Japanese have often taken technology they learned in America and sent it back to us, creating what the Japanese now call the "boomerang effect." But the reasons why these joint ventures have not prospered need to be examined. Perhaps the Japanese were too focused on market strategies and took advantage of American companies that were too naive. Often, however, Americans have not put enough effort into learning how to operate with the Japanese, and the control of the joint ventures, therefore, went by default to the Japanese. For instance, while much of the production work was done by Japanese workers, using the Japanese language, we did not have Americans at the factory site who were conversant with the language and the Japanese firm's environment. We need to place a greater emphasis not only on training people in the Japanese language, literature, and history but, more generally, on preparing them to operate effectively in the hypercompetitive global environment, as well as to monitor the Japanese technical and commercial evolution.

Before World War II, the United States trained its Ph.D. students in the German and French languages to enable them to follow the European scientific literature. After World War II, most publications were written in English, and we lost the incentive to monitor foreign journals. It is true that most Japanese scientific literature is available in English and that much of the rest can be translated, but to follow the latest developments within Japanese companies and laboratories, more Americans need to learn the language and become part of the personal networks that link Japanese scientists.

Although we live in a competitive environment, we are not at war. This fundamental difference must be recognized if we are to successfully manage this complex relationship with Japan as our ally, friend, and competitor.

SELECTED BIBLIOGRAPHY ON JAPANESE BUSINESS, GOVERNMENT-BUSINESS RELATIONS, AND NATIONAL ECONOMIC STRATEGY

Abeggien, James C., and George Stalk, Jr. 1985. *Kaisha: The Japanese Corporation*. New York: Basic Books. An analysis of marketing, capital, and manpower strategy by long-time business consultants.

Bronte, Stephen. 1982. *Japanese Finance*. London: Euromoney Publications. An analysis of Japanese financial markets and their institutions.

Clark, Rodney. 1979. *The Japanese Company*. New Haven, Conn.: Yale, University Press. An analysis of the Japanese company and company networks, by a social scientist turned businessman.

Cole, Robert E. 1979. *Work, Mobility, and Participation*. Berkeley: University of California Press. An analysis of industrial practices, by a social scientist.

Dore, Ronald. 1973. *British Factory#Japanese Factory*. University of California Press. Based on field work in factories in both countries, by a leading social scientist.

Fields, George. 1983. *From Bonsai to Levi's*. New York: Macmillan. Accounts by an experienced American advertiser in Japan.

Hirschmeier, Johannes, and Tsunehito Yui. 1981. *The Development of Japanese Business*. London: Allen and Unwin. A historical overview.

Johnson, Chalmers. 1982. *MITI and the Japanese Miracle*. Stanford, Calif.: Stanford University Press. A historical account of the organizational and personal changes in what is now the Ministry of International Trade and Industry.

Kaplan, Eugene. 1972. *Japan: The Government-Business Relationship*. U.S. Department of Commerce. An introductory guide for American businessmen, drawing on work by the Boston Consulting Group.

Magaziner, Ira C., and Thomas M. Hout. 1980. *Japanese Industrial Policy*. London: Policy Studies Institute. An analysis of several key industrial sectors, by business consultants.

Ojimi, Y. 1972. *The Industrial Policy of Japan*. Paris: Organization for Economic Cooperation and Development. The classic statement of Japanese industrial policy, prepared by MITI upon joining the OECD.

Patrick, Hugh, and Henry Rosovsky, eds. 1976. *Asia's New Giant*. Washington, D.C.: The Brookings Institution. A collection of analyses by pairs of leading American and Japanese economists.

Pempel, T. J.. 1977. *Policymaking in Contemporary Japan*. Ithaca, N.Y.: Cornell University Press. The role of political and bureaucratic leaders in certain key areas.

Reischauer, Edwin O. 1977. *The Japanese*. Cambridge, Mass.: Harvard University Press. An overview of the Japanese by a leading historian who served as ambassador to Japan in the early 1960s.

Rohlen, Thomas. 1974. *For Harmony and Strength*. Berkeley: University of California Press. An account of life in a Japanese bank.

Rohlen, Thomas. 1983. *Japan's High Schools*. Berkeley: University of California Press. An account of Japanese high school education, with consideration of education's role in preparing adults for society.

Schonberger, Richard. 1982. *Japanese Manufacturing Techniques*. New York: Free Press. An account by an American industrial engineer.

Scott, Bruce R., and George C. Lodge. 1985. *U.S. Competitiveness in the World Economy*. Boston: Harvard Business School. A collection of papers from a Harvard Business School colloquium on the international competitive environment, especially regarding Japan and East Asia.

Taylor, Jared. 1983. *Shadows of the Rising Sun*. New York: William Morrow & Co. A critical view of Japan by an American businessman who grew up in Japan as a child of missionaries.

Vogel, Ezra F. 1985. *Comeback*. New York: Simon and Schuster. Includes an account of Japanese shipbuilding, machine tools, coal retrenchment, and information industry sectors.

Vogel, Ezra F. 1979. *Japan as Number One*. New York: Harper & Row. An effort to explain the social, political, and economic basis of Japanese success.

Yoshino, M. Y., and Thomas Lifson. 1986. *The Invisible Link*. Cambridge, Mass.: MIT Press. A study of the general trading company by two business school professors.

4 THE FOURTH INDUSTRIAL REVOLUTION AND AMERICAN SOCIETY
Some Reflections on the Past for the Future

Walt W. Rostow

I am engaged in an effort to elaborate a final statement of my theory of economic growth. I begin by reviewing theories of growth from the eighteenth century to the present. As I look ahead from that perspective, the hero of the story turns out to be David Hume. As I think you will, in the end, agree, he came closer to defining the central problem of our time than any other economist of the past two-and-a-half centuries.

I shall proceed as follows. First, I will define my notion of the ''Fourth Industrial Revolution''; second, I will briefly relate it to the short-run, familiar economic and security problems we face; third, I will introduce David Hume's 1758 definition of the ''rich country-poor country'' problem and discuss its contemporary relevance. Finally, I shall try to explore the meaning of that central problem for U.S. politics and U.S. society in the widest sense, posing the question: Is the United States capable of making the adjustments required to meet our challenges? I will close with a few words on the implications of this analysis for foreign policy.

THE FOURTH INDUSTRIAL REVOLUTION

Round about the mid-1970s, a technological revolution emerged from invention to innovation. We all know its dimensions; that is, microelectronics and genetic engineering, the new industrial materials, the revolution in communications, lasers, robots, and all the rest.

This is the fourth major grouping of innovations in modern history. The notion that innovations come in groups and clusters has been familiar to economic historians for quite a long time. Joseph Schumpeter seized on and dramatized the phenomenon, which mainstream economists have systematically ignored. It is to be taken seriously, but not too seriously, because not all substantial innovations are to be found in these four clusters. Nevertheless, they are real enough. The first embraced cotton textiles manufactured with machines, the fabrication of good iron with coke rather than charcoal, and Watt's steam engine with a separate condenser, which subsequently went through rapid incremental change as it was brought into production and use. The second cluster revolved around the railroad, which helped, in turn, to stimulate the breakthroughs in the 1980s in cheap steel. The third group picked up momentum on either side of the turn of the century: electricity, a batch of new chemicals, and the internal-combustion engine. If you are willing to trace the internal-combustion engine in the jet engine, the development of electricity in the radio, the color television, and the early computers, and chemical breakthroughs in synthetic fibers, plastics, and modern pharmaceuticals, the unfolding third batch dominates the scene down to the mid-1960s, when deceleration is quite marked. There was an interval of about ten years in which some thoughtful analysts feared we had finally come to a time of diminishing returns from science and technology. Then came the new batch, obviously germinating for quite a long time, but emerging on stage only about a decade ago.

There are four characteristics a historian (at least this historian) would assert about the current revolution that make it, in degree at least, different from the other three.

First, the current revolution is rooted in areas of fundamental science that are undergoing rapid, revolutionary change, so that the scientist himself must be a working member of the innovational and production team. The scientist has been an extremely important character all the way back to the first, modern technological revolution, but his influence has mainly been oblique. This time it is more direct because of the paths and the pace at which basic science is moving.

The second characteristic of the Fourth Industrial Revolution is that its impact will be ubiquitous. It will suffuse the old basic industries— agriculture, animal husbandry, forestry, and, of course, all the services. Social scientists did the world a bad turn when they began to talk about a postindustrial society. We will find that most of these innovations, perhaps, will have their most important applications in raising productivity in the old basic industries. The notion that you can run a society successfully by having people talk to each other over computers never really had much sense in it. But, in any case, it is not going to be like that at all. The new technologies are producing—and will increasingly produce—revolutionary change across the board, including the old basic industries.

The new technologies will also prove to be immediately relevant, in different degree, to all the developing regions. Obviously, the degree of relevance is quite different in Africa, south of the Sahara, or Bangladesh than in, say, South Korea, Taiwan, or southern Brazil. I believe that, properly handled, the relevance of these technologies to the developing regions should be one of the pillars in a reconstructed partnership between the North and the South, which was broken up in the early seventies and never adequately repaired.

The fourth characteristic of this revolution is that the new technologies are so diversified that no single country is likely to dominate, as, for example, Britain did in the early stages of the cotton textile revolution, or we did in the early stages of the mass-produced automobile. Each of the fields that I have defined as part of the Fourth Industrial Revolution is so diversified that comparative advantage is likely to emerge in different places. There will be a great deal of international trade in high technology and a great many deals across boundaries as business leaders exploit comparative advantage by bringing together international teams to do highly specialized jobs in particular places.

Now those, I think, are the basic characteristics of the Fourth Industrial Revolution. The United States has a great advantage in the ease, when we are so minded, with which we put together teams embracing basic research, engineering, the entrepreneur, and the working force. Our greatest weakness is that, by historical accident, entrepreneurs in a quite wide array of American sectors have found it extremely awkward to talk to their own R&D people and exploit innovational possibilities. We generated entrepreneurs—in steel, automobiles, machine tools, farm machinery, textiles—who were good at many things: advertising, finance, lobbying in Congress, or whatever. But they were complacent about technology in the postwar period and were hit heavily by a series of blind-side blocks in the form of effective foreign competition, to which they responded sluggishly. The pressure started in the late 1950s and, as we all know, became progressively more acute. I think there is a beginning of a regeneration of creative entrepreneurship, which would bring scientist, engineer, entrepreneur, and worker together into effective teams. The question is: Are we moving far enough, fast enough? This is a theme to which I shall return.

THE FAMILIAR IMMEDIATE PROBLEMS

Now let us shift gears. We all know that we have an array of short-run problems. The conventional way of running through them is something like this. We have a balance of payments deficit that we are not dealing with. In part, that is due to abnormally high real-interest rates, which have yielded, until recently, an overvalued dollar. In turn, this process was mainly a result of the high federal budget deficit. We are doing something with the exchange rate, not much about the deficit. Our real-interest rates, despite some decline, are still too high. This has caused a much slower rate of growth than we should have.

This mixture of problems—especially the slow rate of growth and the high real-interest rates—has slowed down the rate of diffusion of the new technologies because most substitution of new technology for old takes place as capital is maintained. That is why I have always been skeptical of the concept of net investment. Most investment in new technology is embedded in gross investment, and that kind of investment takes place most rapidly when firms are pushing up against full capacity. If you run the society at 75, 80, 85 percent full capacity, you are not going to get the pace of technological change that you want. I will come back to some of the other implications of these short-run problems; but if I were a national security advisor now, I would be concerned about the nuclear problems we face, about the terrorist problem, and about the instability in Southeast Asia, the Middle East, the Caribbean, Africa, and the other obvious points of danger. But I would put our economic situation in the world as the number one national security problem. Why? Because the weakening of our competitive position draws down, in the long run, our capacity to project our power as a stabilizing force into areas where stabilization is in our interest and in the interest of others who rely on us to help. In addition, the slow rate of growth of the United States endangers the developing regions, whose debts are going to get paid off only if we run a high rate of growth and they can export to the us, Western Europe, and Japan. Otherwise, we are going to have dangerous problems. We are going to slow up growth in the developing regions at a time when they have a tremendous outpouring of young people into the work force. This socially explosive problem can only be rendered manageable if they run high rates of growth, but that comes back to our rate of growth and maintaining open U.S. markets.

Finally, the way we are now managing the economy puts military and social expenditures in conflict with each other. They need not be if we were running a high and steady rate of growth and balancing our books. We are doing neither.

DAVID HUME'S GREAT INSIGHT

I touch on these familiar problems because I believe in the end we have to relate them to the problem—the rich country-poor country problem—that David Hume defined in the eighteenth century.

Let me briefly evoke the setting. We are talking about 1758, a quarter of a century before the new technologies of the First Industrial Revolution came on stream in the 1780s. There were some improvements in what Hume called the "mechanic arts"; and through trade, the widening of the market, and specialization of function, certain countries were moving ahead. This was the century during which, even before the industrial revolution, Britain and France moved ahead of the Dutch, who had come to primacy in the world economy in the seventeenth century. It was clear that there were leaders and followers; countries around the world were at different stages of growth, even within the framework of a commercial and handicraft manufacturing society. What Hume perceived in that setting was that the more advanced countries might well stir up what he called a "fermentation" among the less advanced countries, who would pick up the tricks of productivity and, with the benefit of lower money wage rates, move into areas that would compete effectively with the more advanced. He asked the question: What is the correct policy of the more advanced towards the less advanced countries in such circumstances?

Hume lived in a mercantilist age. He, Adam Smith, and others were fighting against the mercantilist instinct, which was to throttle the infants in their cradles. He argued that this was not the right answer.

> Nor need any state entertain apprehensions, that their neighbors will improve to such a degree in every art and manufacture, as to have no demand from them. Nature, by giving a diversity of geniuses, climates, and soils, to different nations, has secured their mutual intercourse and commerce,

as long as they all remain industrious and civilized. Nay, the more the arts increase in any state, the more will be its demands from its industrious neighbors.[1]

Hume went on to argue that, as the poorer country came up in the world, two things would happen. First, there would be an increase in trade between the poorer country and the richer countries. Second, the poorer country coming up would compete successfully in certain sectors, but if the richer country adjusted its use of resources, there were other sectors into which it could move; its advantages would permit it to maintain its position at the head of the line. Modern economists might subsume Hume's description of the structural adjustment required under the heading of a high "elasticity of substitution."

HUME UPDATED

That was the doctrine of David Hume. By example, the more advanced would stir up competition among the less advanced. The less advanced would come on, trade would increase both ways, and critically important structural adjustments would be required if the more advanced were to maintain their position. These adjustments were quite possible if the rich countries remained, in his rather splendid phrase, "industrious and civilized."

Incidentally, I used that quotation at the Tsukuba high-tech world fair in Japan last year when I spoke on the day set aside in honor of the Asian Development Bank. I concluded that Hume's was the appropriate doctrine for the next century in the Pacific Basin. I believe my Asian colleagues understood. But it is not going to be all that easy. It is not simply a question of the Japanese. Behind Japan are South Korea, Taiwan, and the other vital, rapidly developing countries. Behind them are India and China, Brazil and Mexico. They are going to come along. Do not be misled by the gravity of their present debt and other problems.

I am about to quote some World Bank statistics that bear on that assertion and reflect a real revolution. In the United States, the proportion of the population enrolled in higher education is 20 to 24 percent; in what the World Bank calls "lower middle income" countries, that proportion rose from 3 to 10 percent between 1960 and 1982. For "upper middle income" countries, the increase was from 4 to 14 percent. The increase in India—with a low income per capita but a vital educational system—was from 3 to 9 percent; and now I am told it is over 10 percent. To understand the quantitative meaning of these figures, it should be recalled that in 1960 the proportion for Great Britain was 9 percent, and Japan 10 percent. There has also been a radical shift toward science and engineering. In India, for example, the pool of scientists and engineers has increased from about 190,000 in 1960 to 2.4 million in 1984, a critical mass only exceeded in the United States and the Soviet Union. In Mexico the annual average increase, up until 1973, in graduates in natural science was only about 3 percent, and in engineering, 5 percent. But from 1973 to 1981 the comparable figures were 14 percent in natural sciences and 24 percent in engineering. That is an astonishing, almost fivefold acceleration.

I believe this is the general direction of the sudden educational surge that is taking place in the more advanced parts of the developing world. The Chinese were, of course, gravely set back by the Cultural Revolution; even before, they did not have as solid an educational system as India. But we also know they are going to drive, and drive effectively, in these new directions.

What does this mean? What it means, I think, is that the technological absorptive capacity of the advanced developing regions is rising, and we are in for the kind of challenge that was faced by Great Britain after 1870.

Great Britain produced about one-third of the world's industrial output in 1870. It was down to 14 percent in 1913, 4 percent on the eve of the Second World War. The United States, Germany, Russia, and Japan rose over this interval, relative to Great Britain. Japan did not make the cut in 1870, only two years beyond the Meiji restoration; but it contained 4 percent of the world's industrial production in the late 1930s, when Russia had 19 percent and the United States 32 percent. Clearly, there was a radical shift in the locus of industry and technology in the seventy years after 1870, which had profound power repercussions. I believe we are in for that kind of a shift again in the time ahead.

IMPLICATIONS FOR U.S. POLITICS

I turn now to the meaning of all this for U.S. and West European politics. I have come to believe it is useful to look at the last two centuries in the following way. The first century of modern growth ran from about the mideighteenth century down to, say, 1870—a century that begins with David Hume and Adam Smith and ends with John Stuart Mill and Karl Marx. That was the century during which growth was the central issue. Mill and Marx were the hinge on which you turn from the first to the second century because each, in a quite different way, assumed that growth was an ongoing process in the advanced industrial world and that the key question was how the fruits of growth should be shared. Marx, as all know well, prescribed a bloody transition to socialism—Mill, a kind of mild welfare state, democratic socialism, and an environmentalist's limits to growth. But from the 1870s down to the 1970s, the central issue of politics in the advanced industrial countries was how an automatically expanding pie should be divided, including a wide range of welfare issues.

Thus, the politics of the West European societies and the United States, starting with Bismarck's social legislation of the 1870s and 1880s, consisted of a relatively civilized zero-sum struggle over the division of the pie, centered on civilizing and rendering humane an industrial system that, in 1870, was not all that humane. It had its climax between 1960 and 1975 in an astonishing shift in the advanced industrial countries of the proportion of GNP going to welfare—from about 14 percent to 24 percent. Now that is a pace of reallocation that obviously could not go on. At just about the time it was reaching a kind of natural limit, welfare allocations were hit by the slowdown in growth, with the first oil price jump.

We have been wallowing around since without a clear sense of direction. We have been and still are victims of a time lag between our political vocabulary and reality—a time lag that seems to be particularly marked in the minds of economists, who seem to be experiencing great difficulty adjusting to current reality. A great deal of our politics right down to the 1984 and 1986 elections consisted in the debate of getting the government off the neck of the private sector versus equity. Finding the right balance in a democratic society is a great issue; and no such issue wholly disappears. In fact, virtually every national election in the United States since 1896 has been conducted around that issue. But that is not the issue now.

The issue before our society is the following (and it will be the central issue of the next fifty to seventy-five years, perhaps longer): Are we capable of working together in such a way as to continue to expand the pie, in the face of the competition that we already face and will increasingly face? Are we capable of getting the scientist and the engineer, the businessman and the worker—plus whatever role is appropriate for government—to work together to keep this great continental community at the head of the queue, so that we can meet our obligations to ourselves and to the world in the face of intensified competition? That is, I am confident, the issue now and for the foreseeable time ahead. Neither the economists nor the politicians of the West have faced up to the tasks and concepts required to answer these questions positively.

When I have argued that we must make a swift transition to the politics of partnership and call on those strands in our tradition that are consistent with such a partnership, my friends tend to respond: "You used to be quite a practical fellow when I knew you in Washington, but living out here under the big blue sky of Texas you have really gone off the deep end. Don't you know what is going on in Washington? Do you know what they are arguing about in Washington? What is the matter with you?"

My answer is that if you look at our country now—not at what is going on in Washington but at what is happening in the cities and states—you will see that a new politics is emerging. It should be recalled that, historically, new patterns of national politics first appear in the states: the Jacksonian coalition, the slavery issue, the progressive movement that let up to Teddy Roosevelt and Woodrow Wilson. There were many foreshadowings of the New Deal in the states. And there were many foreshadowings of the effort to put a ceiling on public budgets, Proposition 13 in California being simply the most prominent example.

Now what would I cite as evidence of a transition to the politics of partnership? First, there is a real revolution going on in business-labor relations. There is a growing awareness that Dr. Johnson's dictum applies to both business and labor: "Depend upon it, sir, when a man knows he is to be hanged in a fortnight, it concentrates his mind wonderfully." Business and labor are beginning to cooperate in wholly new ways because they know that the survival of their firms and jobs depends upon that kind of cooperation. In politics we have a governor of New Jersey, a Republican, who gets 70 percent or so of the black vote. We have Chuck Robb emerging from Virginia with a mixture of compassion and courage in facing up to rough problems. Look at the cities and their mayors: they have to balance their books, and they know they can only do that if they pull the community together behind their programs. Henry Cisneros, the dynamic Mayor of San Antonio, puts that strategy this way: "The real answers are not found in confrontation, obstruction, or denying access, but rather, in inclusion, cooperation, providing facts, and in trying to build a common stake in the future." I do believe that is the heart of the coming doctrine in American politics. Some time—and before too long—it is going to emerge on the national scene as the doctrine for the next generation. I think it is the only way that we are going to survive and look after our interests; and I do believe that we are basically a resilient continental society that is capable of surviving.

A WORD ABOUT NATIONAL SECURITY

Now a final word about the meaning of this view of affairs for foreign policy. I would recall a difficult spring a quarter of a century ago, in President Kennedy's time. It so happened that Mac Bundy and I split the crises at the beginning of 1961. We inherited plenty of them. He, for his sins, had Cuba, among others; and I, for my sins, had Southeast Asia, among others. But when the Bay of Pigs failed, I volunteered to help mop up. And I sometimes think that the three weeks or so that I spent with President Kennedy at this stage was as useful a public service as I ever performed. At one point he said something I have never forgotten. "We can't afford to have a nervous breakdown. The British could take over Suez and we could cover for them; the French could take over Algeria. But there is nobody behind us." Turning to the problem of our competitive viability, if we fail it is going to corrode our security position in the world, and the United States has no source of security except itself. There is no one to cover for us.

The larger point is this. I evoked earlier the post-1879 redistribution of industrial, technological, and military power. That process generated two German wars—with the Japanese joining the second time around—plus a cold war with Russia where we still have to work our way through to a soft landing. The kind of readjustments that will take place are thoroughly capable of rendering this an extremely dangerous mercantilist world in a nuclear age in which the trick of making nuclear weapons is now accessible to a great many powers, with still more just down the road. We owe it to ourselves—and to our rather special place in the world community—to maintain the strength and poise, not merely to protect ourselves in the military sense, which we have to do, but to also play a constructive and stabilizing role so that this readjustment takes place in peace. To that end, there is a great deal to be done. For example, building a vital Pacific Basin organization with our partners is one of the great potential enterprises in the next fifty years—building a new partnership in that hemisphere. Taking a junior partnership role, we can also encourage the Europeans to work with Africa, where the Europeans have special intersts.

There are many constructive possibilities as well as dangers in the transition. We simply cannot afford a raw, mercantilist struggle in this kind of nuclear age. Therefore, we had better take David Hume's advice and work steadily together to generate and sustain an America that is "industrious and civilized."

NOTE

1.   David Hume, "Of the Jealousy of Trade," in Eugene Rotwein, ed., *David Hume: Writings on Economics* (Madison: University of Wisconsin Press, 1955), pp. 78–79.

5 BACK TO THE FUTURE
Collaboration and Competition in a New World

Joseph D. Duffey

Perhaps we could gain some perspective on how we have become what we are today if we could go back to the future—if we could revisit the fairly recent past with our present knowledge of how things will turn out.

The year is 1952, April of 1952 to be exact, just thirty-six years ago. Peter Drucker is writing in the journal *Nation's Business*. The article is entitled, "Productivity Is an Attitude."

Drucker begins as follows: "During the past few years, the American business system has been examined, probed, and dissected as no other economic system has ever been looked over before" (Drucker 1952). He goes on to point out how "businessmen, technicians, educators, workers, and union officials have come to the United States from every country of Western Europe" to find out for themselves what causes American productivity.

These were the famous "productivity teams." Some 200 of them were organized under the Marshall Plan in the early 1950s, mostly financed by funds from the European governments themselves. They came to visit "foundries, textile mills, business schools, breweries, printing companies, and labor unions, spending sometimes weeks on location." The teams were seeking to find the causes of America's remarkable productivity in techniques and processes.

Drucker wrote, "I know of no team that did not speedily discover for itself that techniques are not the really important thing and certainly not the real cause of our productivity."

Drucker then quotes from a report of a team of British businessmen, primarily in the printing industries. They wrote, "In America, productivity is an attitude of mind." Drucker observes that a number of the teams were reporting the same thing. "Attitudes, social organization and moral values: these underlie and explain America's industrial achievement." Drucker continues: "Even in such a seemingly 'technical' area as the use of machinery the visitors see the main cause for America's lead in attitudes rather than in the abundance of capital, the lack of wartime destruction, etc."

Drucker concludes the article with a list of those aspects of the American scene in business and industry that contrast with the European nations: (1) the discovery of management, (2) productivity as a social principle, (3) the attitude toward the market, (4) productivity based upon diversity and experimentation, and (5) the importance of the human being.

Of the last point Drucker writes, "Even our labor relations seem [to these visitors] . . . to be based upon deep respect for human beings."

Peter Drucker concludes this remarkable 1952 article: "What it adds up to in the minds of . . . foreign visitors is that this country avails itself of a much larger percentage of its human resources than their own" (Drucker 1952).

Thirty-six years ago, when Peter Drucker wrote these words, the United States was the master gear in the world economic machine. We were the world's chief producer of goods and the world's chief lender of money. We were also the world's chief innovator of new technology and the principal peacekeeper. But today our output lags behind the rest of the industrial world. We have become, for the first time in our history, a debtor nation. We still lead the world in certain technological areas, but we transfer as much technology abroad as we commercially apply here at home. We do remain the primary peacekeeper for the free world, although our new concept of that role, as manifested in Central America and Libya, is today more controversial than at any time in more than a decade. The burden of our assumed role as arms supplier and defender of much of the world has freed our friends and allies to accelerate their own nondefense research and economic development.

The United States is still the largest consumer marketplace on earth. But we are buying more from the world than the world buys from us. We are still free traders in a world that is substantially mercantilist and restrictive.

It is a common notion in this country that we are a trading nation. We are not, and never have been. We used to pull out our order books and satisfy the demands of others. We even gave away surpluses in basic commodities as a means of pump-priming or subsidizing faltering foreign economies. We still cover the debts of other nations, thus ensuring that they can trade enough to stay afloat and repay what they owe us.

We do all these things, but we are not traders in the conventional sense of the word. We keep referring to our friends in the industrial world as our "trading partners." Today they are more appropriately our competitors or a source of cheaper labor and subsidized supply. Partners they are not, except in the arcane terminology of treaties.

If we were to turn the clock back to the early 1960s, we might be able to comprehend the forces that shaped the current world marketplace. Those same forces exist today and will influence the course of global economics well into the twenty-first century. They are fivefold.

First, there is geography. The globe has simply shrunk in terms of our ability to move goods, money, and ideas. Transportation and communications have helped to shorten distances and expedite transactions. There is also the matter of geographic alignment. The East-West and North-South distinctions are not only geopolitical but essentially geoeconomic. The United States, Japan, and Western Europe comprise what Kenichi Ohmae calls "triad power." Lumped together, these sectors control so much that the only game is to be on the inside of the triad or be left in the dust.

Second, there is the force of capital. Capital used to be the primary source of developing industrial growth. Today capital is rivaled by knowledge. Brainpower and information are increasingly the bedrock of economic strength. As the authors of *Global Stakes* argue, "America's leadership has failed to recognize the shift from a capital-intensive economy that downplays education to a knowledge-intensive economy that requires educated and trained human resources" (Bodtkin et al. 1982:30).

The third force is technology. We have a fabulous record on invention. We do not do as well, however, when it comes to taking our ideas from the drawing board or test tube to the marketplace. At the same time, we are exporting our technology for others to convert into tangible goods and services. We have permitted ourselves to become the labelers and marketers of products developed elsewhere and sold here. The trend is toward what *Business Week* once referred to as the "hollow corporations": companies more comfortable in packaging than in producing. This is a comparatively dangerous trend from the standpoint of our competitiveness.

Some argue that our future rests in the service sector, and that we can afford to lose our manufacturing industries to cheap-labor nations overseas. That is a dangerous illusion. How will we be able to invent the software if we lose the knack for making the computers?

The fourth force is what we refer to as "quality of life." The industrialized world has created abundance and commensurate standards of living. Our generosity after World War II was designed to shore up the world's ravaged economy as well as to bolster our own. Our altruism, however, unleashed a tidal wave of higher expectation throughout the world and created a new class of competitors. At the same time, the rising prosperity of many has increased the gaps between the haves and the have-nots. Those of us in the developed world must deal with this disparity.

Finally, the fifth force deals with the politics of the macro- and microeconomic rules that play a key role in dragging and shaping a nation's economy. These rules cover the mechanisms of budgets and taxes and the laws and regulations, ranging from antitrust to patents. Whereas other nations have managed to harmonize their mechanisms and have gained consensus from the public and private sectors about strategic directions, the United States continues to flounder around with a patchwork quilt of ad hoc, piecemeal, and sometimes contradictory policies.

Our piecemeal approach is not altogether mad, mind you. After all, it is our flexibility that leads to the innovation and entrepreneurship that are our greatest strengths. Nevertheless, from a policy standpoint, we are still adjusting valves, while other countries are rebuilding engines.

If we could state a vision—what we want for the American economy in the future—and then work our way back to an agenda of tasks and responsibilities, I would propose to rebuild a national economy that will sustain noninflationary growth with strong high employment and a rising standard of living for an expanding population. Such a goal would involve renewal of our rural areas, revitalization of urban centers, opportunities for upward mobility for young people, an expanding job market, aid to the poor and disadvantaged, a measure of security for our less privileged older citizens, a safe environment, quality education at all levels, and strong cultural institutions.

It is not an unrealistic aspiration. In fact, it is the essential goal of a free and democratic society.

There is one essential condition, however, to reach this goal in America. America must become more competitive in the world economy.

The irony and frustration of the present situation is our lack of a national consensus about the issue of competitiveness. Over the past few years, nearly two dozen reports have been issued on the subject from prestigious groups such as the Business Higher-Education Forum and the President's Commission on Industrial Competitiveness.

Dr. Paula Stern, who chairs the U.S. International Trade Commission, recently put the issues correctly when she said, "U.S. power in the world has become as much a function of the balance of trade as of the balance of terror, and our future depends as surely on our grain silos as on our missile silos" (Stern 1986). I believe that Dr. Stern is right. Policies of international trade and their effect on U.S. competitiveness have become matters of national security. Strategic thinking and strategic planning for defense and national security must begin with a consideration of the strength of the U.S. economy.

Many knowledgeable persons today question whether we have a trade policy that reflects our true national interest.

The present administration's approach to the problem of export controls, for example, has injured American industry far more than it has restricted the flow of technology to the Soviet Union. The current policies serve ideological zeal, but they have diminished our already shrinking share of world markets in high-technology products. At the same time, major export deals involving barter arrangements, especially military sales, often make advantaged competitors of our trading partners because of carelessness in protecting patents and manufacturing licenses.

Our trade policy mechanisms are out-of-date. Policy-making authority is dispersed among more than two dozen departments and agencies in the executive branch and among nineteen committees and subcommittees in the Congress.

We need to merge the Department of Commerce with the Office of the Special Trade Representative and bring our trade policies under a strategic calculation that holds as a priority American competitiveness in world markets.

Our tax policies also need to be examined in the light of the competitive challenge. Reuben Mettler of TRW has pointed out that "tax bills proposed by the Administration and under consideration by the Congress today contain some worthwhile features: a broader tax base and lower marginal rates, for example. But they do not seem to be designed with a high priority on competitiveness."[1]

The most striking feature of all tax proposals being discussed at the present moment is that they do not seem to create the major incentives for savings and investment that are vital to our productivity and our ability to compete. In fact, many provisions being advocated by members of both parties would punish companies and industries in international competition, while being more favorable to companies and industries with primarily domestic competitors. In the present tax code, there is a provision not widely understood that substantially reduces taxes for multinational corporations if they move their research and development facilities out of U.S. laboratories and universities and locate them overseas.[2]

The available legal protection at the moment for the intellectual property of American companies—patents, copyrights, and know-how—is weak and relatively ineffective against foreign competitors. There are, fortunately, some signs that the administration is prepared to correct this.

There is a lack of balance between the United States and Japan in the matter of reciprocal access to scientific and engineering research in the two countries.

Current U.S. antitrust statutes and their interpretation work to the distinct disadvantage of U.S. companies in our own domestic markets. They unfairly restrict American companies in foreign markets.

I cite these illustrations to underscore my argument about the lack of a national priority on the issue of U.S. industrial competitiveness. I believe that a sense of priority is needed. I believe that it will come in time. Each of us can, however, begin now to act individually and collectively on this important question.

If we are educators, we can work with our colleagues from all disciplines to ensure that our students understand the kind of world that they will enter when they graduate. Historians, creative artists, and teachers of economics and literature all have a role in raising the national level of awareness about the importance of U.S. competitiveness in world markets.

Most economics departments and business schools in the United States still teach what Ruben Mettler calls the eighteenth-century "wine and wool" concept of comparative advantage in international trade based upon climate and natural resources. In the modern world, however, comparative or, perhaps we should say, competitive advantage is being created by technology, investment, and worldwide marketing, as demonstrated not only by Japan but by other Pacific Basin nations. These new concepts lead to very different public and private policies. We need more emphasis on language studies and cultural understanding.

Our society is in the midst of a significant transition. We have enormous strengths: an intelligent and skilled work force, the energy and ideals of a democratic society that respects diversity, spectacular inventive genius, and capacity for basic research, applied research, and innovation not only in the basic sciences and in engineering but in the social sciences and important areas of human understanding.

In the early 1920s, after World War I, Walter Lippmann wrote:

> We are living through the closing chapters of an established and traditional way of life. We are in the early beginnings of a struggle to remake our civilization which will probably last for generations. This is not a good time for politicians. It is a time for prophets and leaders and explorers and inventors and pioneers . . . and for those who are willing to plant trees for their children to sit under (Steel 1982:510).

Walter Lippmann was describing a particularly pivotal time at the moment of history in which he lived. He was also describing the time in which we live, and the challenge that we face.

NOTES

1. The major weakness of most recent revisions of the federal income tax codes, including the comprehensive tax legislation of 1986, remains the failure to address issues related to the competitiveness of the American economy.
2. I am indebted to Reuben Mettler and Pat Choate at several points in this paper. Mettler is chief executive officer of TRW, and Pat Choate heads TRW's research office. Mettler and Choate began to raise the issues of American productivity and competitiveness, particularly in the manufacturing sector, before many others were aware of the problem. Their writings and leadership in this area put us all in their debt.

REFERENCES

Bodtkin, James; Dan Dimancescu; and Ray Stata. 1982. *Global Stakes: The Future of High Technology in America*. New York: Harper and Row.

Drucker, Peter. 1952. "Productivity Is an Attitude." *Nation's Business*. April 15.

Steel, Ronald C. 1982. *Walter Lippmann and the American Century*. Boston: Little, Brown and Company.

Stern, Paula. 1986. Remarks before a meeting of the Business Higher-Education Forum, Clifton Forge, Virginia, April 22.

III NATIONAL STRATEGIES

6 A NATIONAL RESEARCH STRATEGY

Erich Bloch

The quality and diversity of U.S. research in science and technology remains unmatched by any other nation.[1] This success results from a unique combination of factors. Clearly, the magnitude of the federal commitment to basic research since World War II has contributed significantly. But the productivity of U.S. science and engineering owes an equal debt to the research community's adherence to standards of excellence and to institutional arrangements that have encouraged innovation. The close coupling of research and education in the university setting—a uniquely American invention—and the academic ethos of autonomy, integrity, and pluralism have provided a singularly stimulating climate for research.

However, the very success of this system—and the recognition that science and technology are vital to U.S. economic competitiveness and to national security—has thrown into sharp relief not only its accomplishments, but also its weaknesses and the need for change. Some worrisome trends have surfaced, and, as a result, the national research system has become the subject of serious concern and close scrutiny. The House Science and Technology Committee has undertaken a

Editor's Note: Reprinted with permission from Erich Bloch, "Managing for Challenging Times: A National Research Strategy," *Issues in Science and Technology* 2 (Winter 1986). Copyright 1986, by the National Academy of Sciences, Washington, D.C. The postscript has been written by Mr. Bloch especially for this volume.

two-year review of science policy, and several federal and professional organizations are examining the health of the research infrastructure.[2] Peer review and our ways of setting priorities among disciplines are being questioned, as is the appropriate balance of funding between basic and applied research and between large facilities and individual investigators.

Pressure for change in our research system comes from three sources: first, from problems relating to research infrastructure; second, from the larger budgetary, economic, and political environment for research; and third, from developments in the nature and conduct of research itself.

Research Infrastructure

The U.S. research system lacks adequate mechanisms and resources to maintain its infrastructure. Cumulative neglect has led to shortages of manpower, equipment, and facilities, in turn leading to policy-making and remedial action under crisis rather than to thoughtful planning for the future.

We are short of advanced-degree engineers to staff our universities and government and industry laboratories, and our production of Ph.D. engineers has been declining since 1976 (NSF 1983:272).[3] Only now are there signs that this trend is reversing. Moreover, since 1981, foreign nationals have received over half of the U.S. doctoral degrees in engineering, an increase of more than 100 percent since 1959 (NSF 1983:228).

The proportion of R&D scientists and engineers in this country has also dropped; while we were once far ahead of other industrialized nations, we now have only a slight lead over Western Europe and Japan. Both Japan and the Soviet Union produce proportionately more engineers than the United States (NSF 1983:6). Over the next decade, this gap could widen as the size of the U.S. college-age population drops, unless a larger proportion of college students decides to major in mathematics, engineering, and the sciences (NSF 1983:78).[4]

The shortage of university research equipment is also cause for concern. Meeting current requirements for new equipment would require approximately $4 billion, and some estimates run as high as $10 billion. Spending on academic research equipment and instrumentation, which declined 78 percent in constant dollars from 1966 to 1983, is now about $1 billion a year (AAU 1985:15).[5]

A problem of similar proportions is the deterioration and obsolescence of university buildings and laboratory facilities. A major conference on the topic, held in 1984, concluded that between $15 billion
and $20 billion is now needed to build or renovate such facilities.[6]

Budgetary and Political Environment

We are also confronting major changes in the budgetary and political
environment affecting research. For the past five years, federal R&D
budgets have fared relatively well, but there is little prospect of significant increases in the immediate or medium term. Meanwhile, the total
R&D share of gross national product in the United States has fallen
in comparison with every other industrialized nation. Twenty years
ago we enjoyed a substantial lead; now other nations are drawing even.
Moreover, the defense component of U.S. R&D, already larger than in
other industrialized democracies, has been the largest beneficiary of
recent increases in federal R&D spending. As a result, civilian R&D
in the United States now constitutes a smaller share of gross national
product than in either West Germany or Japan.

While total federal spending for basic research has increased 48 percent in constant dollars since 1972, federal support for basic research
at universities has grown only slightly more than the inflation rate.
Despite sizable increases in total R&D funds during the current administration, for instance, the National Science Foundation (NSF) budget has
remained essentially the same in constant dollars since the mid-1960s.

Meanwhile, demands on the civilian R&D budget for fundamental
research have grown. Federal support has nourished university research
establishments and, sometimes deliberately (as in the institutional development programs of the 1960s and 1970s), has increased the number
of research universities competing for constrained resources.[7] Undergraduate colleges and institutions on the periphery of the research system are also demanding attention. Recently, for example, a group of
liberal arts colleges joined in the so-called *Oberlin Report*, which
pointed out their vital role in producing science and mathematics
majors and urged greater recognition and financial support (Davis-Van
Atta, Carrier, and Frankfort 1985:9–13).

In light of these trends and the deteriorating position of the United
States in international trade, the nation's research priorities need reex-
amination. Defense, energy, and health applications will continue to

occupy a prominent place among federal research priorities. We need to balance this emphasis with greater attention to the role of civilian basic research, including fundamental research and the training of scientists and engineers, in supporting these applications and expanding the knowledge base.[8]

The research system's political environment is also changing. As Don Price, former dean of Harvard University's John F. Kennedy School of Government, has pointed out, the research system is a victim of its own successes (Price 1976:34). As the public and its representatives realize that scientific discovery leads to practical benefits, political demands on science intensify. Over the past two decades, state and local governments have come to see science and technology as a key to economic development. Following the example of California's Silicon Valley, Boston's Route 128, North Carolina's Research Triangle Park, and Austin's recent buildup in electronics, many states have adopted active, technology-based development strategies, and they are leading current efforts to improve the quality of public science and mathematics education.

Not surprisingly, members of Congress have been showing more interest in appropriations for university research facilities and in the geographic distribution of federal research funds. Their interest has coincided with a new political activism among universities, which, in order to address their shortage of research facilities, are seeking funds directly from Congress, bypassing the traditional process of merit review. In the long run, this activism could damage the research enterprise, whose success has been based on self-discipline within the scientific community and on willingness to compete in scientific arenas while remaining aloof from the scramble for political spoils.

Nature and Conduct of Research

Pressure for reassessment and change of our research system also stems from an evolution in the substance and practice of research. The traditional boundaries between scientific disciplines have become blurred, and research that crosses these boundaries has led to some of the most important recent advances. Attention and energy must be focused on these multidisciplinary developments, while protecting the viability of important basic disciplines.

The practice of research has changed in another way. Disciplines long dominated by single investigators in self-sufficient laboratories now require elaborate and expensive instruments that, by financial necessity, must be shared by many investigators. This trend is already familiar in high-energy physics. Its impact on other areas—for example, the reliance of mathematics on computer technology, particularly on supercomputers—is newer but equally significant. These new arrangements are altering the culture and social fabric of these disciplines in profound ways, still not fully understood.

Research is producing new knowledge at an accelerating pace, and the time lag between basic research and applied technology is becoming shorter. In response, cooperation between universities and industries is expanding in such areas as biotechnology, microelectronics, computer hardware and software, and new materials. These new cooperative arrangements benefit both parties, but also cause strains within the research system. Private industry's concern over proprietary rights, for example, must be balanced against the importance to academia of unfettered communication.

A related change is that defense and civilian research are no longer as discrete and separable as they once were. Moreover, in dual-use technologies that have both military and commercial applications, the private sector, more often than not, provides the stimulus for their development and initial use. One result is that unclassified research at universities now has major military implications. Defining policies that appropriately accommodate national security considerations with concerns for academic freedom and scientific and technical productivity will require open minds and recognition of new realities.

To meet these needs and challenges, the scientific community must devise new strategies to manage our research enterprise and then get on with the job. In doing so, the following agenda must be addressed.

A RESEARCH STRATEGY

1. Allocate More of Our R&D Resources to Basic Research and to the Science and Engineering Infrastructure. The administration has been shifting support from civilian-applied R&D to basic research. Between 1980 and 1984, government support for nondefense-applied R&D fell, but its support for civilian basic research rose 50 percent (NSF 1983:40). This moved us in the right direction, but not far enough. As the relevance of science and technology increases, the fraction of support devoted to basic research must also increase. Similarly, while industry's support for university research has grown in the last few years, more is needed.[9] Total national funding for basic research amounts to only about $13.3 billion, less than 12 percent of the national total for all R&D (NSF Forthcoming). Total funds for basic research should be increased by at least 50 percent, and the federal government should double its share.

The case for this increase is compelling. The opportunities now available in science and engineering research are greater than ever before. Breakthroughs in instrumentation, computation, experimentation, and theory seem to be occurring in every discipline, and multidisciplinary research offers particularly exciting opportunities. Biologists, chemists, and physicists have made major advances in biotechnology, especially in genetic engineering. Materials research brings to bear the insights of physics, chemistry, and engineering to develop substances of high strength, corrosion resistance, or special electrical characteristics. Drawing on the talents of computer scientists, psychologists, and linguists, information science research is revealing a common theoretical ground that enriches all disciplines. The resulting knowledge provides new insights into both human and artificial intelligence.

We cannot afford to pass up these opportunities.

2. Reallocate Funds from Less Productive Uses to Basic Research and Infrastructure Support.

Increased funding for basic research need not require an increase in the federal budget. Instead, some federal resources for the support of other R&D areas must be reallocated to basic research. This will require a determined leadership willing to support new initiatives that will often have to be funded at the expense of programs that are still highly productive but of secondary priority.

Increased support for basic research could come from our national laboratories, which represent an annual federal investment of close to $18 billion. In pursuing the missions of sponsoring government agencies, the national laboratories have expanded scientific and technical frontiers. Recently, however, their vitality and productivity have been cause for concern. A White House Science Council panel, headed by David Packard, chairman of the board of Hewlett-Packard, found that many laboratories have lost a clear sense of their mission and that the quality of their research has declined (White House Science Council 1983).

We should recast or expand the missions of some national laboratories to enhance support for basic research and to provide better access for university and industry researchers to the laboratories' major instruments and facilities. In line with past experience, these laboratories should continue to focus on multidisciplinary activities, such as environmental, health, and nuclear research.

3. Rebuild the Research Infrastructure of Trained Scientists and Engineers, Instrumentation, and Facilities.   Several aspects of our research infrastructure require particular attention: the quality of undergraduate science and engineering education, the limited enrollment in both undergraduate and graduate science and engineering, and the state of university research equipment and facilities.

We need to improve undergraduate science and engineering education throughout the United States. Only a minority of our future scientists and engineers receive their undergraduate training at the major research universities. These universities tend to provide incentives and foster attitudes that value research over teaching. The undergraduate institutions, which place the highest priority on teaching, are hard pressed to buy increasingly expensive research instruments and facilities. Such equipment and facilities are important, however, in attracting faculty to these institutions, in keeping faculty abreast of their teaching fields, and in exposing students to the process of research. Enrollment in science and engineering will decline along with the size of the college-age population unless we attract a larger proportion of individuals to these disciplines. Women and minorities are a rich source of new talent and are underrepresented in the sciences and engineering. These groups need innovative programs emphasizing early exposure to science and engineering, continuous attention to necessary skills, and encouragement throughout their educational careers.

At the graduate level, we must substantially raise the number of U.S. citizens receiving doctoral degrees in the sciences and engineering, reversing a long-term downward trend. We must reduce our overdependence on foreign nationals, whose availability can be seriously affected by foreign policy changes. An adequate supply of advanced-degree scientists and engineers is a national imperative and must be so recognized.

The financing of R&D facilities must also be put on a realistic basis. The current shortage and obsolescence of research facilities and equipment arguably results from past shortsightedness. In the 1970s, some universities apparently chose to defer building and renovation in order to subsidize tuition costs and to maintain student enrollment and faculty levels (Doyle and Hartle 1985). Recent steep increases in tuition reflect the universities' recognition that they cannot continue shortchanging their research infrastructure. The government, too, chose to ignore the true cost of replenishing these assets and now faces difficult short-term funding demands. These demands might have been avoided by a better balance of research support among research, equipment, and facilities and by realistic depreciation and amortization charges—which still seem the only satisfactory long-term solution.

4. Leverage the Effect of Federal Research Resources by Stimulating Increased Support from Industry, State, and Local Government, and other Institutions.   The magnitude of the tasks outlined here and current constraints on the federal budget mean that responsibility for supporting research and the research infrastructure must be shared by all who stand to gain from them. Increasingly, the federal government will be a catalyst, instead of the sole provider, to facilitate research and lower its financial risk. We can use limited federal funds to help remove obstacles to cooperation between university researchers and industry and to activate private support for research. We can then set research priorities by taking into account our aggregate national research assets.

Programs that combine federal funds with matching resources from industry—such as the National Science Foundation's Presidential Young Investigator Awards, engineering research centers, and supercomputer centers—have attracted additional funding from both industry and state and local governments.

Similarly, the enhanced federal tax deduction that encourages corporate equipment donations to universities has helped alleviate the shortage of university research instrumentation. Clearly, such techniques will also be an important policy tool for raising private funds to complement federal dollars for the construction and renovation of research facilities.

5. Reform the Federal Organization for Research Support.   Effective support for science and technology requires improved coherence in federal policies and practices. Most support for science and technology now comes from the mission agencies (for example, the Department of Energy and the National Aeronautics and Space Administration). The National Science Foundation is the only agency charged with overall responsibility for the health of science and engineering.

An alternative proposed from time to time is a Department of Science and Technology. This department might share responsibility with existing mission agencies and complement their primary orientation toward applied research with more systematic attention to basic research and the overall health of the research system. As one recent study suggests, such a department could focus government activities more effectively; encourage interaction among government, industry, and academia; and improve the application of science and technology to national and international needs and issues (President's Commission 1985).

This proposal continues to receive conflicting evaluations both from Washington and from the scientific community. The wisdom of establishing such a department depends on the details of its organization and responsibilities and on whether efficiency and coherence could be gained without undue loss of flexibility and pluralism.

The president's science adviser and his Office of Science and Technology Policy are responsible for providing leadership in effective management of the research enterprise. This leadership can also come from single-agency initiatives and from collaboration among agencies. One recent example is the joint Department of Energy and National Science Foundation plan under which the Argonne National Laboratory would make some of its resources and facilities available to university researchers. Another is the current effort involving the major federal research agencies to increase support for university instrumentation and equipment.

6. Improve Relations and Communication among Disciplines, Institutions, and Industries Interested in Research.

How effectively we seize our scientific opportunities and redress deficiencies in the research infrastructure depends, in large part, on how well the nation's research community develops cooperative attitudes and relationships. Within and outside the government, adversarial attitudes that block cooperation must be overcome—but without sacrificing our creative, competitive drive or the distinctiveness of individual institutions. We should continue building relationships among universities, industries, and governments to enhance the flow of people and research results, thereby raising the productivity of the research system.

This premise has prompted the National Science Foundation to devise programs that cross traditional institutional and disciplinary boundaries in such areas as biotechnology, materials science and systems engineering, and computational science and engineering. Arrangements bringing together a variety of actors are not new, although they used to be peripheral to the main research strategy. In the future such strategies will become central.

New technologies will also help break down institutional barriers. Electronic networking, in particular, will allow easy communication across geographic distances and institutional walls. The National Science Foundation is working with the Defense Advanced Research Projects Agency and the university community to plan a nationwide science network.

New roles for diverse institutions, and more cooperative and innovative relationships among them, will require alteration of some deeply ingrained political attitudes. Since these attitudes are frequently reflected in laws and regulations, some of them, too, will need to be changed. For example, until recently antitrust laws were construed as restricting industry collaboration in research. This was clarified by the Joint Research and Development Act of 1984, which promotes joint research ventures. The Mansfield Amendment to the 1970 Defense Authorization Act (which was incorporated the following year into the Military Procurement Authorization Act) also inhibits cooperative research by prohibiting DOD support for nondefense-related research at universities. It needs to be reexamined as well.

As universities and industries collaborate in technology-related research, intellectual property rights must be sorted out. Increased industrial investment in university research and collaboration between industry and university researchers, moreover, may cause some worry that the normally unfettered exchange of information among academic researchers could be curtailed and research priorities distorted. These concerns should not, however, cause us to underestimate the integrity of the universities and their commitment to their traditional role, or industry's appreciation that open academic inquiry is in the best interest of both the university and industry.

7. Enhance the Responsiveness of the Research Enterprise to Public Concerns while Maintaining the Integrity and Excellence of Standards in Research.   Public demands on science and technology will intensify because of their increasing impact on the nation's economy and security and their influence on the public's work, health, and leisure.[10] The research community must persist in its resolve to sustain standards of scientific excellence in the face of heightened political interest. Failure to do so would squander resources and undermine research productivity. The research community must also exercise self-discipline and adhere to the ethic of excellence and merit competition. To date, its autonomy and freedom from political manipulation have been based on its neutrality and on the promise of an eventual payoff. These will continue to be the most effective bases for a relationship between the scientific community and the public.

In light of the greater expectations for practical results from our research system, scientists and engineers will have to be increasingly sensitive to the public and political environment. This will require a different type of political involvement than that motivated by the pursuit of research funds. As Daniel Yankelovich has observed, we hear much about how the public must learn about science, yet "little is said about what science must learn about the public" (Yankelovich 1984:11). The point is not so much to improve scientific public relations as to reduce the isolation of scientists from public attitudes and from political debates about science, technology, and their consequences.

The science and engineering enterprise has been called on in the past to address problems of extreme complexity and national importance, such as development of the atomic bomb during World War II and the Apollo program during the 1960s. Circumstances outside the research system drove the extraordinary scientific and engineering accomplishments in these instances. Today there are no such visible, compelling, and unifying issues.

Today's problems, such as economic competition, while strongly dependent on science and engineering for their solution, are more diffuse and less likely to lead to consensus and concerted action. Thus, the research community must construct its own rallying point to sustain the success of U.S. science and engineering. We dare not take our accomplishments for granted.

The agenda proposed here is ambitious but achievable. Our nation does not lack the material, organizational, or intellectual resources to secure the health and productivity of the research system. To bring those resources to bear and to manage them effectively, however, will require tough management, innovative policies, and vigorous leadership.

POSTSCRIPT

Since "Managing for Challenging Times" was published one-and-a-half years ago, there has been a wide-ranging national debate on our economic competitiveness. Concern over the deterioration of our leadership position in the world has provided a particularly urgent reason for assessing the issues raised in this article.

The discussion on competitiveness has broadened beyond the inner policy circles of Washington to encompass academic, industrial, and state government leadership. In the process, it has produced a consensus on two points. One is that this nation is indeed confronting an unprecedented challenge. The mounting trade deficit, which now for the first time includes a negative balance in high-technology products, is just one indication of the steady deterioration of our competitive position in the world markets.

A consensus has also emerged on the critical importance of science and engineering research and education to our ability to compete effectively in the world arena. Innovation in products and processes is the single largest determinant of productivity. The new knowledge that makes innovation possible depends on fresh ideas and highly educated technical talent.

The concerns raised by this article are, if anything, even more pressing today. The health of our research infrastructure and its ability to respond to challenges and opportunities will determine the viability of our industries and the excellence of our universities.

Significant steps have been taken to address the specific problems discussed in the article. Today, as a result of an NSF survey, we know a great deal more about the facilities needs of universities and have moved to make known our willingness to support facilities within the context of research effort. Several bills have been introduced in Congress to establish programs to support modernization and construction of research facilities at universities.

NSF has provided funding for thirteen engineering research centers (ERCs), which support multidisciplinary cooperative research with potential economic importance. The foundation will expand its support for ERCs and, in a parallel program, fund science and technology centers in many areas of science. These centers provide university investigators with an opportunity to work in some of the most exciting research areas. Simultaneously, the involvement and support of industry exposes university researchers to real industrial perspectives. Industry benefits as well through access to new ideas and talented researchers.

There has been progress in education as well. The flood of studies documenting the decline of standards and substance in our educational system has elicited an impressive response from around the country.

State governments, individually and through the National Governors' Association, have worked to raise standards, improve curricula, and develop training programs and models. NSF, whose role in education is largely catalytic, has focused primarily on increasing the availability of fellowships for graduate, undergraduate, and precollege students and on developing models for teacher training and curriculum development in the sciences and mathematics. Increasingly, states are also investing in research centers based on cooperation between industry and universities.

Nevertheless, the problems identified in the article remain. Although total federal support for R&D has increased substantially, as a percentage of gross national product (GNP), it has remained flat—just 2.8 percent—over a long period of time, while Japan's R&D spending has doubled and Germany's has tripled in the last twenty-five years. If we consider civilian R&D alone, both these nations make a larger investment than our 1.8 percent—2.7 percent and 2.5 percent, respectively—and despite yearly increases since 1981, basic research as a percentage of total federal R&D has been dropping over the last three years. Similarly, federal support to universities has been dropping one percentage point per year.

To make matters worse, the moderate gains of the last few years, far from being consolidated, are in danger of erosion. Despite severe budget constraints, the administration had proposed doubling the budget of the National Science Foundation by 1992, beginning with a 17 percent increase for the 1988 fiscal year. Unfortunately, congressional action on the FY1988 budget has provided no real growth for this important area.

Despite a heightened awareness, the outlook for assuring an adequate supply of educated individuals for our economy is not reassuring. The number of college students interested in pursuing graduate work and careers in the sciences and engineering is declining, and the void is being filled by large numbers of foreign students who, in the long run, represent an uncertain source of supply. Demographic trends will make matters worse. Even if the proportion of students interested in the sciences and engineering remains the same, the number of such majors will decline as the college-age population declines in the years ahead. The education of a graduate scientist or engineer is a long-term, cumulative process that begins in primary school. It is clear that we still have an enormous task ahead of us to avoid shortages of technically skilled manpower.

As we continue to struggle with budgetary constraints and the very real pressures caused by economic dislocations and resource limitations, it becomes more difficult to keep in mind the long-term requirements for our scientific, technological, and economic competitiveness. Nevertheless, as the gravity of our situation becomes more obvious, the strategies put forth in "Managing for Challenging Times" not only retain their value, but become more urgent.

Simply put, we must significantly increase support for basic research and place greater priority on civilian research within federal R&D. We must attend systematically to the health of the research infrastructure. That means providing for research equipment and facilities, but above all, it means providing support for people and ensuring an adequate supply of scientists and engineers for our future. We must support cooperation between university and industry researchers and develop an institutional framework hospitable to the kind of multidisciplinary and cooperative research that enhances the transfer of new knowledge to commercial use.

Finally, we must continue to develop a policy environment conducive to marshaling the energies and investments of government, industry, and universities to make the most effective use of our total national assets. This includes a continuous dialogue on goals, needs, and approaches and a commitment to cooperation for the purpose of maximizing our resources.

NOTES

1. The author wishes to acknowledge the assistance of Marta Cehelsky in the preparation of this article.
2. The debate ranges through a number of recent activities and publications. The most notable are the science policy review by the Science Policy Task Force, established by Representative Don Fuqua, chairman of the House Science and Technology Committee; the White House Science Council Task Force on Federal/University Relationships; the White House Science Council Panel on Federal Laboratory Review, which published an initial report in 1983 and a follow-up review on the implementation of its recommendations in July 1984; the National Science Board's February 1985 report on excellence in science and engineering education, which addressed the problem of direct congressional funding of research facilities; and the November 1984 conference on academic research facilities sponsored by the National Academy of Sciences, the

National Science Board, and the White House Office of Science and Technology Policy. Sections of the report of the President's Commission on Industrial Competitiveness (1985) also bear on research conduct in the United States.

3. Testimony by Simon Ramo before the House Science and Technology Committee's science policy task force, 25 July 1985, contains a valuable review of manpower shortages in key areas of science and engineering and their implications.

4. See also Davis-Van Atta, Carrier, and Frankfort 1985:7–8. Major reports on the declining quality of U.S. education include U.S. Education Department 1983, and National Science Board 1983.

5. For recent trends, see also NSF 1985.

6. Conference on Academic Research Facilities, Washington, D.C., 22–23 November 1984, sponsored by the National Academy of Sciences' Government, University, Industry Research Roundtable, the National Science Board, and the White House Office of Science and Technology Policy.

7. NSF and the Department of Health, Education, and Welfare had the largest programs, although NASA and the Department of Energy also provided some institutional development support for universities. The NSF programs peaked in 1966 and were eliminated by 1972.

8. See discussion of this point in the recent testimony by Lewis Branscomb, former National Science Board chairman, before the Senate Commerce, Science, and Transportation Subcommittee on Science, Technology, and Space, 2 May 1985.

9. The United States had the lowest percentage of industry-funded R&D among the industrialized nations in 1970. By 1979, U.S. industry had increased its investment in R&D to 67 percent, second only to the French private-sector investment in R&D of 71 percent. (NSF 1983:10).

10. Public opinion surveys conducted over a number of years by NSF and the National Science Board indicate a steady increase in public awareness of science and technology issues (NSF 1983).

REFERENCES

Association of American Universities; National Association of State and Land-Grant Colleges; and Council on Government Relations. 1985. *Financing and Managing University Research Equipment*. Washington, D.C.: Association of American Universities.

Davis-Van Atta, David; Sam C. Carrier; and Frank Frankfort. 1985. *Educating America's Scientists: The Role of the Research Colleges*. Report of the Oberlin Conference on the Future of Science at Liberal Arts Colleges, June 9–10. Oberlin, Ohio: Oberlin College (May).

Doyle, Denis P., and Tery W. Hartle. 1985. "It Costs a Small Fortune." *Washington Post* (1 September).

National Science Board Commission on Precollege Education in Mathematics, Science, and Technology. 1983. *Educating Americans for the 21st Century*. Washington, D.C.: National Science Board.

National Science Foundation. 1985. *National Academic Research Equipment in Selected Science/Engineering Fields, 1982–83*. Washington, D.C.: National Science Foundation.

———. Forthcoming. *National Patterns of Science and Technology Resources*. Washington, D.C.: National Science Board.

———. 1983. *Science Indicators 1982*. Washington, D.C.: National Science Board.

President's Commission on Industrial Competitiveness. 1985. *Global Competition: The New Reality*. Washington, D.C.: Government Printing Office.

Price, Don K. 1976. "Endless Frontier or Bureaucratic Morass?" In *Science and the Public: The Changing Relationship*, edited by Gerald Holton and William A. Blanpied. Boston Studies in the Philosophy of Science 33. Boston: D. Reidel Publishing Company.

U.S. Department of Education. Commission on Excellence in Education. 1983. *A Nation at Risk: The Imperative for Educational Reform*. Washington, D.C.: Government Printing Office.

White House Science Council. 1983. *Report of the White House Science Council Federal Laboratory Review Panel*. Washington, D.C.: Office of Science and Technology Policy (May).

Yankelovich, Daniel. 1984. "Science and the Public Process." *Issues in Science and Technology* (Fall).

7 THE RESEARCH AGENDA ON COMPETITIVENESS
A Program of Research for the Nation's Business Schools

Peter T. Jones and David J. Teece

The President's Commission on Industrial Competitiveness and historians, statesmen, and executives here and abroad have independently warned this nation that our declining ability to compete in world markets is symptomatic not only of current macroeconomic policy problems, but also of deeper structural, organizational, and infrastructural problems, which threaten American and international economic welfare and possibly certain social and political institutions as well. These problems have been long in the making, and some will take decades to overcome. They must and can be overcome in a responsible manner, however, to the positive sum benefit of the U.S. and the global economy.

An important prerequisite is the availability of scholarship that digs deep into the nature of the problems and their remedies. Since business must be a major part of the solution, researchers in the nation's business schools are well positioned to assist this process by furnishing studies that identify the big issues, researching those issues thoroughly, and furnishing managers, policymakers, and the work force with the evidence necessary to formulate effective remedies to the U.S. dilemma. The nation's business schools are also able to help identify companies that have responded successfully to the challenge and can make such experience available in the classroom as well as to other corporations.

While there is already considerable research available on the issues, the experts agree that only a rudimentary beginning has been made.

In particular, the problems have been documented more thoroughly than the solutions. An action plan for the private sector has been sketched only in faint outline.

Faculty in the nation's business schools can be at the center of a research program because of the broad range of disciplinary skills they collectively represent; the growing capacity demonstrated in bringing an interdisciplinary focus to complex business phenomena such as technological innovation; and their contact with executives and a student body that will be tomorrow's managers. Spillovers from research to student and executive education are a necessary and important component of the proposed program.

THE ISSUES

The research issues outlined include topics in innovation, manufacturing, organizational behavior, finance, industrial relations, compensation, business history, institutions, and law. No policy institute has more than one or two of these areas among its set of competencies. The nation's business schools are, therefore, positioned to make a unique research contribution, complementing the work of other institutes and university faculties with whom business schools should collaborate.

A program of research will take from three to five years for substantial progress to be made. Since most of the issues are core policy issues, research on many of the issues will need to be pursued for a much longer period. Representative topics that have a bearing on decision-making within firms, among firms, and in government at the federal, state, and local levels, roughly prioritized by the order in which they are presented, include:

The Corporation

- How can firms convert technological prowess into a sustainable marketplace advantage? What distinctive competencies are American firms lacking vis-à-vis their international rivals? In particular, to what extent is integration into the manufacturing function necessary to capture value from innovation? Put differently, what dysfunction, if any, can be expected from the "hollowing" of the American corporation?

- How can human resources be more effectively developed and utilized in the American corporation? As evidence mounts, both here and abroad, that methods of work organization, motivation, compensation, and training can make enormous differences to productivity, the implications for corporate structure and management and labor practices are in need of explication.
- How can successful methods of work organization already employed in the United States, especially by the Japanese, be diffused more rapidly? What are the managerial and labor barriers to change, and how can they be overcome?
- To what extent are conventional accounting and finance investment evaluation techniques faulted as sufficient guides for managerial decisions when difficult-to-quantify issues, such as product quality, flexibility, and responsiveness, are at stake?

Industry

- Is the concept of a strategic industry economically meaningful? What aspect of marketplace performance, if any, leads to underinvestment in such industries? Is firm size and industrial market structure of importance for U.S. competitiveness? Should the manufacturing and services sectors be viewed differently with respect to their qualitative importance to competitiveness?
- Are telecommunications as important to the business infrastructure today as the railroads were in the nineteenth century? If so, what are the implications?
- Do new forms of cooperative behavior within industries, such as strategic alliances, enable innovators to commercialize technology more quickly, with attendant competitive advantages? To what extent is cooperative behavior within firms in a nation a prerequisite for competitive success at the national level?
- What are some of the differences in the ways in which business institutions operate internationally? What, if anything, is to be learned from the structure and performance of the Japanese industrial groups and trading companies?
- What can be learned from the performance of Japanese-owned and/or -managed manufacturing operations in the United States? In particular, is the experience of U.S.-Japanese joint ventures, such as GM-Toyota NUMI, transferable? If so, how?

- Does vertical integration yield diseconomies in fast-moving environments? In particular, is the vertical disintegration of U.S. industry driven by the inefficiencies associated with vertical structures, or is it driven by low-cost, offshore out-sourcing opportunities?

Federal Government

- Must U.S. trade and exchange-rate policy be significantly changed to restore competitiveness? If so, how?
- Why do U.S. multinationals exhibit higher export competitiveness than the U.S. economy? What does this tell us about U.S. management, U.S. technology, and the U.S. economy as a site for operations?
- In what ways do U.S. intellectual property, antitrust, and bankruptcy laws promote or impede U.S. competitiveness? By promoting price competition over competition from new products and processes, does antitrust impede competitiveness? What kind of competition policy does today's business environment require?
- How does the institutional structure of U.S. credit markets impact savings? What modifications to existing credit regulations would promote savings? To what extent are U.S. investment decisions decoupled from U.S. savings decisions?
- What aspects of the tax code are particularly important to U.S. competitiveness? Which revenue-neutral changes would most positively impact U.S. competitive performance?
- Are U.S. science, technology, and educational practices and policies in need of fundamental restructuring? What are the implications of current demographic and educational trends for U.S. competitiveness?
- Can SEC disclosure policy be modified to yield information, such as productivity and product quality, more relevant to assessing a firm's economic performance? What impact, if any, would such disclosures have on managerial incentives and firms' performance?

State and Local Government

- What is the impact of product liability law on international trade? What can the states do about it?
- What state policies have had the most beneficial and the most negative consequences on competitiveness? In particular, should the efforts of states to attract foreign investment be coordinated?

- What directions must educational reform take to best serve com-petitiveness goals? How can technology transfer from state univer-sities to local industry proceed most expeditiously and efficiently without having a deleterious impact on academic research? Should universities engage in joint ventures with industry?

The Nation

- What are the geopolitical and economic implications of the failure of the United States to grow as fast as other leading industrial nations?
- How can the United States mount a response to the newly rising foreign competition after 1970 more energetic and successful than Britain's after 1870?
- What are the institutional, social, political, and intellectual forces that lie at the root of the U.S. failure to sustain a growth-oriented and internationalist economic policy?

Technology and organizational behavior issues are at the core, where the expertise of business school faculties is pertinent. We firmly believe that no other institutions can do a better job on these key issues than the business schools, particularly in joint ventures with other university departments, including engineering, economics, political science, law, and history.

For full effectiveness, a research program of the kind just outlined must be coupled with curriculum modifications and outreach. Both will be markedly assisted by the availability of studies that identify the roots of key productivity and competitiveness issues. More, how-ever, is obviously needed. To offer a better perspective on the scope, importance, and urgency of the research agenda we just summarized, the meaning of competitiveness, its present state in the United States, and the need for further research are presented in the pages that follow. For a more detailed discussion of the "Corporation," "Industry," and "Government" issues, the reader is referred to the appendix of this volume, "What We Know and Don't Know About Competitiveness."

Toward a Definition of Competitiveness

America is being challenged as if she were at war. It is not national borders that are being breached, although profound geopolitical issues do lie ahead. Rather, it is American levels of living and the viability of a liberal international order that are at stake. In order to respond to this challenge, the United States must regain its international competitiveness.

Competitiveness is not measured simply by economic growth, as economic growth can be fueled by foreign borrowing. Nor is it measured by the balance of trade or the current account balance, as a nation's external balance can be improved by devaluing its currency. If a nation has to bring the trade sector into balance by discounting the price of its exports and increasing the price of the goods and services it imports, it is improving its trade balance, but only through lowering the real incomes of its citizens. Lying behind international competitiveness is more than just productivity. Productivity—which measures the rate at which the quantity of inputs needed to produce a defined unit of output changes—does not easily accommodate factors such as product innovation. Moreover, productivity does not measure or account for the pricing of a nation's internationally traded commodities, which is often a function of product quality and the degree to which a nation can capture value from its product innovations. Thus, if a nation is producing customized and differentiated goods, productivity measures alone are unlikely to capture the essence of international competitiveness. Moreover, productivity does not reflect the strategic significance and growth opportunities of a nation. A country that had the highest productivity in the manufacture of buggy whips in 1910 would not have had quite the prospects of a nation that had the highest productivity in automobiles.

Competitiveness will be defined here as a relativist concept because it is recognized that declining relative performance from parity involves very significant economic, political, and social adjustment costs. This definition rejects the notion that a nation can be competitive if it is not keeping abreast of its principal trading rivals.

Competitiveness is a new concept, which deliberately does not bear a close relationship to standard measures of economic performance. This is because it is increasingly apparent that the spillovers and interdependencies in the international economic system are now enormous; a hybrid concept has had to be invented to capture the richness of the performance concept most relevant in today's world. This discussion of competitiveness is being deliberately undertaken without a definition. We are not sure that one precise definition can be offered, nor that it is needed.

The language of competitiveness is new only to the present generation of Americans. Ironically, it was common usage in the United States
in an earlier period, and competitiveness is an age-old topic of discussion among policymakers and businessmen abroad. Certainly it is not
an unfamiliar term to the Japanese or to Europeans. It is a developmental
term, and it slides into disuse when a nation's economic preeminence
is not at issue. There admittedly is a degree of vagueness to the term,
which should not be all that surprising. Complex problems involving
interdependencies are difficult to sense, let alone define and solve
(Mason and Mitroff 1981). Only simple problems have a one-dimensional
goal structure that guides the solution. Separability, reducibility, and
one-dimensional goal structures mean that simple problems can be
bounded, managed, and "tamed."[1]

The problems of competitiveness are all highly interrelated and,
hence, cannot be easily tamed. Competitiveness problems fall into a
class that has been called "wicked" (Rittle 1972). *Wicked problems
have no definitive formulation*, and understanding the problem is
almost synonymous with identifying solutions. Such problems never
have closure, they go on forever, as there is always room for improvement. Defining the problem of competitiveness is thus a research problem in and of itself. Following Lawrence (1986), three distinct notions
can be identified:

1. One concept is that competitiveness refers to the comparative per-
    formance of the United States versus other nations. "We take certain
    criteria that we consider desirable objectives for an economy—
    most noteworthy and commonly used would be output per man
    hour or total productivity—and then compare how we are doing
    in relation to other nations" (Lawrence 1986:17).
2. A second concept relates to U.S. performance in international trade,
    such as the current account balance.
3. A third notion, which Lawrence believes to be the most impor-
    tant, has to do with efficiency. "Are we doing the best we can?"
    (Lawrence 1986:18).

The third notion is clearly not a relativist formulation of the problem.
One is tempted to comment that, to the extent that different economies
have similar potential and are not politically constrained, the best way
to ascertain whether an economy is doing the best it can is to look

at its growth history and the performance of other advanced industrial nations with which it trades. This formulation of the nation brings one back very close to the first concept.

How one defines the problem of competitiveness is partly a consequence of how one perceives national goals. We take it as axiomatic that Americans want to maintain economic growth commensurate with other key industrial countries at similar levels of per capita income. We assume that American society must experience economic growth in order to maintain its social contract. A demographically and ethnically diverse society, we assume, can best flourish when opportunities for economic advancement are constantly created and no group is locked into the status quo by lack of opportunity. We also take it as axiomatic that an open world trading system, in addition to economic growth in the West, is an important prerequisite for the maintenance and furtherance of democratic societies worldwide. In short, should the American economy decline relative to the rest of the world in the way the British economy has in this century, we see the stability and viability of democratic institutions everywhere being placed at risk.

With this in mind we offer the following definitions:

1. Competitiveness is the ability of an economy's GNP and GNP per capita to grow as fast as any other major economy.
2. Competitiveness is the degree to which a nation, in a world of open markets, produces goods and services that meet the tests of the marketplace while simultaneously expanding GNP and GNP per capita at least as fast as any other major trading economy.
3. Finally, we offer a third definition from the President's Commission on Industrial Competitiveness (1985): "Competitiveness is the degree to which a nation can, under free and fair market conditions, produce goods and services that meet the test of international markets while simultaneously maintaining or expanding the real incomes of its citizens."[2]

We do not find any of these definitions ideal, though we favor definitions that have a relativist performance component. The reason for the latter is that we believe that the nature of technological development is such that there are large costs for the United States in falling behind other trading economies. For one, U.S. military strength depends on a qualitative rather than a quantitative edge. If the United States loses control over key technologies that have military significance, and those technologies are exposed to the risk of early transfer to adversaries, then, in order to maintain the balance of power, the United States must follow the Soviet strategy of diverting a substantially larger share of GNP into defense. We do not believe that the latter strategy is viable in a peacetime democratic society. Needless to say, there are also economic and social risks associated with falling behind.

THE PRESENT STATE OF U.S. COMPETITIVENESS

In January of 1985, the President's Commission on Industrial Competitiveness issued its report, *Global Competition: The New Reality*, which evaluated the state of U.S. competitiveness in the international economy. The commission unanimously and forcefully concluded that the United States faced a serious competitiveness problem requiring both public and private remedies. Other eminent observers have gone further, with one noting that "future historians may well mark the mid-1980s as the time when Japan surpassed the United States to become the world's dominant economic power" (Vogel 1986:752).[3] Relevant indices of competitiveness include the trade balance, U.S. shares of world trade in manufactured goods—especially high-technology exports—and gross domestic product (GDP) per capita.

Competitiveness is not an end in itself. It is a means to an end. It is a measure of a nation's economic capability and potential in the world economy. Nations that are competitive are in a position to fully capture the benefits of a liberal international order. They are also in a position to fashion it and to meet domestic social and economic goals as well. Nations that were once internationally competitive, but then lose that position, face wrenching economic, political, and social adjustments.

The United States has lost the internationally competitive station that it occupied for much of this century. The American people have been insulated from all but an inkling of the direct impact of this process by massive foreign borrowings that have propped up levels of living. Unless U.S. international competitiveness expands quickly and dramatically in this decade, painful adjustments will be experienced over the decades ahead, with attendant damage to the economic, political, and social infrastructure of the nation and of nations that are interdependent with us.

The U.S. economy has slightly improved its performance on these indices in some respects since *Global Competition* was issued, but the competitive problems the commission identified still remain. Inflation and interest rates have fallen, the stock market remains close to historic highs, but the trade deficit and the level of U.S. indebtedness to the rest of the world has expanded. The U.S. trade deficit in 1986 was the largest in world history (approximately $150 billion). The United States took nearly seventy years to accumulate a peak creditor position of almost $150 billion in 1982, but the rapid deterioration in trade and current account balances that began in 1983 dissipated this position in only three years (U.S. Commerce Department 1986). In every subsequent year, net indebtedness has increased. Deleterious trends recognized by the commission have continued largely unabated, despite a significant devaluation of the dollar against several key currencies since about September 1985.

Especially troublesome is the dramatic decline in U.S. high technology trade (Finan, Quick, and Sanberg 1986). These industries, which include computers, scientific instruments, aircraft, and specialty chemicals (but exclude low-research-intensive, consumer electronics like televisions, stereos, and videocassette recorders), possessed a strong export position until recent years.[4] More complacent observers of the U.S. trade situation have argued that the trade deficit is part of an inevitable process of restructuring the American and international economies; old "smokestack" industries in the United States naturally lose their competitive edge to producers in countries with lower labor costs and cheaper raw materials, while the U.S. industrial base shifts to high-technology industries where, it is argued, there is a natural comparative advantage, owing to a large and productive research base. Recent trade trends indicate, however, that the United States has not been maintaining, much less increasing, its relative or absolute position in high-technology trade. In fact, the substantial trade surpluses once experienced in this sector had slid into deficit by 1986.

The persistence of the trade deficit, despite significant dollar devaluation, is disturbing. Even if export values increase and import values decrease by an amount sufficient to bring trade into balance, which is highly unlikely in the near term, the picture is still troubling in that it suggests that the United States must resort to devaluing its way out of trade deficits. Obviously, the United States would be better off if balance could be achieved through lowering domestic costs through new technology and greater efficiency. Ominously, U.S. productivity growth since 1982 has not improved by more than is usually associated with an upswing in the business cycle, thereby suggesting that the United States will continue to lag behind Japan, Germany, and other countries on this critical index of competitiveness.

Unless U.S. competitiveness improves, the dollar will continue to drift lower against the currencies of Japan, West Germany, Switzerland, and other nations whose competitive performance is superior to that of the United States. A historical progression similar to that which Britain experienced through much of this century may then be upon the United States.

RESPONSES TO THE PRESIDENT'S COMMISSION AND THE NEED FOR FURTHER RESEARCH

The President's Commission called upon both government and the private sector to respond. The responses have been muted. The Reagan administration ignored the commission that it had appointed; and the major legislative initiative since the report was filed—the tax bill— did not even recognize the commission's recommendations.

A major contention here is that, although competitiveness concerns have now commonly surfaced in the press and in Congress, and although as a result of the work of the President's Commission and many other organizations and scholars our understanding of the U.S. dilemma is considerably better than it was just a year or two ago, vast areas of ignorance remain. We contend that understanding the challenges requires new paradigms of trade and investment, new paradigms of management and organization, and new paradigms of capital markets and business-government relations.

All of this indicates that the intellectual battle has not been won, that important processes are not well understood, and that proposed solutions are either opaque or unappealing to important interest groups able to forestall change. Hence, the need for a major research program to sense the problems, clarify the issues, diagnose the problems, quantify the stakes, and outline the solutions.

We do not mean to imply that all aspects of competitiveness need to be researched and that answers do not exist to many important questions. It does appear to us, however, that many important issues are inadequately understood and that, moreover, an important group of decisionmakers lacks the important facts, analyses, and syntheses that could provide the foundations for action.

Such a research program must be coupled with outreach efforts so that the research culminates in action. The measure of success of the research program will be more than the publications it engenders and the national dialogue it stimulates. It will also include the affirmative responses it triggers. In this sense, the research program we have in mind is more than the typical academic exercise. Besides the research publications, it hopes to assist curriculum improvement in business schools, attitude and behavioral changes in labor and management, and policy changes at the local, state, and federal levels of government.

The program being proposed is to be housed in the nation's business schools for several critical reasons:

1. Business school faculty have the interdisciplinary and broad-based skills that can help elucidate competitiveness issues. In some ways, a well-balanced business school is a miniuniversity, with several major disciplines represented. These typically include economics, sociology, psychology, mathematics and statistics, history, and computer science. Many fields of business, such as international business, industrial relations, marketing finance, the management of innovation, information systems, and public policy, draw on and integrate these disciplines in ways that may prove useful for a comprehensive analysis of competitiveness issues. To this end, business school faculty also are well positioned to collaborate with faculty in other university departments and with professional schools such as law and, especially, engineering.

2. Business schools may well be part of the problem, through the design of curriculum and the pursuit of research styles that in some cases pay such great attention to theoretical elegance and minutiae that relevance is torpedoed. In other instances, research has a level of specificity that is so great—as with the case study—that no meaningful induction or deduction is possible. In short, the middle ground needed between the highly abstract and the highly particular may be imperfectly represented. It is this middle ground that we propose to promote. In any event, the President's Commission challenged the nation's business schools "to undertake a systematic and comprehensive academic response to the changing competitive environment" (President's Commission 1985:56).

3. Business schools can surely be part of the solution. The framers of this proposal believe that the primary response to the competitiveness challenge lies in private hands, though government is also

important. Business schools are well positioned to build the kind of partnership with business and labor that is needed to provide the intellectual and pragmatic case for change.

4. Business schools, as well as other parts of the university, also have access to government and have the credibility to be heard. To the extent that policy initiatives are required that lack an articulate constituency, academic personnel can make an effective contribution by getting critical national issues on the legislative agenda.

5. Research in business schools necessarily impacts teaching, not only because most academic researchers are also teachers but because research findings inform the design and content of instruction provided to tomorrow's managers.

The agenda of a competitiveness program is necessarily broad. We want to make it clear, however, that we understand that the nub of the problem and the focus of the proposed program lie with the processes of innovation, which we believe are strongly systemic. We believe it to be uncontroversial that industrial competitiveness depends on the process by which new products and processes are continually introduced, improved, produced, and replaced. The effects of this are seen clearly not only in the familiar pattern of industrial growth and decline, but also in the changing patterns of employment as new skills are created and old ones become redundant.

For purposes of analysis and in spite of important overlaps, it is useful to think of decisionmakers in at least four different institutional settings as having access to the levers that control U.S. competitiveness: the firm, the industry, state and local government, and the federal government. Accordingly, research issues categorized under each of these institutions are presented in the appendix at the end of this volume.

Needless to say, this research agenda, even in its more detailed formulation in the appendix, is necessarily incomplete as to subject matter, and particularly as to methodology. In fact, there is no attempt here to specify the most suitable methodologies, although it is our belief that the most productive approaches are likely to involve a mixture of theory building and theory testing, with emphasis on the empirical dimension of the research activity. To the extent that theoretical efforts are employed, we believe that eclectic approaches that are decidedly heterodox show the most promise. Clearly, we also favor comparative institutional research and the gathering of field evidence. This is where academic research has underinvested in the past, and in our judgment it is where the greatest challenge, but also the greatest "pay dirt," lies.

NOTES

1. Even complex problems can be "tamed" if the variables are not interconnected.
2. This was originally put forward in Cohen et al. 1984.
3. For an alternative view, and one that suggests that Japan will not provide the economic challenge in the future that it has in the past, see Krugman 1986. Early reviews of the state of U.S. competitiveness include Lawrence 1984 and Scott and Lodge 1985.
4. In 1980, the high-technology industries as defined by the Department of Commerce "DOC3" produced a trade surplus of $27 billion, but have declined in every year since.

REFERENCES

Cohen, S.; D. Teece; L. Tyson; and J. Zysman. 1984. "Competitiveness." Published as Vol. 3 of *Global Competition: The New Reality*, Report of the President's Commission on Industrial Competitiveness. Washington, D.C.: Government Printing Office.

Finan, W.; P. Quick; and K. Sandberg. 1986. "The High U.S. Trade Position in High Technology: 1980–86." Report prepared for the Joint Economic Committee of the U.S. Congress.

Krugman, Paul. 1986. "Introduction: New Thinking about Trade Policy." In *Strategic Trade Policy and the New International Economics*, edited by Paul Krugman. Cambridge, Mass.: MIT Press.

Lawrence, R.Z. 1984. *Can America Compete?* Washington, D.C.: The Brookings Institution.

Lawrence, R.Z. 1986. "Perspectives on Technology and Industrial Competitiveness." Edited transcript of a National Academy of Engineering roundtable. Washington, D.C.: NAE (August).

Mason, R. and I. Mitroff. 1981. *Challenging Strategic Planning Assumptions*. New York: John Wiley & Sons.

President's Commission on Industrial Competitiveness. 1985. *Global Competition: The New Reality*. Washington, D.C.: Government Printing Office.

Rittle, H. 1972. "On the Planning Crisis: Systems Analysis of the First and Second Generations." *Bedriftsokonomen* (NR8: 390–396).

Scott, B. and G. Lodge. 1985. *U.S. Competitiveness in the World Economy*. Boston: Harvard Business School Press.

U.S. Department of Commerce. 1986. *U.S. Trade: Performance in 1985 and Outlook*. Washington, D.C.: International Trade Administration (October).

Vogel, E. 1986. "Pax Nipponica?" *Foreign Affairs* (Spring): 752–767.

IV INDUSTRY STRATEGIES

8 THE TRANSFORMATION OF MANUFACTURING AS A NATIONAL PRIORITY

John W. Rouse

"The age of U.S. industrial supremacy has clearly ended, and a new period of head-to-head competition has begun," wrote Wickham Skinner (1985:viii). U.S. industry is now competing in a new game, against strong opposition, and with a different set of rules.

THE PROBLEM

We are not doing well. Our imbalance of trade is dangerously high and worsening every year. For the first time in over fifty years, the United States is a debtor nation. American products are being beaten by superior quality, service, and reliability and by lower prices. According to Skinner (1985:71), "Loss of market shares to international competition in dozens of industries refutes any optimistic view of U.S. industrial performance."

The challenge facing U.S. industry is to rapidly regain a competitive position in international markets via a greatly enhanced manufacturing capability. The magnitude of the task is enormous. The importance of the effort is beyond measure. The progress toward the goal is uneven: spectacular in some areas, dismal in others. We lack a satisfactory game plan, adequate technology, appropriate performance criteria, and most importantly, we lack people with the skills and experience to get the job done.

The present state of affairs developed with surprising suddenness. The U.S. electronics industry, for example, dominated world markets until very recently, and the often cited crisis in the U.S. automobile industry is less than a decade old. It is perhaps because of the newness of the problem, and the lingering disbelief that it could happen here or be long-lasting, that acceptable solutions are evolving so slowly.

In the meantime, the situation—that is, the trade imbalance, deteriorating domestic markets, etc.—is worsening quarter by quarter. At least it now has our attention. Harvard professor Harvey Brooks (1985) noted that "American competitiveness in the world economy has now become the highest priority item of public discussion, and almost every government policy is being assessed for its impact on the rate and quality of industrial innovation and competitive performance."

SEARCHING FOR ANSWERS

Despite the public clamor for government action to curtail foreign imports or otherwise improve the competitive advantages of U.S. producers, such actions do not represent long-term solutions to this nation's poor market performance. The fundamental causes of our problems are lurking inside U.S. companies. That is where the answers must be found.

The search for answers has focused a great deal of attention on the executive suite. Shortsighted capital investment strategies driven by the need to maximize quarterly profit sheets are being blamed for many of the most serious problems. The "MBA mentality" favoring short-term optimization of "return on investment" is frequently cited as a major failure of conventional business practices. It has become disturbingly clear that the "market" driving the decisionmaking processes in many large corporations is only loosely related to the market in which their products must compete.

There is also a growing awareness that the accounting practices that provide the data upon which critical capital investment and production decisions are made are either inadequate or inappropriate to support the development of manufacturing systems on a par with the Japanese. It seems to many people that there is something unwise about the "conventional wisdom" employed in compiling, interpreting, and basing decisions on these data.

It may be that the answers to our problems lie somewhere among the management practices of modern companies. Certainly part of the solution is there, but there are also serious problems on the factory floor. The U.S. product design, production, and performance parameters that determine customer acceptance, market share, and profits are too often being bettered by foreign competition.

The United States is the world leader in innovation skills, but that capability is not proving adequate to control product markets. Indeed, products of our own inventions, produced better and cheaper abroad, are becoming our toughest competition.

The situation on the production line is now getting the level of attention it has needed for some time. Manufacturing has come to the forefront in corporate decisionmaking like never before in the last twenty years. For better or for worse, the government and universities have also joined in the effort. Suggestions for new approaches are coming from every quarter.

The approaches favored by experienced production managers, who have to live with the decisions, are generally of three types: (1) fine-tune the present production system; (2) return to the production concepts that worked in the past; (3) develop entirely new principles of manufacturing.

It is clear that "fine-tuning" is the dominant theme of most of the activity now under way in our nation's factories. Very few companies appear to have the money or the courage to undertake implementation of completely new manufacturing concepts.

In their defense, it should be noted that there is an alarming shortage of viable new manufacturing concepts that might be tried. As Erich Bloch (1985a), director of the National Science Foundation, recently commented, "Manufacturing science is in its infancy."

Nevertheless, many companies are making a serious attempt to strengthen their manufacturing capabilities to meet the competition. Many corporate executives are relying on the emerging automation, robotics, and computer technologies to upgrade existing production facilities. There is a growing market for new automated machinery and new information-handling systems. We are hearing new terminology like "computer-integrated manufacturing" and "computer-aided engineering." Robots, computer-aided design computer-aided manufacturing (CAD/CAM) systems, computerized inventory control, etc. are becoming increasingly familiar sights on the factory floor.

These are healthy signs that U.S. industry has awakened to the seriousness of the problem, and that it is mobilizing its considerable resources to regain its once dominant position in world markets. New research is being initiated in universities and federal laboratories, and new research centers and revised curricula are blossoming on campuses from coast to coast as the momentum for change gathers steam.

DISTURBING REALITIES

Some of the new "advanced manufacturing facilities" implemented during the last few years have been spectacular successes. Production man-hours have been reduced, cycle-times shortened, product quality improved, sales expanded, and profits increased. Such success stories as the General Electric diesel engine and the Maytag refrigerator are the stuff that the dreams of investors in robotics are made of.

Unfortunately, some of these "modern" facilities have been complete failures. The list of failed attempts to adapt automation and robotics technologies is growing at a disheartening rate. Much of the almost new factory automation equipment now in instructional laboratories at our engineering schools represents the tax write-off from aborted efforts to upgrade assembly lines.

The troubling aspect of most of these fine-tuning approaches is that it is extremely difficult to quantify the causes of the successes or the failures by either a priori or postmortem evaluations. In the final analysis, manufacturing in its present form is an art. The quality of performance of a production operation is most often a direct function of the talent of its designer. That's fine for companies with an abundance of such "artists," but it is a disquieting prospect for a nation in need of a massive upgrading of its manufacturing capabilities.

In general, these fine-tuning activities, particularly those that focus on substituting high-tech equipment for manpower, are of the "quick fix" variety that contribute little to our understanding of the underlying issues that manufacturers must eventually face.

BASIC ISSUES

In Skinner's analysis of this situation, he offered the following insightful observations:

The assumptions on which manufacturing is conventionally managed are out of date. . . . Manufacturing implicitly has a new manufacturing task but continues the old manufacturing policies and structure. . . . Few executives realize the existence of trade-offs in designing and operating a production system. . . . Industry is clinging to the myth that the main criteria for evaluating factory performance are efficiency and cost. . . . The mistake of considering low cost and high efficiencies as the key manufacturing objectives is typical of the oversimplified concept of good manufacturing operation. . . . We are beaten more often by superior product quality, service and reliability than by lower prices. . . . Mass production as we have known it is an outmoded concept" (Skinner 1985:59, 33, 54, 210, and 9).

The problems troubling manufacturing in this country appear to be too deep-seated, too fundamentally a part of our corporate culture, to be resolved by merely fine-tuning existing production systems, regardless of the sophistication of the technologies being employed in the process. According to Skinner (1985:56), "What is needed is changes in thinking, not changes in technology."

A return to the production practices of the golden post-World War II era likewise does not appear to offer much promise for success. An objective analysis of that period clearly shows that it was the golden postwar markets, not superior production methods, that yielded the exceptional profits. Those market conditions disappeared more than a decade ago.

NEW APPROACHES

There exists now throughout our country a stimulating environment for change. There is an exciting vitality within the manufacturing community; people are anxious to try new ideas, implement new technologies, and experiment with new production methods, new curricula, new management strategies.

Many companies are receptive to change, and they are optimistic about the future. What we lack are the tools with which to accomplish the transformation of manufacturing into the competitive force this nation must have.

Erich Bloch (1985b:11–13) observed, "The problem is to develop a genuine science of manufacturing. . . . In manufacturing today we have a primitive technology analogous to Watt's steam engine. . . . We are far from ready to address sufficiently the change to the new manufacturing age. . . . We do not have the people we need to do the research and planning, to build and staff the factories of the future.''

The challenge is to elevate manufacturing from an art form to a science; to define its structure and quantify the associated decision rules; to formulate evaluation criteria and measures of success.

One approach to meet this challenge might be a concept known as "product engineering" (also known by the name "unified life-cycle engineering" [U.S. Air Force 1986]). Product engineering encompasses the engineering expertise associated with the design, production, testing, marketing, and maintenance of technology-based products as a holistic, integrated process.

Manufacturing can be described as a process of transforming information and materials into useful products (Lardner 1986). In this context, product engineering is the formulation, quantification, management, and evaluation of the information involved in the total product generation cycle. It is an activity that characterizes the product generation cycle as a continuum, which, when optimally implemented, results in successful, competitive products.

The distinguishing characteristic of the product engineering viewpoint is that the measures of performance of the product design, production, maintenance, etc. are consistently product-based. That is, the basic principle of the product engineering method is that every activity associated with a product, every decision made relative to it, must be determined, evaluated, and verified in relation to the corporate strategy for achieving a competitive position for that product.

Manufacturing executives like to think their present production systems meet these criteria. Most do not. Consider, for example, the typical engineering design process. In traditional product development, the engineering design is an iterative process involving, usually in sequential order, a number of "experts," each at different nodes in the process, to check, refine, and/or modify a product as deemed appropriate relative to the expert's particular functional area of responsibility.

In addition to being unacceptable in terms of lag-time to market, this process is costly and frequently causes the designer to lose control. That is, this method compounds the problem of incorporating and maintaining the performance, producibility, reliability, maintainability, etc. features that are critical to achieving a competitive product.

The premise upon which the product engineering concept is based is that the design and production of competitive products requires a thorough knowledge of the interrelationships of each of the distinct steps in the process. For example, the design engineer must understand the manufacturing options and trade-offs in addition to the characteristics of the product that enhance customer acceptance, and these features must be basic to the design.

The task of quantifying the many interrelated factors that influence the competitive potential and profitability of products is overwhelming. Therefore, approaching engineering design and manufacturing from the viewpoint of product competitiveness and compatibility with corporate strategies and resources is usually beyond the scope of activity of most engineers engaged in the various segments of the product generation cycle.

The Texas Instruments wristwatch is a classic example of a product with superb design and production, but with neither activity adequately interrelated and in association with critical factors that customers accept.

The problem of accounting for all of the elements involved in the generation of competitive products is compounded by the fact that many companies have deliberately segregated engineering and business operations into distinct compartments, such as design, manufacturing, accounting, marketing, etc. This trend has been aided and abetted by the increasing specialization of university curricula in science, engineering, and business administration.

Many U.S. manufacturers attempt to overcome these problems by employing ''design teams'' that include not only representatives from the several disciplines required in the development of modern technology-based products but manufacturing engineers, quality control engineers, and marketing specialists. Products such as the MacIntosh computer and the General Dynamics F-16 fighter aircraft are excellent examples of how effective this approach can be. Unfortunately, there are far more examples where the approach failed, for example, in the automobile industry.

In general, our understanding of the interrelationships of the principal components of the product generation cycle, and of the criteria they must satisfy to be considered ''optimum,'' is so limited that we are unable to employ them effectively. Yet, based on what we see happening abroad, it appears that our competition has gained a sufficient knowledge and appreciation of these relationships to employ them to their competitive advantage.

Some believe that the practice of some Japanese companies of requiring that design engineers have extensive hands-on experience in manufacturing, quality control, etc. before undertaking product design provides the Japanese designers with a better understanding of the overall product generation cycle than that possessed by their U.S. counterparts (Davidson 1984). This may be one cause of the advantage the Japanese have in lag-time to market and in overall product competitiveness.

A methodology such as that embodied in the product engineering concept might provide a foundation for evolving the principles of a useful manufacturing science. Unfortunately, such total-system concepts constitute extremely complex and difficult research topics, and product engineering has remained as yet merely an abstract concept. As a result, the attention of most of the ongoing research activity in this country is focused on the separate components of the product generation cycle, that is, on design, manufacturing, logistics, etc. The traditional American belief that the optimum system is one composed of optimum subsystems still dominates the thinking of much of the manufacturing community, despite the criticism of Skinner and many others.

LOOKING AHEAD

The President's Commission on Industrial Competitiveness (1985) found that an essential reason for our country's loss of vital, high-growth markets is that "the United States has failed to apply its own technology to manufacturing."

This failure is certainly not due to an unwillingness on the part of corporate executives and production managers to try new ideas and new technologies. Rather, it is the scarcity of proven ideas and tested technologies that is handicapping the effort. These deficiencies leave us without adequate criteria upon which to base the prerequisite investment decisions that could eventually lead to the desired transformation of manufacturing.

What would help us most are good role models. After giving special attention to Japan in the hope of learning from their examples just what needs to be done here, it has been generally concluded that Japan's models are not readily transferable to our industrial culture. We must develop our own models.

By tedious and expensive trial and error methods, the United States is beginning to accumulate the knowledge of how to produce products that can compete and win in international markets. Multimillion-dollar experiments by major corporations such as General Electric, General Dynamics, IBM, Texas Instruments, and Chrysler are showing the way into a new era of manufacturing in this country. Some of the results are encouraging.

It is too early to formulate blueprints of how this transformation can be made to happen, but among the lessons being learned are that product quality is a paramount issue in today's markets, and that automation techniques are generally superior to manual labor in ensuring uniform quality of product.

We also know that to absorb the cost of implementing quality-dictated automation equipment and still keep the product price within the market tolerances, the cost of labor per product must be reduced to an absolute minimum. Not only must direct labor costs be decreased, but the white-collar labor costs that have mushroomed in recent years must be drastically reduced.

This fact has caused great concern among economists and sociologists, who warn that the decoupling of industrial growth from employment opportunities will introduce serious socioeconomic problems in this country. Clearly, one measure of the success of implementing automation technologies is the reduction of labor cost per product. To conclude, however, that having done so the number of jobs will be proportionately reduced, does not appear to be valid. The reason is that the cost of implementing automation technologies cannot be offset by labor costs alone, except in a few high-labor-rate industries, such as automobiles and steel. The corporate investment decision process leading to automating manufacturing must include the probability of expanded markets. In most cases where automated manufacturing has proven effective as a corporate strategy, the market growth has offset the reduced labor cost per unit of production, and the number of employees has increased, not decreased.

SUMMARY

There is no doubt that the transformation of our manufacturing capability from the present tradition-bound factories to efficient, competitive production facilities is a high priority concern in the United States. The status and progress of this effort is summarized in the following observations.

First, we are clearly on the threshold of a major revolution in U.S. manufacturing that will result in sweeping changes throughout the country during the next decade. The most visible indicators of these changes will be the new technology incorporated into manufacturing systems—robotics, CAD/CAM, computerized inventory control, etc. The most significant indicators, however, will likely be found within the product design process. Holistic design methodologies providing closer coupling between product design and the other principal activities of the product generation cycle, including corporate marketing strategies, will emerge and mature as a primary factor in product competitiveness.

Second, there is a sense of urgency about this movement, yet there are many significant barriers to implementing the necessary changes in our factories. The most troublesome is the lack of enough knowledgeable people to make the changes in an intelligent, cost-effective manner. The primary talent pool upon which the nation must draw for this task is composed of the very people who fashioned the manufacturing systems we now consider inadequate. The new talent emerging from our universities is inexperienced and untested, and the curricula through which they passed are still experimental. Fortunately, professional groups, such as the Society of Manufacturing Engineers, and many large corporations have initiated aggressive programs to upgrade the capabilities of our technical labor force. Their efforts, complemented by improved university curricula, should overcome the personnel barrier to the development of competitive product production capabilities in this country. We also suffer, however, from a lack of accepted criteria against which to optimize the production process. What are the appropriate measures of "goodness" of a manufacturing operation? When a critic like Wickham Skinner labels as "myth" the time-honored criterion of efficiency and places cost as the primary objective for factory performance, he attacks the heart of conventional production optimization procedures. But then, what quantifiable measures are we to use? We are yet to arrive at a uniformly acceptable set of alternative standards.

Third, the current generation of automation and robotic devices and computer software are inadequate to meet our needs. Direct replacement of manual labor with currently available technology has not proven cost-effective, except in a few specialized manufacturing situations. It appears that a total-system approach is necessary to make automation pay, including appropriate redesigning of the product. This approach is expensive, particularly since we are yet to define and master the methodologies of total-system automation.

Fourth, computers appear to offer enormous potential for increased productivity, but in too many instances we are not asking the right questions before incorporating computers into the production process. The cases where the introduction of computerized procedures has actually increased the cost of production constitute an alarmingly high percentage of the total number of applications.

Finally, advanced manufacturing technologies will evolve at an ever accelerating rate. Inevitably, within the next decade virtually every manufacturer in this country will be forced to incorporate aspects of these new processes in order to remain competitive. Yet, as a nation, we are not properly prepared to undertake that challenge.

Despite the many problems we are experiencing today in the international marketplace, I share the growing optimism that during the next few years we are going to see significant and positive changes throughout the manufacturing community. We will regain a dominant competitive position in world markets. And that is not just a goal worth pursuing, it is a challenge we cannot afford to ignore.

REFERENCES

Bloch, Erich. 1985a. "Rebuilding the Research and Education Base for Manufacturing." Engineering Education (October).

———. 1985b. "Manufacturing Technologies." *The Bridge* (Fall): 11–13.

Brooks, Harvey. 1985. Speech presented at symposium on economy and technology, National Academy of Engineering, Stanford University, Stanford, California, March 17–19.

Davidson, William H. 1984. *The Amazing Race: Winning the Technorivalry With Japan*. New York: John Wiley & Sons.

Goldstayn, A.B. 1986. *U.S. Air Force Systems Command*. "Military Needs and Forecast 2." Washington, D.C.: Government Printing Office (July).

Lardner, James F. 1986. "Computer Integrated Manufacturing and the Complexity Index." The Bridge (Spring):10–16.

President's Commission on Industrial Competitiveness. 1985. Vol. 1 of *Global Competitiveness: The New Reality*. Washington, D.C.: Government Printing Office.

Skinner, Wickham. 1985. *Manufacturing: The Formidable Competitive Weapon*. New York: John Wiley & Sons.

9 MANUFACTURING AS A COMPETITIVE STRATEGY

William P. Weber

U.S. industry is undergoing fundamental changes whose full impact on the economy may not be seen for many years. In industry after industry, manufacturers are either going out of business or giving up on the United States as a suitable place to make their products.

ECONOMIC FACTORS AFFECTING MANUFACTURING

The symptoms of the decline of U.S. manufacturing are clear and unmistakable. By most measures, the manufacturing sector has collapsed from a peak of 30 percent of U.S. gross national product in the early 1950s to about 20 percent in 1985, with much of the decline coming in the last two decades. (See Figure 9-1.) No single statistic exemplifies the troubles of American industry as much as our manufacturing trade balance. After several decades of surplus or near equilibrium, the U.S. trade balance for manufactured goods plunged to a $40 billion deficit in 1983, $80 billion in 1984, and $110 billion in 1985. (See Figure 9-2.)

The ability of the United States to keep pace in world markets is slipping not only in traditional manufacturing areas but even in high-technology industries—a sector in which we have always taken our leadership for granted. In the computer industry, the flagship of

Figure 9-1. U.S. Manufacturing as a Percentage of GNP (Current Dollars).

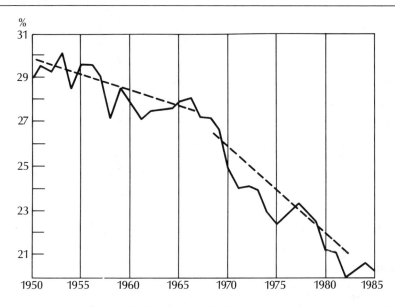

Source: U.S. Department Commerce, Bureau of Economic Analysis, *Survey of Current Business*, various issues.

Figure 9-2. U.S. Manufacturing Trade Balance (Billions of Dollars).

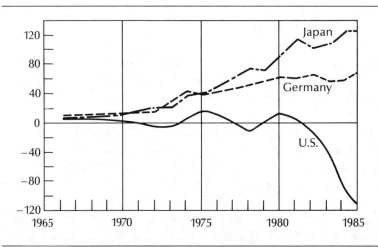

Source: U.S. Department of Commerce, Bureau of the Census, *Highlights of U.S. Export and Import Trade*, various issues; and Organization for Economic Cooperation and Development, *Monthly Statistics of Foreign Trade*, various issues.

America's high-technology sector, import penetration has increased by a factor of nine in the last six years. Communications and instruments have also suffered large losses in market share. (See Figure 9-3.)

Cost-of-Capital Differential

What are the forces weakening U.S. manufacturing, and what strategies could reverse this decline? First, the United States has been handicapped by a tax code that has encouraged a low propensity to save and intensified the cost of doing business relative to Japan. Trade barriers are not the secret to Japan's success, nor is superior technology. Instead, Japan's performance is in large part the result of financial advantages that have been translated into market advantages. High savings rates in Japan, and close ties between banks and industry, have favored highly leveraged financial structures. Debt is less expensive than equity, and Japanese firms have exploited that fact with debt-equity ratios that are much higher than comparable ratios in the United States. The combination of low-cost debt and high debt-equity ratios has provided Japanese firms with a 2:1 cost-of-capital advantage over U.S. firms.

Figure 9-3.   Import Penetration of U.S. Markets (Percentage).

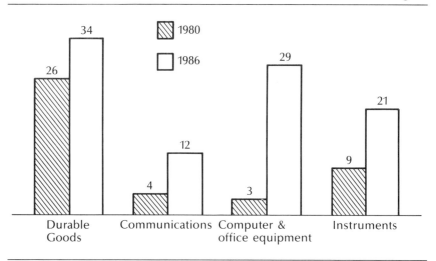

Source: U.S. Department of Commerce, *M-3 Current Industrial Reports, Manufacturers Shipments, Inventories, and Orders*; and Electronic Industries Association, *Market Data Book* various issues.

Furthermore, Japanese companies benefit from a tax system that effectively exempts from taxation most dividend income, interest income, and capital gains on stock. The result, shown by the gap between the two curves in Figure 9-4, is that even if debt-equity ratios were the same in Japan and the United States, the Japanese would still enjoy a cost-of-capital advantage.

Lower cost of capital and different earnings standards of the financial community have allowed Japanese firms to succeed with only 1 or 2 percent after-tax profit on sales, compared with the 5 or 6 percent required in the United States. This difference in acceptable profit margins means more cash available to our Japanese competitors for additional capital investment and research. If this disparity is allowed to continue, Japan's technology will become superior to ours, because U.S. companies will not be able to keep up with Japanese investments.

The recent U.S tax reform, instead of narrowing the cost-of-capital gap between the United States and Japan, actually widened that gap by repealing the investment tax credit and raising the capital gains tax

Figure 9-4. Cost of Capital, U.S. vs. Japanese Companies (Texas Instruments vs. NEC Corporation).

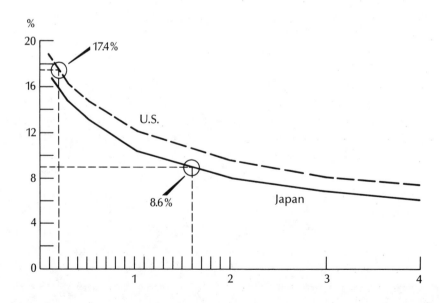

Source: Texas Instruments' internally developed financial models for cost-of-capital analysis.

on investment income. The new tax bill still does not adequately address the major issues that are needed to make this country more competitive. It encourages consumption rather than saving; it does not go far enough in promoting R&D investment; and it penalizes manufacturing industries while providing a tax windfall to services. A more thoughtful reform of the U.S. tax code would encourage savings, discourage consumption, and provide incentives for private R&D.

Educational Gap

A second force weakening U.S. manufacturing has been our disregard for quality education and our neglect of engineering programs. With a national commitment to excellence in education, the Japanese are raising a whole population to a standard currently inconceivable in the United States. Meanwhile, we are for the first time in our history producing a generation less educated than its predecessor.[1]

With a population only about half that of the United States, the Japanese are projected to graduate over 10,000 more engineers per year than we are for the remainder of this decade. (See Figure 9-5.) On top of this quantitative advantage, the starting salary of a Japanese electrical engineer with a bachelor's degree is roughly 70 percent of the salary of a comparable U.S. engineer.[2] Also, the Japanese practices of on-the-job training, exposure to manufacturing operations, and job rotation enhance their productivity.

Although figures on U.S. engineering graduates show some improvement, recent increases in the number of bachelor's degrees awarded are deceptive. Projections of engineering graduates suggest that we neared a peak level in 1986, and that we face a downturn over the next decade because of a drop in the available college-age population.[3] These trends are worrisome for a nation accustomed to carrying the banner of world technological leadership.

Low Productivity Growth

A third reason for weakness in manufacturing is a combination of low productivity growth, relative to other countries, and inability to translate ideas into production quickly and efficiently. Since 1960, Japan's

Figure 9-5. U.S. vs. Japanese Engineering Graduates

Half the population . . . 1986 (millions)	One-third the graduates . . .* 1984 (thousands)	But more engineers 1984 (% of graduates)
U.S. 240 Japan 121	U.S. 1037 Japan 383	U.S. 7 Japan 23

*Bachelor degrees

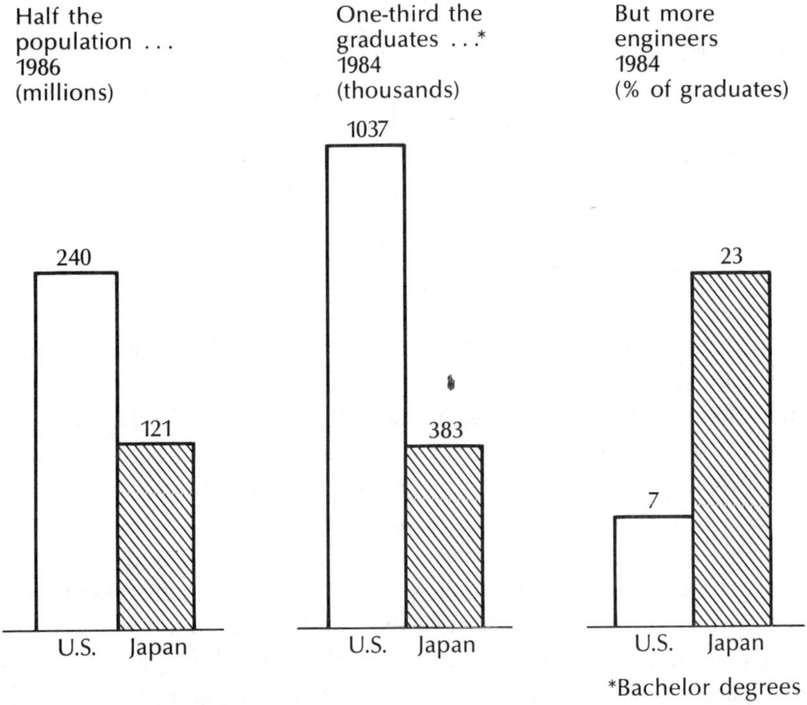

Source: Texas Instruments estimates, based on Engineering Manpower Commission, *Engineering Manpower Bulletin* (July 1984), and National Science Foundation, *Source Book on Engineers and Engineering Graduates* (1982).

productivity in manufacturing has increased three times faster than Europe's and seven times faster than that of the United States. (See Figure 9-6.)

The major causes of lagging productivity growth in the United States have been decreasing R&D as a percentage of GNP, insufficient capital formation, deterioration in work ethic, deterioration in education, and increasing energy costs. Although many of these negative factors have now turned in a more positive direction, much improvement is still needed.

Taking a product through all the steps between the prototype stage and full-scale production is often a more complex process than the initial product development itself. The Japanese recognized some time ago the importance of this critical phase in manufacturing and devoted a high percentage of their R&D to this area. As a result of their commitment of more people and resources, they are able to take ideas into

Figure 9-6. U.S., European, and Japanese Productivity Growth in Manufacturing (Billions of Dollars).

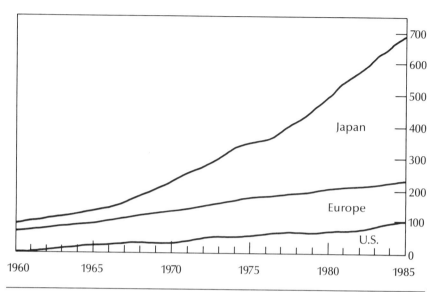

Source: U.S. Department of Labor, Bureau of Labor Statistics, *International Comparisons of Manufacturing Productivity and Labor Cost Trends* (1986).

volume production in only half the time we require.[4] We cannot expect to offset Japan's strengths by looking to them for changes. Instead, we need a strategy that creates our own advantages.

A WINNING MANUFACTURING STRATEGY

Many have suggested that high-technology industry could take up the slack caused by the deterioration of the U.S. manufacturing sector. Even though the rate of growth in technology-intensive industries is higher than in the traditional goods-producing sector, the absolute level of output and employment in high-technology industries is not enough to offset the impact of declines in the manufacturing sector.

A much greater economic benefit will be realized if we begin to think of high technology not only as an industry, but as a powerful set of tools that can revitalize our traditional industries. The revitalization of the U.S. manufacturing sector depends on changing the way we think about manufacturing.

The manufacturing strategy of the future must be geared toward more than just substituting machine functions for human functions. Success or failure in meeting the Japanese challenge will depend on how well we understand the manufacturing process, restructure the manufacturing process, and make manufacturing an integral part of our total product and marketing strategy.

Understanding the Process

How well we can integrate the manufacturing process, and incorporate it into the overall business strategy, will depend upon how well we understand the process itself.

In order to understand the process, we must be able to quantify, measure, and analyze the process, and we must have access to complete information. Nothing should move, change, or be processed in a factory without being captured electronically in a data base. This is where semiconductor and computer technologies can have a major impact.

Traditional approaches to analyzing the manufacturing process include systems engineering, operations research, modeling, and simulation. These approaches are not wrong; the reason they have not been as effective as we would like is that the systems engineers and operations researchers do not have access to sufficient information and could address only a part of the problem. Continuous performance and cost improvements in semiconductor logic and memory are leading to a proliferation of affordable "smart" devices on the factory floor. We now have the potential for accessing more and better information through artificial intelligence, distributed computing power, and communications networks. These emerging tools, coupled with the existing tools of modeling and simulation, will enable us to take a systems approach to enhancing the overall process, using hard data.

One example of better information access through distributed computing power is in controlling the environment of the clean rooms where semiconductors are produced. The newest generation of semiconductors, with 1.25-micron geometries, are 40 percent smaller than their predecessors, and the environments in which they are produced must be much more stringently controlled.

In Texas Instruments' newly designed clean room, a series of programmable controllers monitors each phase of the process, allowing us to collect data continually from 900 different sensors, instead of the 100 measurements every four hours with our earlier system. In addition, the new system provides a window into the entire process, so that the operator can quickly spot a problem as it develops and correct it before it causes a shutdown. Since installation of the new control system several years ago, monthly downtime costs have been reduced about 50 percent. And because it takes significantly fewer people to maintain the clean room to required specifications, monthly quality control and facilities wages have dropped by about half.

In attempting to gain more information about the manufacturing process, we are not limited to data gathered from measuring devices. Some of the most critical information is qualitative knowledge that only humans possess, so-called "expert knowledge." The era of computational plenty has given us the key to unlock this source of information through a branch of computer science called "artificial intelligence." This technology allows computers to address problems that require humanlike reasoning and intelligence, opens a new dimension in data processing, and will change the way we think about factory automation.

In addition to new tools for gathering and analyzing information, we now have the technology for tying this information together and distributing it to the user. Local area networks give us the technology needed to integrate all of our different sources of process information. From factory floor to corporate mainframe, we can link together our cell controllers, computer-aided design terminals, artificial intelligence workstations, and minicomputers with compatible and consistent data bases. With this linkage, we can collect, organize, and analyze information about the manufacturing process as a complete system.

For the first time, we can now have access to complete and consistent information wherever needed in the manufacturing hierarchy, and we can consider any problem in terms of its impact on the total process. Consistency assures us that the information presents the same conditions at the same time.

Restructuring the Process

With access to both real-time information and empirical knowledge, we can greatly enhance our understanding of the manufacturing process and design ways to improve it.

Often, in the process of restructuring the manufacturing process, a number of problems will come to light. Some are technical—existing tooling is inadequate, or not enough systems engineering has gone into the design of the new process. But the principal barriers to changing the system will be cultural. People are threatened by new and unfamiliar technology. Change creates new pressures on supervisors and requires operators to be more flexible. Changing the culture of the workplace requires significant attitude adjustments. For example, someone with an ingrained "more is better" attitude will not easily accept a manufacturing system geared to producing small quantities of a product quickly and with "zero" defects.

The fact that every individual has a vested interest in his or her part of the process can be a significant barrier to change, but it is also the key to implementing a new manufacturing strategy while increasing worker involvement. The same technology that allows us to gather data about the manufacturing process also makes it possible for the operator on the factory floor to control the process, experiment with it, and make it better. Each employee should be seen as a source of ideas, not just a pair of hands. Management can create the best environment for change by involving individual operators in planning and controlling his or her part of the process, along with giving operators the responsibility and the recognition for making improvements.

Manufacturing Strategy

The biggest attitude adjustment required is a recognition of the importance of manufacturing itself, and of the interaction between manufacturing and all other aspects of a business. An essential element in the revival of the U.S. industrial sector is the infusion of a stronger manufacturing culture in boardrooms and executive offices across the country, leading to the development of strategic plans that incorporate manufacturing as an integral part of a total business strategy.

Most strategic planning focuses on financial numbers, basic research, and designing products to meet market demand. Only rarely does it focus on manufacturing. This has produced a mentality that has caused manufacturing to be considered a process separate from design and distribution, and automation strategies have concentrated on improving isolated pieces of the manufacturing process. For the future, we must broaden this perspective and look on manufacturing as an integrated process.

"Integrated" means two things. First, manufacturing must be an equal partner with R&D and marketing and must become an integral part of a total business strategy.

Second, the manufacturing process itself must be treated in its totality. The most efficient use of resources requires looking at the process as an integrated system, and then investing in the resources necessary to optimize that system.

CHALLENGES FOR THE FUTURE

The U.S. government should take the lead in highlighting the importance of competitiveness and productivity. Our government should provide stable fiscal and monetary policies that ensure noninflationary growth, an environment that nurtures and protects technological innovation, an educational system that prepares our people for the future, a fair trading environment, and policies that help American firms and workers respond to the changing economic landscape.

But governments cannot legislate success. The ability to compete lies primarily within the private sector. Business must establish world leadership in the commercialization of product and process technology, raise investment levels in productive assets and in the development of employees, and broaden its perspective to include the opportunities offered by the global environment.

We have the means available to make manufacturing technology a competitive advantage for the United States. The challenge now is to put it to use.

NOTES

1. Standard Aptitude Test (SAT) average scores are 20 to 35 points below the levels achieved in 1967: from average scores of 466 and 492 on verbal and math components, respectively, in 1967—to 431 and 475, respectively, in 1985 (Educational Testing Service).
2. Texas Instruments, estimate of this figure is based on data provided by the Engineering Manpower Commission, *Engineering Manpower Bulletin* (1983), and National Science Foundation, *Source Book on Engineers and Engineering Graduates* (1982).
3. See note 2 above.
4. According to a 1976 special report by the National Science Foundation, *Indicators of International Trends in Technological Innovation*, the lapse of time from invention to market is 7.4 years in the United States, 6.5 years in Europe, and 3.5 years in Japan.

10 BIOTECHNOLOGY
Promise Redeemed

Douglas McCormick

Biotechnology isn't an industry. It isn't even a technology—not a single technology anyway. It's a collection of techniques for manipulating life. Biotechnology rests squarely on the knowledge we've gained over thirty years of basic research into the fundamental processes of life. And nearly all of the techniques we use have sprung directly out of methods developed in the laboratory to push back those frontiers of basic knowledge. The tools are very powerful. A look at the cross section of *Bio/Technology*'s readers indicates how diverse the biotechnologies are—they are developing human diagnostics and therapeutics and veterinary products, developing new plants, inventing replacements for agricultural chemicals, investigating alternative energy sources, producing flavors and fragrances, manufacturing commodity chemicals, and doing many other things impossible to catalog.

Space doesn't permit a review of the key underlying biotechnologies—recombinant DNA technology, monoclonal antibodies, fermentation and cell culture techniques, and the strategies for separation and purification. Anyone who needs a good introduction should get hold of the epic *Commercial Biotechnology*, just reissued by the Office of Technology Assessment (OTA). It is still as comprehensive and understandable an introduction as one is likely to find.

FREE RELEASE AND THE U.S. REGULATORY MESS

Since 1986, the regulatory situation in the biotechnology sector has clarified considerably. There is little doubt that biotechnology needs firm and credible regulation. But for too long the United States seemed in danger of dithering itself to commercial death. Thanks in part to a judicious, if in retrospect overcautious, concern on the part of scientists themselves, and in part to a dogmatic, metaphysical opposition from a single, high-profile opponent (Jeremy Rifkin and his one-man Foundation on Economic Trends), we were in danger of throwing our scientific lead away while we contemplated our regulatory navel—seemingly so determined to do everything so absolutely right that we were in danger of doing nothing at all. Meanwhile, we lost tens of millions of dollars a year to pseudorabies in pigs, billions of dollars a year to frost damage, and millions of lives to disease.

There is a gene in a leaf bacteria (*Pseudomonas syringae*) that makes a protein that helps ice crystallize at $-1.5\,^{\circ}C$ (Hirano 1985). That's about three degrees warmer than ice would otherwise form at. If you snip the "ice nucleating" gene out, the bacteria can't start ice crystals at these relatively high temperatures. Populate a field with those organisms and there is no room left for the bugs that do promote freezing. The field survives marginal frosts that would have killed it before.

There is a herpesvirus disease sweeping through U.S. swine. It kills piglets agonizingly and quickly. If you snip out one enzyme gene, the virus can't reproduce and spread, but it still produces a strong immune reaction when it's injected into a pig. The pig is protected against the virus without running any danger of getting the disease.

Both genetically engineered solutions were blocked by court challenges from Mr. Rifkin, even though the engineered organisms are nearly identical to their wild cousins. Some scientists would not call these deletion mutants "recombinant" at all. But because of the precise procedural requirements of U.S. environmental laws, it was possible for opponents to make victory on a procedural challenge look like a decision on the safety of the recombinant organism. This is what happened in May of 1984 when a U.S. district court enjoined researchers from continuing with field tests of ice-minus bacteria, tests that the National Institutes of Health (NIH) had approved as safe. But NIH had failed to toe the line and file an environmental impact statement. I learned long ago as a political reporter that a thorough knowledge of

Robert's Rules of Order can be more important than a knowledge of right and wrong.

Since then, existing laws have been stretched to cover biotechnology, producing a maze of regulation that is more complicated than ever, with jurisdiction split among the Environmental Protection Agency, the Department of Agriculture, and the Food and Drug Administration, under the 1976 Toxic Substances Control Act (ToSCA); the 1972 Federal Insecticide, Fungicide, and Rodenticide Act (FIFRA); the 1957 Federal Plant Pest Act; the 1974 Noxious Weed Act; and the Food, Drug and Cosmetic Act, among others.

FACTORS AFFECTING COMMERCIALIZATION

In *Commercial Biotechnology*, OTA labeled ten factors affecting the commercialization of biotechnology: personnel availability and training; government funding of basic and applied research; financing and tax incentives for firms; health, safety, and environmental regulation; intellectual property law; university-industry relationships; public perception; national targeting policies; international technology transfer, investment, and trade; and antitrust law. (See Figure 10-1.)

We've already discussed the regulatory mess; originally, OTA called this a secondary issue. Now, we'll turn to some of the other factors.

Financing

This critical aspect seems to be taking care of itself. It is interesting, though, to look at how the market is voting on biotechnology, using some figures put together by James R. Murray (1986), president of Policy Research Corporation.

The total private investment (TPI) in U.S.-based biotechnology through the end of 1985 was $4.003 billion. Of that amount, most interesting is the already mentioned $1.72 billion (43% of TPI) invested in cancer therapeutics (see Figure 10-2), followed by other human therapeutics ($773 million—19%) and diagnostics ($519 million—13%). The combined totals for all kinds of agricultural biotechnology—crop improvement, agrichemicals, and animal health—equal $713 million—18%. Specialty chemicals ($163 million—4%) and research supply ($136 million—3%) finish further back.

Figure 10-1. Relative Importance of Factors Affecting the Commercialization of Biotechnology.

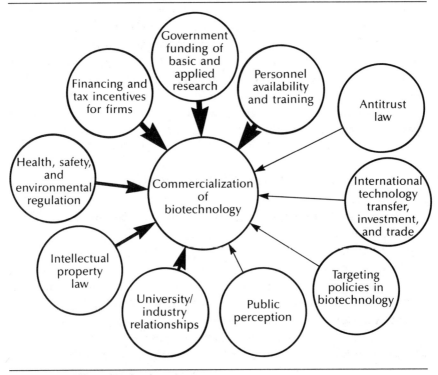

Source: U.S. Office of Technology Assessment.

Figure 10-2. Cumulative Investment in Biotechnology (through 1985) and Percent of Total Investment ($4.003 billion) by Application, Form of Transaction, and Technology.

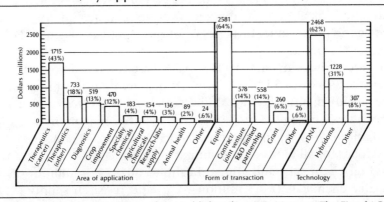

Source: Reprinted by permission of the publisher, from J.R. Murray, "The First $4 Billion Is the Hardest," *Bio/Technology* 4 (April 1986).

Investors have voted overwhelmingly to support recombinant DNA technologies ($2.47 billion—62% of TPI) over hybridoma technology ($1.23 billion—31%), though it is interesting to note that most of the biotech products producing profits are monoclonal antibodies; that's plain from the big jumps in recent years. (See Figures 10-3, 10-4, and 10-5.) Finally, private investment in U.S. biotechnology has been over-whelmingly American by a factor of 10. (See Figure 10-6.)

Despite much repeated predictions of a biotechnology shakeout, in-vestor confidence in biotechnology remains high. On 1 April 1987, Inter-national Plant Resources Inc. became the first company I've ever known to get out of bankruptcy through a public stock offering (for a successor company, Escagen). A little later, the nearly moribund Genex was rescued by an infusion of cash from a consortium of venture capitalists.

Federal Research Funding

This is a continual cause for concern. According to the historical tables of the U.S. budget, the administration proposed to spend a little under

Figure 10-3. Private Investment from all Sources: Major Product Application Areas.[1]

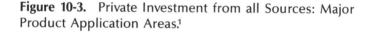

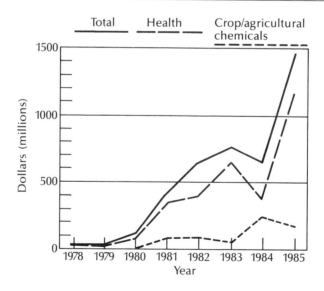

Source: Reprinted by permission of the publisher, from J.R. Murray, "The First $4 Billion Is the Hardest," *Bio/Technology* 4 (April 1986).

Figure 10-4.   Investment in Technologies: Cumulated Over Applications.

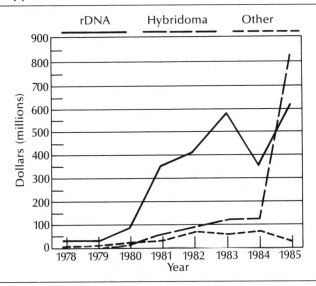

Source: Reprinted by permission of the publisher, from J.R. Murray, "The First $4 Billion Is the Hardest," *Bio/Technology* 4 (April 1986).

Figure 10-5.   Source of Investment: Cumulated Over Technology and Applications.[2]

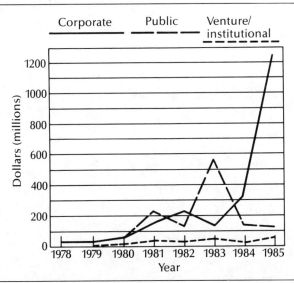

Source: Reprinted by permission of the publisher, from J.R. Murray, "The First $4 Billion Is the Hardest," *Bio/Technology* 4 (April 1986).

Figure 10-6. Country of Private Investor: Cumulative Investment.

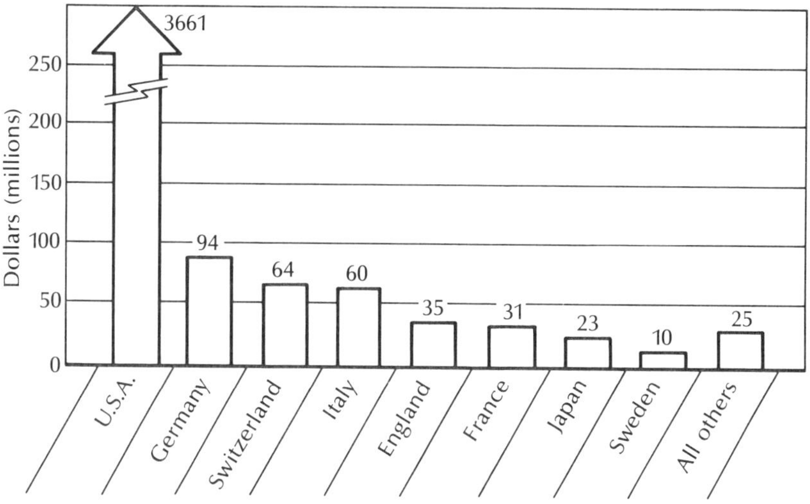

Source: Reprinted by permission of the publisher, from J.R. Murray, "The First $4 Billion Is the Hardest," *Bio/Technology* 4 (April 1986).

$5 billion a year on NIH (the primary support of life-science research) in fiscal years 1986 and 1987. The Gramm-Rudman dip in the 1987 allotment is worrisome, but not tragic. Look at the healthy increases over the last ten, twenty, and thirty years. (See Figure 10-7.) That growth looks much less healthy if you translate it into constant dollars or a share of GNP—essentially static at about $3.5 billion in 1982 dollars, or about .001 percent of the U.S. GNP.

Right now, NIH has allotted some $692 million for "generic applied" research in biotechnology, with $1.2 billion for related basic research (Perpich 1986).

The National Science Foundation (NSF) is running one $5 million-center in bioprocesses at MIT. And NSF's 1987 budget includes $20 million for two or three more biotech centers, with another $10 million for other biotech research. There is also a proposal on the books for a massive $500 million project for new NSF research centers in all fields, with a hefty share to go to biotechnology. And NSF, USDA, and the Department of Energy are looking at Office of Science and Technology Policy proposals to add $250 million for five years of research in plant biotechnology. Finally, the Department of Defense will fund three biotechnology centers for five years at a total of $45 million.

Figure 10-7. Outlay of Federal Support of Life-Science Research (Millions of Dollars).

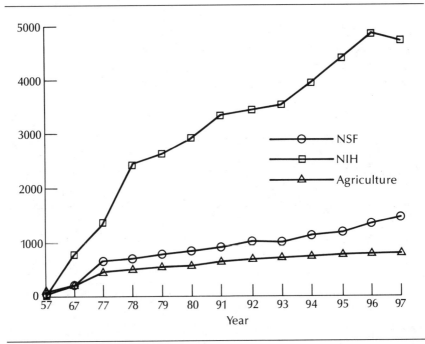

Source: U.S. Ofice of Management and Budget.

People

The United States has done an extraordinary job of training life scientists and attracting top talent from abroad. We need to remember, though, that "fewer than 20 U.S. universities have meaningful biochemical engineering programs. . . training fewer than 60 doctoral and masters graduates annually. The U.S. will need about two to three times that number (Perpich 1986:523).

I've seen fashions come and go in technical education. I've seen a drought in mechanical engineers followed by swelling enrollments—and a wholesale exodus of potential professional faculty into industry, drawn by outlandish supply-and-demand salaries. I've seen the same thing happen in the computer industry. And I'd bet a pretty penny that the same thing will happen, if it hasn't already, to life-science teaching in the United States.

INTERDISCIPLINARY AND INTERNATIONAL:
BIOTECHNOLOGY CROSSES ALL BOUNDARIES

It is interesting to glance over the public product portfolios of two leading biotechnology companies with a common bias towards pharmaceuticals. These lists show the true breadth of the technology. Interferon, interleukin, anti-infectives, cancer tests, VD tests, sickle-cell anemia tests, AIDS tests, vaccines against herpes and hepatitis, blood-clot dissolvers, blood-clotting agents, insulin, human growth hormones, liquid-handling instruments, herbicide-resistant plants, vaccines for porcine scours and foot-and-mouth disease, animal growth hormones, food additives, and wood derivatives.

They also show the number of Japanese partners intimately involved with the commercialization of biotechnology products at the world's top biotechnology companies. Biotechnology is not the sole preserve of any one nation. Most products are developed and sold by scientific and marketing talent drawn from several continents. It is therefore necessary to take a brief and oversimplified look at how things are progressing in some other parts of the world.

Japan

The Japanese have obviously made biotechnology a national priority. The national legislature boasts a Society of Diet Members for the Development and Protection of Biotechnology, chaired by the minister of finance (Cape 1986).

The government also maintains the bioindustry office in its Ministry of International Trade and Industry (MITI). MITI, as part of its "Next-Generation Technology" project, runs several biotechnology projects—in bioreactors, recombinant DNA, biomass conversion, and mass cell culture.[3] Other government agencies, notably the Science and Technology Agency, the Ministry of Education, and the Ministry of Agriculture, Forestry, and Fisheries, have programs of their own.

And there is the nonprofit Bioindustry Development Center (BIDEC), maintained by the Japanese Association of Industrial Fermentation; BIDEC collects and exchanges information on new trends, promotes international cooperation, and helps researchers travel overseas.

Overall, says Masami Tanaka (1985:176), director of MITI's Bioindustry Office, "Japanese biotechnology remains very close to more traditional technologies, like fermentation and enzymology, in which the country has accumulated considerable know-how. Industry is integrating this inherited strength with the new techniques of genetic engineering. This gives Japanese biotechnology one of its most distinguishing features."

(This inherited strength is real: Genex, one of the original "Big Four" of biotechnology, was one of the few biotechnology companies with a positive cash flow. It supplied most of the phenylalanine from which G.D. Searle made its sweetener, aspartame. When Searle licensed production technology from Japan and canceled its Genex orders, Genex all but closed up shop.)

The conventional wisdom in this country has been that the Japanese are very strong in the production technologies like fermentation—just as they are very strong in automotive and electronic production—but that the country is weak in basic science. "That," Pat Gage said at a roundtable dinner we had in the fall of 1985, "is an easy thing to say, but there may be a myth there. If you look at the new chemical entities in the drug area in the last few years, you'll find that a lot of them come out of Japan, and you'll find that they are getting a lot more bang for their buck in terms of new drugs approved... In our collaborations with Japanese companies, they have proven quite capable. They can produce recombinant proteins; they can clone them; and they can isolate them" (Klausner and McCormick 1986:21). Gage is vice president for exploratory research at Hoffmann-La Roche, USA and deals frequently with Japanese scientists.

Still, the Japanese seem to acknowledge some sort of weakness in basic research—and they seem determined to correct it (Anderson 1985). Even now, I'm afraid that Westerners tend to underestimate some of the strength of their basic science.

Much is made of the Japanese ability to mobilize towards stated goals, but little is said in biotech circles about the agents of that mobilization in international trade: the great *sogo shosha*, or trading companies: Mitsubishi, Mitsui, Marubeni, C. Itoh, Sumitomo, and Nissho Iwai. While they appear to be great and diverse producers, they are in fact middlemen. Although they began as brokers of bulk commodities, they are now turning to commerce in high technology (Itoh 1984), in the products and in the technology itself. Thus, MITI has to deal with a relatively small number of companies handling nearly a trillion yen (nearly $6 billion) annually. Implementing a biotechnology policy is thus relatively easy, at least compared with the situation in the United States.

Europe and the Organization for Economic Cooperation and Development (OECD)

The OECD released its guidelines for biotechnology safety after a lot of wrangling and dramatic confrontations (Henderson 1985a; Henderson 1985b; Sun 1985b). The OECD accords seem destined to be the nucleus of any international standardization in biotechnology; the governments of Japan and Europe have postponed issuing their own regulations on the key area of environmental release until the OECD document is available (Walgate 1985; Itoh 1985). Despite official government programs to promote biotechnology (Yanchinski 1984), Germany in particular seems beset by dogmatic, anti-biotechnology activists whose stated aim is to put a stop to the new science on the grounds that it is either unnatural or politically incorrect (pick one) (Walgate 1985).[4]

The OECD has a role in normalizing patent rules. The group has paid special attention to biotechnology patents; a suggestive result is that the countries that have been most aggressive in protecting patent rights—the United States and Japan foremost among them—are getting the lion's share of biotech investment. A special problem here is the tension between business demands and researchers' academic habits; scientists in the United States can publish their results and still patent their ideas—they can't in Europe.

The importance of patent protection has been underscored dramatically in a series of patent suits that have undermined the positions of some of the front-runners. In 1987, for example, Genentech had its European patent on the blood-clot dissolver, the tissue-type plasminogen activator (t-PA) disallowed, and Amgen lost a challenge to its rights to erythropoietin.

Export Laws

Congress passed a bill allowing export of pharmaceuticals not yet licensed for sale in the United States, if the importing country has duly approved the drug or if another ''approved'' developed nation has given its own go-ahead. Such a development could have three positive effects and one possible negative effect.

Fledgling biotech companies could develop much needed cash flow from foreign markets. They would then have an incentive to develop products—a malaria vaccine, for example—not needed here but badly needed abroad. And they could stop doing what many are doing now: striking licensing arrangements with foreign companies and exporting not drugs but the know-how for making the drugs.

The negative effect of a bill allowing the export of unapproved drugs could be the appearance—or the fact—of "dumping" dangerous or substandard pharmaceuticals on unsuspecting Third World populations.

THE BIOTECHNOLOGY PROMISE

Near-Term—Human Therapeutics: Heart Disease.   Heart disease is responsible for 34 percent of all U.S. deaths, the leading cause (U.S. Census Bureau 1986). Companies like Genentech expect their blood-clot dissolvers—t-PA and prouruokinase most prominent among them—to be their ticket to the pharmaceutical big time (McCormick 1987a, 1987b).

Cancer.   Each year, cancer causes 23 percent of all deaths. Investigators are pursuing virtually every conceivable cancer therapy. They have attacked malignancies with all kinds of monoclonal antibodies: "naked," toxin-linked (to kill the tumors), or tricked out with markers (radioactive or autofluorescent compounds that help doctors locate and diagnose tumors) (Klausner 1986). They have used immune modifiers like cell-wall skeletons and interleukin-2 to marshal the body's own defenses against tumors.

Others.   Biotechnologists are also making strides in mastering the systems that regulate blood pressure (Nakanishi et al. 1985). Implanting functional islet-of-Langerhans cells in porous capsules could "cure" diabetes with naturally regulated insulin.

Near-Term—Vaccines.   It would be cavalier to call vaccine development "routine." But it nearly is. Bacteria and yeasts can be made to produce key antigens from hepatitis, herpes (Valenzuela et al. 1985), and probably even HTLV viruses. More complex organisms—even the malaria parasite, which has made an evolutionary career of suborning the body's defense mechanisms and does it successfully enough to kill two million people a year (Ravetch et al. 1985)—are yielding their immunological secrets.

Near Term—Agriculture.   Right now, the most visible research efforts are aimed at engineering herbicide resistance into plants—a fairly straightforward task that will, first, secure lasting markets for the manufacturers of generally nontoxic, broad-spectrum herbicides like glyphosate and, second, increase productivity for those farmers who can meet the start-up costs (Fillatti et al. 1987). Most recently, genetic engineers have achieved insect resistance in plants, including the insertion into tomato plants of a natural bacterial compound that is harmless to humans (Fischoff et al. 1987). Beyond that, researchers are focusing on fundamental problems of genetic manipulation: how to get genes into plants; how to regenerate the recombinant plant tissue.

Harnessing nitrogen fixation is in the more distant future. Nitrogen-fixing bacteria, of course, associate with legumes and (of about equal importance ecologically, though not economically) with trees and grasses (Elmerich 1984).

Long-Term—Human Gene Therapy and Genetic Testing.   Most observers had expected approvals of the first human gene therapy protocols before now.

As has been pointed out many times, there are two distinct kinds of gene therapy—somatic and germline. Both use some agent—usually a retrovirus like Moloney murine leukemia virus—to insert a selected gene into the chromosome of a cell extracted from the patient.

Right now, all reputable researchers are proposing somatic cell therapies—that is, alteration of some selected tissues of an individual already formed. Current proposals are to insert, into the patient's bone marrow, genes encoding an enzyme that the patient lacks because his own DNA is damaged. In the future, however, the inserted sequences could include regulatory sequences and the genes for metabolic intermediaries for a variety of maladies. Only bone marrow, skin, and some liver tissues could be manipulated in this way.

Protein Design.   As we learn more about the tertiary structure of proteins—how proteins fold to produce it, how it affects biological activity—we will be able to design compounds that never existed in nature and act in ways nature never intended. We are still decades away from any practical capability here; researchers are just beginning to cobble together simple combinations of alpha helices and beta sheets (Van Brunt 1986a). Most of the time, it is a great victory if the thing merely folds into the expected shape, though Kaiser has produced an artificial molecule that not only mimics the performance of salmon calcitonin, but outperforms the natural compound (Van Brunt 1986b). The ability to design proteins, and eventually the ability to design non-protein molecules that will control living processes, is the key to a really controlled application of biotechnology.

Biochips.   Semiconductor electronics are reaching within an order of magnitude of their theoretical performance limits. The wavelengths of light put a lower limit on the size of structures that can be etched on silicon. Field effects limit how close circuits can be packed together without interfering with one another.

It is possible then, that when better computing machinery is made in the early twenty-first century, we will make it the old-fashioned way: we will grow it. Researchers have proposed several mechanisms for growing biologically based logic circuits (Van Brunt 1985). Any practical progress, though, is several decades away.

Energy.   Coming generations will have many more questions to answer. When the world's supply of oil dries up, will we still have access to the biological technologies developed over the past decade? I have seen some elegant technical approaches to producing alcohol, methane, and other fuels from materials nobody wants. The problem is that they never quite make economic sense. Will our society, so fixed on quarterly earnings statements, have the sense to preserve these solutions for the inevitable dry day?

Artificial Organs.   Developmental biology seems to be the real frontier of the laboratory life sciences now. When its puzzles are solved—and I'm betting that many will be—it will open the way to making replacement organs to order as the original equipment wears out. What kinds of expenses will the medical establishment face then? What will be the challenges of vastly elongated life spans?

Neurobiotechnology.   Increasingly sophisticated understanding of receptor function and of the structure of the nervous system opens the doors to research that will reveal the mechanisms of mental processes as clearly as earlier molecular biology revealed the function of the immune and hematopoietic systems.

The stage is set; the play has barely begun. No ringing curtain speeches are yet appropriate. Certainly the possibilities are vast. But what is important now are the choices we make today.

NOTES

1. The quantity of funds committed to agricultural applications has increased as a consequence of technological advance. Also, the percentage of funds committed to agricultural areas increased from 6 percent of total private investment in 1983 to 12 percent of TPI in 1985.
2. The cumulative investment provided by corporations in 1985 was $2.24 billion, or 56 percent of total private investment. Venture and other fund managers contributed $500 million, or 12 percent of TPI, and the public market made available $1.26 billion, or 31 percent of TPI.
3. MITI's budget, though, is just $130 million for a ten-year program, as noted in Sun 1985a, p. 791.
4. See also Dickson 1985, p. 13. Also, for a real horror story, see Klein, Corea, and Hubbard 1985. It reports on a meeting whose manifesto includes statements like, ''We declare that we do not want this [genetic and reproductive] technology and that we shall combat it in its true form: a declaration of war against women and nature'' (p. 6).

REFERENCES

Anderson, A. 1985. ''More Creativity Wanted: Japanese Research.'' *Nature* 313 (17 January).

Cape, R.E. 1986. ''Who Will You Blame When the Other Guy Wins?'' *Bio/Technology* 4 (April).

Dickson, D. 1985. ''Gene-Splicing Debate Heats Up in Germany.'' *Science* (April 4).

Elmerich, C. 1984. ''Molecular Biology and Ecology of Diazotrophs Associated With Non-Leguminous Plants.'' *Bio/Technology* 2 (November).

Fillatti, J.J.; J. Kiser; R. Rose; and L. Comai. 1987. ''Efficient Transfer of a Glyphosate Tolerance Gene Into Tomato Using a Binary Agrobacteria Tumefaciens Vector.'' *Bio/Technology* 5 (July).

Fischoff, D.A.; K.S. Bowdish; F.J. Perlak; P.G. Marrone; S.M. McCormick; J.G. Niedermeyer; D.A. Dean; K. Rusano-Kretzmer; S.G. Mayer; D.E. Rochester; S.G. Rogers; and R.T. Fraley. 1987. ''Insect Tolerant Tranogenic Tomato Plants.'' *Bio/Technology* 5 (August).

Henderson, N. 1985a. ''24-Nation Group Adopts Draft Gene-Splicing.'' *Washington Post* (December 7).

———. 1985b. ''Uncertainties of Biotech Rules Hold Up Global Marketing Plans.'' *Washington Post* (December 1).

Hirano, S. 1985. ''Ecology and Physiology of *Pseudomonas syringae*.'' *Bio/Technology* 3 (December).

Itoh, T. 1984. ''Trading Companies Have Many Biotech Roles.'' *Bio/Technology* 2 (December).

———. 1985. "Japan: Release a Long Way Off." *Bio/Technology* 3 (December).

Klausner, A. 1986. "Taking Aim at Cancer With Monoclonals." *Bio/Technology* 4 (March).

———, and D. McCormick. 1986. "The *Bio/Technology* Roundtable on Commercialization." *Bio/Technology* 4 (January).

Klein, R. D.; G. Corea; and R. Hubbard. 1985. "German Women Oppose New Technologies." *Gene Watch* (Boston) (September-October).

McCormick, D. 1987a. "Every Six Minutes." *Bio/Technology* 5 (July).

———. 1987b. "Genentech Bound." *Bio/Technology* 5 (August).

Murray, J.R. 1986. "The First $4 Billion Is the Hardest." *Bio/Technology* 4 (April).

Nakanishi, S.; N. Kitamura; and H. Ohkubo. "Structure, Regulation and Evolution of the Genes for the Renin-Angiotensin and the Kallikrein-Kinin Systems." *Bio/Technology* 3 (December).

Perpich, J. 1986. "A Federal Strategy for International Industrial Competitiveness." *Bio/Technology* 4 (June).

Ravetch, J.V.; J. Young; and G. Poste. "Molecular Genetic Strategies for the Development of Anti-Malaria Vaccines." *Bio/Technology* 3 (August).

Sun, M. 1985a. "The Japanese Challenge in Biotechnology." *Science* (November 15:791).

———. 1985b. "Administration Drafts Biotech Plan for OECD." *Science* (November 22).

Tanaka, M. 1985. "A Japanese View of Japanese Biotechnology." *Bio/Technology* 3 (February).

U.S. Department of Commerce. Bureau of Census. 1986. *1986 Statistical Abstract of the United States.* Washington, D.C.: Government Printing Office.

U.S. Office of Technology Assessment. [1984] 1987. *Commercial Biotechnology: An International Analysis.* Washington, D.C.: Government Printing Office.

Valenzuela, P.; D. Coit; M.A. Medina-Selby; C.H. Kuo; G. Vannest; R.L. Burke; M.S. Urdea; and P.V. Graves. "Synthesis and Assembly in Yeast of Hepatitis B Surface Antigen Particles Containing the Polyalbumin Receptor," and "Antigen Engineering in Yeast: Synthesis and Assembly of Hybrid Hepatitis B Surface Antigen-Herpes Simplex 1gD Particles." *Bio/Technology* 3 (April).

Van Brunt, J. 1985. "Biochips: The Ultimate Computer." *Bio/Technology* 3 (March).

———. 1986a. "Protein Architecture: Designing from the Ground Up." *Bio/Technology* 4 (April).

———. 1986b. "Neuropeptides: The Brain's Special Messengers." *Bio/Technology* 4 (February).

Walgate, R. 1985. "Europe: A Few Too Many." *Bio/Technology* 3 (December).

Yanchinski, S. 1984. "Biotechnology Taking Root in West Germany—Could It Challenge U.S.?" *Bio/Technology* 2 (April).

11 | SUSTAINING AND AUGMENTING COMPETITIVE ADVANTAGE IN EMERGING INDUSTRIES IN A GLOBAL ENVIRONMENT

Alfred J. Stein and Somshankar Das

The emergence of a global sphere of activity for several industries over the last decade and a half has very much become a fact of life. Nowhere is this more prevalent than in the emerging information-based industries. For the United States, this has created several challenges, the most significant of which is how to sustain and augment technical and commercial advantages. In the past, U.S. industries possessed, and virtually took for granted, these advantages. The new global environment, however, calls for a new set of skills to deal with the much wider and more discriminating customer base and a host of competitive elements, such as the increasing role of national governments, in promoting competitive advantage.

In the pages that follow, we will examine the factors causing the global expansion of industries, the general implications of this trend, and the challenges faced by management. We will also explore the characteristics of emerging industries and what management needs to do to address the challenges created by this new environment. Since a global perspective is more relevant to the information-intensive industries, the emerging industries referred to in our discussion are high-technology- and information-oriented.

We will conclude with a discussion of the alternatives open to management for retaining and advancing their business enterprises in this new global environment.

THE GLOBAL EXPANSION OF INDUSTRIES

The creation of global industries is characterized by distinct trends and features.

First, the world becomes one marketplace, with increased trade volume crossing national boundaries. Customers are located in all countries, and they may obtain products and services from different sources in different regions of the world. The actual mix of suppliers and products depends on what provides the best benefit-cost ratio to the global companies. In an excellent article in the *Harvard Business Review*, Gary Hamel and C. K. Prahalad (1985) clearly allude to the fact that the truly global competitor will adopt those strategies and organizations that best maximize cash flow from global operations, thereby retaining and advancing a competitive posture.

Secondly, the factors of production are chosen in a worldwide market to optimize their mix relative to cost or productivity. In other words, a company may have its manufacturing plants in Europe and Japan, its basic R&D laboratories in the United States, its product engineering facilities in the Pacific Rim countries, etc. This means that management acquires a global perspective to utilize the synergy possible through the interaction of different company operations in different areas of the world.

In contrast, in a traditional multinational corporation, management sets up self-contained national subsidiaries to cater to national markets. Different national subsidiaries have little interaction with each other and lack a global perspective. This form of international operations was common in the 1950s and 1960s with European corporations operating in developing countries (for example, Philips, Siemens, Imperial Chemical Industries) and U.S. corporations operating in different regions of the world (Ford, General Motors, IBM).

We saw the first signs of a true global corporation in the 1970s when Japanese companies began addressing the world marketplace and sought satisfaction of customer needs through some optimal combination of goods and services produced in different regions.

Factors Accounting for the Global Expansion of Industries

The factors contributing to the global expansion of information-intensive industries are discussed below.

Improved worldwide communication—itself a product of information-intensive industries—has linked different national marketplaces into one, gigantic world marketplace. The result is that economic and political events occurring in one place can, in real time, have immediate impacts on events in many other places.

The same improved communication also allows a corporation to link its worldwide operations and maximize economic benefits by entering into the more profitable markets, by minimizing manufacturing costs through appropriate location policies and by enabling timely responses to the moves of other global competitors.

Another consequence of better communications has been the emergence of a worldwide financial system that closely connects buyers, sellers, and investors across several continents.

Global expansion is obviously prevalent in such high-technology industries as semiconductors, computers, and telecommunications, where information is the key raw material. Since, unlike the traditional industries (steel, chemicals, paper, and engineering), high-technology industries do not depend on fixed natural resources, they have proliferated whenever their true limiting factor, the scarcity of people with the right managerial and technical background, has allowed it.

Recently, new players have aggressively entered the area of technology-based industries on a worldwide basis. Certain countries in the Pacific Rim and Japan have generated huge trade surpluses and, through appropriate government policies, are now investing these surpluses in emerging information-based industries.

The increased competition from new entrants has resulted in companies being forced to, for example, use the low-cost manufacturing in the Far East, have components and systems designed in the United States, and have software developed in India.

Cost is not the only consideration. Companies have also found the need to make their presence felt in certain markets and have made the necessary investments to achieve their goals. According to Hamel and Prahalad (1985), companies that wish to be truly global

> must distinguish between the cost effectiveness based on off-shore sourcing and world-scale plants and the competitive effectiveness based on the ability to retaliate in competitors' key markets. The cash flow available to a global competitor is a function of both total costs and realized prices. Cost advantages alone do not indicate whether a company can sustain a global fight. Price level differences, for example, may provide not only the means but also the motivation for cross-subsidization (p. 145).

Hamel and Prahalad (1985:144) have defined cross-subsidization as "a global company [using] financial resources accumulated in one part of the world to fight a competitive battle in another."

GENERAL IMPLICATIONS OF GLOBAL EXPANSION

There are six key elements of the phenomenon of global expansion that bear the greatest relevance for the management of individual companies. First is the role of national governments as promoters of as well as major players in the growth of high-technology industries.

Second, trade issues are becoming increasingly important. The concept of national sovereignty runs counter to global economic influence and results in trade frictions between countries. An example is offered by the increasing trade disputes between Japan and the United States. At the time of this writing, the dispute has worsened, and stiff tariffs are being imposed by the United States on selected Japanese electronic products.

Third, with more players expanding competition as a consequence of global marketing, many companies traditionally interested mainly in national markets have now arrived on the scene with substantial financial and technological clout, as well as governmental support, to stake out their claims.

Fourth, with the size of markets expanding, customers have become more knowledgeable and demanding, and with the geographic choices of suppliers widening, their bargaining power has increased.

Fifth, the environment in which business decisions are made has become more complex. Management has to simultaneously take into account such factors as the impact of government policies, trade relations and tariff barriers, ease of access to foreign markets, protection of proprietary information, and the impact of different business cultures and different expectations in other parts of the world.

Sixth, even large companies are finding it difficult to operate without appropriate business alliances. Corporate giants are collaborating to keep up with the increasingly competitive marketing environment. A good example of this is the collaboration between Philips and Siemens on the megaproject aimed at developing one-megabit static random access memories (RAMs) for low-power consumer applications (for Philips) and four-megabit dynamic RAMs for data processing equipment (for Siemens). The megaproject is the largest cooperative R&D effort in Europe today. Smaller companies are under even greater pressure to cooperate in R&D.

CHARACTERISTICS OF EMERGING COMPANIES

Some of the characteristics of companies in emerging industries offer important insights into the issues that must be confronted by management facing the global expansion of their industry. Among them is the fact that technological changes, rather than being incremental, are dramatic and repeat themselves in cycles. Another characteristic of companies in emerging industries is that product and technology life cycles tend to be short because the basic raw material being processed is information, rather than site-specific resources such as iron ore, wood, and crude oil.

Also, technology breeds more technology. Thus, a semiconductor company's product, VLSI chips, makes possible more powerful computers, which in turn make possible the development of more complex computer-aided engineering software that is used for the design of more complex VLSI chips.

Finally, the new technology industries are strongly people-oriented. Therefore, they can be set up very rapidly and with less capital investments than are required to establish traditional businesses such as steel mills, petroleum refineries, and paper mills. With lower barriers to entry, new competitors abound in high-technology industries. On the other end, because of the threat of rapid technological obsolescence, market shakeouts and consolidations are more common than in other industries.

CHALLENGES FACED BY MANAGEMENT OF EMERGING INDUSTRIES IN A GLOBAL CONTEXT

Having taken a look at the phenomenon of global expansion and at the basic nature of emerging technology-based industries, let us review the key issues that confront management: (1) How does a company obtain a global presence? (2) How is the optimum mix of factors of production, which will allow the company to remain cost-competitive or distinctive in some other way, identified and attained? (3) How should the company deal with the technological and other changes necessary to remain competitive in the marketplace? (4) How can the additional resources required be obtained?

To address these issues, management must commit to an international business strategy; understand international business cultures and practices; guide the company toward a distinctive competence, either technical or cost-related; and establish cooperation with other companies to ensure maximum efficiency in resource allocation.

The penetration of foreign markets can no longer be considered a secondary task undertaken after satisfying U.S.-based customers. Foreign as well as domestic companies see the United States as the largest and most attractive market, and U.S. management must respond in a proactive manner by shedding their commercial isolationist policies and selling in other countries.

Successful generation of business overseas requires a thorough understanding of a different customer base and of different business styles and practices. This makes management's commitment to an international strategy an area of considerable complexity (Hamel and Prahalad 1985). But let us assume that top management has the vision and the commitment needed to formulate an international business strategy, and turn to the task of developing a distinctive competence for the company.

To illustrate the need for a distinctive competence, we may look at the likely status of the semiconductor industry in the year 2000 A.D.

> The semiconductor world will be divided into two camps, each with its own distinctive set of market characteristics. One will produce high volume commodity parts, and the other the many forms of semicustom chips, including system-, customer-, and application-specific integrated circuits, as well as other parts targeted at low-volume market niches. The commodity side of the industry, which will be in the hands of a relatively few players, will focus more on low cost manufacturing than on interactions with customers. The semicustom side will represent a completely different way of doing business, with especially close customer relationships and high levels of service and support (Weber 1987:60).

For smaller companies, strengths in service and technology or focus on niche markets is absolutely essential for survival. Some examples are Altera, Brooktree, Integrated Device Technology, Weitek, and Vitelic in digital design; Crystal Semiconductor, Micro Linear, and Silicon Systems as leaders in analog design; Performance Semiconductor, Cypress Semiconductor, Mosaic Systems, and Inova Microelectronics having a distinctive competence in process specialization, and VLSI Technology, California Devices, LSI Logic, and Zymos excelling in integrated semicustom capabilities (design, prototyping, and manufacturing).

Without a distinctive technical or marketing advantage, small companies in emerging information-intensive industries will not be able to survive the competitive forces at play in the global environment.

Competitive Advantages for the Small, Semicustom Company

Let us consider the case of VLSI Technology, Inc. We are a semiconductor company, yet we are not in competition with large companies such as Texas Instruments, Motorola, National, or Intel. We have chosen the area of semicustom integrated circuits (ICs)—involving gate array and cell-based designs—which require unique strengths in IC design automation and manufacturing technologies and a strong customer-service orientation. These strengths are less critical for companies producing large-volume off-the-shelf components.

A conscious choice of the application-specific integrated circuit (ASIC) market within the IC industry, backed by strength in IC design technology, has been our key business strategy. We cannot rely, however, on these strengths alone. As more companies have brought sharper design technologies to bear on the ASIC market, it has been necessary for us to offer to our customers additional distinctive competencies. We have addressed this need by developing unique manufacturing systems and methods specific to low-volume semicustom designs and by creating libraries of IC design software elements that are among the most comprehensive in the business. The design software may be compared to a set of paint brushes and the library elements to the colors available to an artist: the greater the range of colors, the greater the creative possibilities for the artist.

This type of business strategy, based on a distinctive competence, has enabled VLSI Technology to weather, during 1985 and 1986, the worst recession in the U.S. semiconductor industry.

Competitive Advantages for the Large, High-Volume Company

Large companies that depend on cost leadership to remain competitive in a global context maintain ultra-efficient manufacturing systems and organizations. Competitiveness based on costs, however, involves more than using low-cost manufacturing locations in the Far East. The effects of such factors as new automated manufacturing technologies, tariff and nontariff barriers, and foreign exchange fluctuations influencing wage rates (in addition to local labor costs) determine the choice between manufacturing and buying a product's components, or choosing a combination of the two.

Large electronic system companies that are vertically integrated, such as AT&T, NCR, Rockwell International, Philips, Signetics, Siemens, and all major Japanese and Korean companies, have greater protection from market downturns than standard IC manufacturers such as Advanced Micro Devices, Intel, Texas Instruments, and National Semiconductor.

The Need for Cooperation

A direct consequence of a tougher competitive environment is the need for cooperation among companies.

The semiconductor industry provides a good example of this phenomenon. No other industry is confronted with faster change in both product and process technologies, accompanied by shorter and shorter life cycles.

Competition is acute between U.S. manufacturers as well as between the Japanese and other Pacific Rim countries. European manufacturers are making major investments and are aggressively positioning themselves in the U.S. market through various means, including acquisition of U.S. companies (for example, Thomson CSF's acquisition of Mostek).

Setting up new fabrication facilities now requires the investment of large sums in R&D, automatic IC design technology, process technology, and new product development. With rapid obsolescence having become a stark reality, the industry no longer tells low-dollar investment stories. Consequently, even large companies are finding it increasingly difficult to stand alone. The result is a plethora of alliances, ranging from joint ventures to second-source agreements and linking giant and small companies among themselves and to one another in closer customer-vendor relationships, R&D cooperatives, and strategic partnerships between competitors.

Closer Customer-Vendor Relationships.   Three conditions usually account for this relationship: the customer represents a major sales opportunity for the vendor, the customer is a leader in its own industry, and the vendor has strategic access to the customer's product development programs. The motivations are greater control over the quality of supplies, better delivery schedules, and timely supply of proprietary products and services.

As companies seek to develop closer ties with their major industrial customers, they must secure access to their product development plans. And the greater the competition, the greater is the need for strategic access to the customer's future product plans.

For example, the growing use of semicustom and custom chips to create computer systems that competitors cannot clone or match induces computer manufacturers to prefer suppliers who produce exclusive, customer-specific devices. In turn, the vendor must have an understanding of the system needs of the manufacturer if it is to be effective in designing and producing the right kinds of chips.

At VLSI Technology, our marketing distinguishes between strategic and other accounts. A strategic account is a customer that has the potential to exceed $50 million in annual sales within five years and has the financial strength, product offering, and the marketing expertise to remain a leader in its market.

Research and Development Cooperatives.   In the past, R&D projects funded by industry were implemented in either industrial or university laboratories but "owned" exclusively by the sponsoring company. When R&D activity was sponsored by traditional trade organizations, it focused on projects not too closely linked to the business strategies of member companies.

Today, with resources shrinking relative to the expanding global environment, even the largest technology-based companies can no longer rely solely on internally generated and financed projects (Fusfeld and Haklisch 1985). Emerging new forms of cooperative R&D are being well endowed, often with research budgets of several tens of millions of dollars.

These newer R&D groups found in high-technology industries emphasize the development of a technological base that promotes a competitive capability named "precompetitiveness," become an integral part of the company's strategy, and receive direct attention from top management.

Large cooperative research projects first occurred in Japan and Europe in the 1970s, under government inducement, in order to compete with the United States. But in the 1970s, the United States was still the unquestioned technology leader, global competition was less obvious, and individual companies did not feel the pressure for cooperation. Also, the influence of government on the private sector was and still is considerably less in this country than in Europe, Japan, or Korea, and the United States lagged behind in forming the new R&D cooperative ventures.

The intense global competition of the 1980s, however, especially from Japan and in the semiconductor industry, has forced American companies to cooperate in R&D. Good examples of the new American trend are the Microelectronics and Computer Technology Corporation (formed in 1983), the Semiconductor Research Corporation (formed in late 1982), and Bell Communications Research (1984). The major difference between these ventures and their overseas counterparts is the role of government: minimal in the United States now, but perhaps increasing in the near future. The recent formation of SEMATECH by the Semiconductor Industry Association to develop world-class semiconductor manufacturing technologies with financial assistance from the U.S. government, is an indication of this new trend.

Difficulties for these programs lie in the prevailing philosophy of business independence from government and in the often elusive boundary between the precompetitive research on technological innovation and product development.

Strategic Partnership Between Competitors.   Unlike the customer-vendor relationships or the cooperative R&D ventures, these alliances take place between competing companies interested in mutually beneficial commercial advantages (such as better products or marketing arrangements) rather than in long-lead-time, basic R&D programs.

These partnerships share some common characteristics. An optimal distance between the market interests of the two companies has to be carefully evaluated before such partnerships can take place. If the interests are too similar, even when the technical personnel of both companies have a good working relationship, it is impossible for the sales forces of the companies to work together. On the other end, if the markets are too different, the technical personnel would not share sufficient common interests to justify their working together.

Each party must supply an essential ingredient or position of the cooperative project and both must have ownership of the whole production resulting from the cooperative work. Relationships are usually organized along horizontal rather than vertical lines but may encompass several different areas, such as technology development, product development, guarantee of manufacturing capacity, buy-sell relationships, or alternate sourcing.

Potential Hazards in Strategic Partnering.   Despite the need for strategic partnering to counter global competition and access sufficient resources, these alliances are very difficult to maintain over the long term. The prevalent causes of partnership failure are uneven levels of commitment by management, changing strategic objectives of the partners, changing market conditions, incompatibility between big and small firms, inadequate incentives for cooperation, insufficient executive guidance, and lack of consensus within each company (Alster 1986 a and b).

How to Select and Maintain a Good Partnership.   First, to ensure top management attention during the execution and implementation of the partnership, the strategic alliance must address vital company objectives. The senior management of both companies must remain involved beyond the early stages of the negotiations by establishing and continuously supporting "alliance champions" and understanding the real or imaginary concerns of the "deal killers." Secondly, there should be provisions in the relationship to handle changes arising from new strategic goals of the partners. Thirdly, companies must understand each other's management style and decisionmaking process.

At VLSI Technology, we have found that we must understand the motivations, priorities, and hidden agenda of our own key people involved in the implementation of partnerships. Before major negotiations, extensive discussions are held in-house to flush out all concerns and to ensure the cooperation and support of middle management. This internal conditioning to the strategic relationships is particularly needed when the alliance is between small and large companies, and broad differences in company management style, culture, decisionmaking processes, and priorities must be overcome.

The main issue is people. Large companies may mistakenly think that they are buying technology or market presence from a smaller partner, but actually they are buying the talent and brainpower of a few key people, and if these people are neglected, the relationship will fail. Domestic companies wishing to enter into alliances with overseas companies face the added challenge of understanding a completely different cultural background.

Successful and rewarding partnerships are the result of attentive and person-oriented management combined with a careful and realistic evaluation of the advantages and disadvantages to be derived from the alliance. The major risks are loss of proprietary information, birth of new competitors, reduced motivation to make strategic investments, national and international political risks, and loss of management control. The benefits of cooperation are cost advantage, better competitive position in new markets, reduced capital-investment requirements, increased returns, lower break-even points through increased leverage, and acquisition of new technologies.

REFERENCES

Alster, Norm. 1986. "Strategic Partners: Seeking the Right Chemistry." *Electronic Business* (May 15).

Fusfeld, Herbert I., and Carmela S. Haklisch. 1985. "Cooperative R&D for Competitors." *Harvard Business Review* (November-December).

Hamel, Gary and C. K. Prahalad. 1985. "Do You Really Have a Global Strategy?" *Harvard Business Review* (July–August).

Weber, Samuel. 1987. "The Look of the Industry in 2000." *Electronics* (special semiconductor issue) (April 2).

FURTHER READING

Barney, Clifford. 1987. "Winds of Change Sweep the Industry." *Electronics* (April 2).

Cohen, Charles L. 1987. "Japan Drives for Strategic Alliances." *Electronics* (April 2).

Cornell, Jon. 1985. "Strategic Partnering: A Tool for Survival." *Engineering Manager.* (April).

Erikson, Arthur. 1987. "A One-World Industry Is Arriving Fast." *Electronics* (April 2).

Ford, David, and Chris Ryan. 1981. "Taking Technology to Market," *Harvard Business Review.* (March–April).

Gluck, Frederick. 1983. "Global Competition in the 1980s," *Journal of Business Strategy.* (Spring).

Gosch, John. 1987. "Europe Pushes Hard for Global Role." *Electronics* (April 2).

Reich, Robert B., and Eric D. Mankin. 1986. "Joint Ventures With Japan Give Away Our Future." *Harvard Business Review* (March–April).

12 TECHNOLOGY MARKETING
The Three-Level Sell and Other Market Developments

Edward A. McCreary

It is all well and good to turn out a technology or a brilliant series of technologies, but if they are not effectively marketed and embodied in products by those who created them, eventually the corporate and national capacity to continue developing useful new technologies is lost.

High Technology, the magazine that sponsored the studies I am here reporting, is written for and read by a special three-level mix of top senior operations and tech-user managers in multiple industries. These managers reside in both companies that develop and companies that buy-and-apply technology. It is indicative of some of the changes under way in technology-stirred industries that one of this magazine's most useful roles for its readers is that of an early warning system: readers use it to track emerging technologies that can affect their businesses.

Since the magazine is directed to both technical and nontechnical readers, it is a combination translation-communications device. Specialists use it to explain technical points to general managers. General managers use it to acquire the background and language tools for asking questions of technical personnel and for making judgments about technology usage.

High Technology's present, essentially self-selected tech-aware readers are among the key persons in shaping their companies' tomorrows. Because of these readers' positioning, they are windows upon

169

current developments in their companies and represent a living, real-time, national data base! It is this data base that, working with the editor at *High Technology* and with certain outside consultants, I am preparing to tap. Thus far, we have only seen interesting reader survey/dialogues on some of the technology developments that these readers are living with. Since marketing is one of the keys to any linkage between the development and the effective diffusion of strategic technologies, I have been conducting background interviews for *High Technology* among selected tech vendors.

TECH MARKETING SURVEY: METHODOLOGY

These tech-marketing interviews were open-ended, in-depth visits with practitioners: people living and directly wrestling with the marketing of their companies' specific products. In all, some forty to forty-five individuals in twenty different companies or divisions of companies were drawn upon. These companies included, among others, Prime Computer, Apollo, Intergraph, Applicon, Xerox, Perkin Elmer, and elements of GE, ITT, IBM, Philips (of Holland, at its Eindhoven headquarters), Siemens, Intel, and in the artificial intelligence (AI) field, Intellicorp, Inference, Symbolics, and Techknowledge Inc. I must note that this was not a formal study. The interviews were not for attribution, and statistics were not collected. As reservoirs of anecdotes and information built up, these visits of from forty-five to ninety minutes' duration more and more became exchanges of information rather than interviews per se. As with the seismic probes that geologists use to try to map subterranean formations, what one listened for were not only the initial but also the secondary and tertiary reflections from a given perspective. Over a series of interviews, what we were mapping along with the standard surface factors were those anomalies or seemingly singular events that, when reported from multiple sources, gave glimpses of underlying patterns. Visits with marketing operations chiefs were followed by corroborative visits with selected market-research and management consultants, such as specialists at Dataquest, Arthur D. Little, and McKinsey and Company, the last in the United States as well as in Holland and West Germany. For our own market study purposes, we were sifting through attitudes, trends, experiences, and perceptions. On an "early-warning radar" basis, we were scanning for those early indicators that later may (or may not) show up as hard statistics in academic studies. We found some of those indicators.

Early Findings

One of the questions indirectly explored was: Although certain basic principles and practices in marketing are constants, is technology marketing different than other kinds of marketing? The answer is yes. Another question was: Are there any underlying rules to the marketing of tech products and services that one could begin to bring to the surface and use consciously? Again, the answer is yes.

In a partial summary of the long-term project, which is still in progress, we found that there is much of the partly conscious, although sometimes totally unconscious, arrogance of the engineer-designer at play in the fields of technology. Ironically, however, there are stages where this is a "best" policy. The common criticism of technology management and marketers is that they are product- and technology-blinded and production-oriented. Confusing better, or more "interesting," technology with better, more usable products, they ignore the real needs and technology-connected difficulties of user-customers.

Nevertheless, it is science- and engineering-focused technology that does initially drive these new-style markets. It is shifts in technologies that keep them in turmoil. It is engineer-inventor-producer entrepreneurs, not marketers, who have generated the new products, the new wealth, and the energetic creativity in which all America now claims pride and credit. What's more, when it is other tech-specialist engineers to whom our marketer-engineers are selling, at least initially, there is enormous logic and marketplace validity to this "techy" approach. It works!

The troubles come later as the products or the systems to which they are tied are accepted and spread throughout a company and industry. This is precisely what's happening among us now. Meanwhile, as we've all seen, one industrial- and consumer-market hotshot after the other, initially brought in to bring "realism" and/or pizazz to technology marketing, has ended up out of the action, with his company out of business.

As John Scully, a successful adapter at Apple, will be the first to admit, you don't sell PCs like you sell Pepsi-Cola. As GE long ago discovered, computers are not sold like locomotives or jet engines. Software is "published," but it is not really sold like books or magazines. Computer-assisted design and manufacturing (CAD/CAM), one of the most powerfully catalytic technology packages in existence, is not successfully sold today in the way that it was sold a mere four or five years ago.

Technology marketing *is* different. Tech marketing is a moving target, a field in flux, where the rules are unknown or unclear because they have not yet been written. They have not been codified because they are still being invented or discovered by the players. This will hold for at least ten years while our industries and society go through changes. Talk to enough key players, however, and you'll find that at different points within their markets, there are emergent patterns that some see clearly and others don't. Although almost all interviewees, of course, profess total confidence in whatever it is they and their managements are doing, tech marketers' awareness levels run the gamut. They range from those who clearly see and preadapt to ride and use evolving patterns to those who can only react to what happens long after it has happened and has become routine. We are tracing some of these patterns.

THE THREE-LEVEL SELL

Take, for one example, the three-level sell. More and more, vendors of tech products and services are discovering that they have to sell to a company simultaneously at the top, the senior operations, and the tech-user management levels.

Only two computer generations ago, in the mainframe-medium-frame era, salespeople covering prospects that IBM was already selling to would come back from a call ruefully shaking their heads to report: "IBM's wrapped around those guys like a blanket." That was the three-level sell in its formative stage; all key bases were covered. It was a two- to three-year sales cycle. Units of sales were in the high six- and seven-figure range. Since then, the world and technology marketing have changed greatly. As multiple, new technology products, processes, and possibilities have developed, the pace of change has accelerated. New, far lower unit prices and the resultant, new, far broader markets have evolved. Ten-thousand-dollar computers now perform at the level of one-million-dollar computers of the early 1970s. Where "real" sales were once made essentially to tech specialists, the "anointed knowledgeables" in specific departments, now more and different sets of managers are becoming knowledgeable—and involved in the decision.

Further, the recognition has finally spread that technology products and "systems" increasingly interact. This means that these different systems should be compatible. It also means more and different groups of people in different departments have had to be drawn into key selection and application processes. As upper-level buyer-company managers recognize that new technologies are inescapable, that they can't be compartmentalized, and that they do involve turf, their personal interest, "need to know," and need to be involved in these matters has zoomed. Meanwhile, as competition for the attention of newly diffuse decision-making groups has spread and sharpened, uncertainty has increased for all sellers.

Today, merely "blanketing" the appropriate specialists and top managers in target companies, as in the previous mainframe era, is something different from and inadequate to the three level sell that has evolved and is crystallizing among us. For marketing success, our contacts report that today you must tread the threefold path.

The Threefold Path

The threefold path is the one sure way of selling to technology-user companies because there are three levels that must be reached. Level one consists of tech-user specialists. On-site tech users are seldom the ultimate decisionmakers. If they don't know or like your product, however, you have a big problem. They can cripple you even after you have "sold" their chiefs and even after you are installed in place. You know the breed. They are most attracted to and "sold" on the basis of equipment specs and range of performance.

Second to none are the upper-middle- and senior-level operations managers. These include the vice presidents of operations, engineering, design, and manufacturing, plus the project leaders who carry the ball for these chieftans. As we all know, the media myth that CEOs and top management make all key decisions is just that, an edifying story based on a kernel of truth. The truth is that top management has the power and authority, but they delegate some of that authority.

For most technology-tied sales, it is here at the second level that most of the sales activity occurs. It happens via recommendations by those who will most closely live with or die from the consequences. Here is where you find your real corporate risk-takers, your in-house white knights and champions-in-waiting, ready for clear input and backing from vendors, ready to "sell" across departmental and division lines, and ready to "sell" up in the heirarchy, sometimes in order to move up within it. These senior and midlevel groups, increasingly forced by technology-driven organizational change to interact and to explain, describe, and coordinate things across, up, and down the company hierarchy, are where it happens.

Third are those veteran, but not deeply technical, top managers and staff who must give projects formal approval. This group wants to understand the essentials. It is vital to these managers that they draw upon but not be swept away or aside by the technology "expertise" of specialist advocates. They want to know context—what questions to ask of the specialists, and how to weigh the answers. They are the corporate "appellate court" that can (and sometimes does) reverse others' prior judgments. You must keep this group continually informed, aware of your plans, and content with your prospects. They don't, however, decide the sale. Who does decide? The three-level sell answers this question.

Living With the Three-Level Sell

With combined puzzlement and resignation, particularly if their product or service is a system or is systems-tied, vendors ruefully report that there is no one identifiable person, group, or department that makes the total buy-no-buy decision. Instead, it is a network, a shifting web of managers, that directly or indirectly becomes a part of the act. What's more, this network is a fluctuating one. That is, its membership changes. What's happening is that various managers whose interests are involved are making their needs known and their weight felt. More important, what's going on is that more and more managers, as they become knowledgeable in technology (and as they recognize the extent of its sweep into their bailiwicks), are determining that technology purchases are too important to be left strictly to the specialists.

The implications and results are multiple.

Because the tech and tech-systems decision groups in target companies are now numerous and diverse, old-style, one-on-one sales visits to key tech people. while still vital, are no longer solely adequate. The total target audience is now too numerous and too diffuse for direct, one-on-one contacts. This means that, especially for system and systems-tied vendors, the right kind of advertising becomes increasingly important. Here, larger companies would seem to have an edge. With their heavyweight budgets, they can cover a spectrum of the trade press, the technical press, and the much higher priced general management press. They can blanket all target managements, but here again, thinking simplistically can backfire expensively. It is not all tech or general managers who get involved in these tech-tied matters. It is *certain* managers. It is those particular managers who, because of their positions and proclivities, are tech-alert and tech-involved in their companies. These have to be sought out. Then they must be presented with the proper messages—in the right ways.

What all this means is that there is still room for the canny marketer who does it right. Doing it right, for one thing, means that expert but narrowly focused, tech-conditioned vendors must learn to explain themselves clearly, with less than the usual jargon, to nontech managers "who need to know!" Important nonspecialists don't want more and more data in the form of glorified technical specifications lists. Neither do they need slogans about how clever or audacious a particular vendor may be. Mostly these nontech managers, who have technical and political situations to face, problems to solve, and decisions to make, want help. Also, they would like some form of reassurance that they are not helpless (from ignorance) in the face of new technologies. They do seem to prefer help in the form of information that lets them feel and be more knowledgeable. That is the crux of the matter.

For technology marketing in really new or change-driven technology fields, the best and most effective sell has been and continues to be an educational sell, and advertising that educates as it reassures is what works particularly well. This last is a genuine problem because, with some exceptions, what advertising agencies don't know about tech advertising could fill a book. One may blame the newness of this emerging area of marketing. Business school courses in technology marketing are not yet offered. The real problems, however, are deeper. Agency people, as a group, are technology-ignorant and technology-frightened, when not technology-hostile. They consistently tend to oversimplify, romanticize, or trivialize tech products rather than explain them. Moreover, agencies are essentially focused on consumer products. For them, consumer markets are where the money and prestige are. What works in consumer ads—meaning, what they are comfortable with—is what agencies tend to apply. Business-to-business ads may be important to the agency, but mind-sets don't change easily. To consumer markets-conditioned account executives and creative-department types, business ads are secondary and déclassé.

When a senior vice president at a Saatchi & Saatchi overseas office describes himself as the technology specialist in his agency because he worked on an armored-vehicles account in Detroit, you know there are serious perception and translation-of-technology problems in the offing for that agency. When the self-admittedly brilliant, young chief of a boutique agency servicing tech companies in Los Angeles caustically refers to his engineer clients as "propeller heads," you know there are attitude problems in place. When a soon-to-be-chastened-in-the-marketplace company like Wang runs ads depicting a helicopter trashing a "Big Blue" office site, you know there is confusion about what's really being sold to whom. When a senior executive at IBM says of a previous, and successful, "science-focused" campaign, "We didn't let the agency write it. . . . They couldn't. . . . Our people wrote it with agency input"—you have just learned something more about IBM and about the "techniques" of marketing technology.

THE KNOWLEDGE VACUUM

Meanwhile, delving just a bit deeper, there is an immense knowledge vacuum at the present stage of technology development and application in U.S. and world industry and business. The minute he learns a little trade jargon, your average manager (and salesperson) talks and sounds like an expert. Far more than half the time in technology fields, behind the facade is a desperate man who is tap dancing. More jargon and glib promos can't help him.

There is deep hunger among buyer-user companies' managers for understanding of technology and of how to use it. Call it "knowledge-hunger." Companies that learn to feed and feed upon this hunger are the companies that learn how to succeed.

The above is why the most powerful sales tool for many tech-product and -service companies is the seminar. In some companies, seminar sessions for existing and potential customers are profit centers! When people to whom you wish to sell a product or service pay out money to have you or some other party explain to them how to use that product or service, it becomes obvious that technology marketing is rather different from other forms of marketing. People want to know things. By using new technologies, most companies are trying to solve perceived problems or grasp new opportunities.

For technology vendors, these needs are the key to living successfully with the three-level sell. The vendor who can effectively translate and explain technology finds open doors for his product or services. Novell, in the presently booming local area network (LAN) field, is an example here. This seller of network tools and software is, not incidentally, a publisher of news and information and one of the few tech companies around that consistently produces clear, crisp reports, brochures, and pamphlets on its field. In the AI field—in the "expert systems" subdivision thereof—Techknowledge Inc. is one of numerous companies making its living not just by selling systems but by "teaching" customers about AI systems, about their usage, and about so-called "knowledge engineering." Similarly, in the robotics field, Dataquest researchers report that more than 50 percent of the "sales" in this area go to independent systems integrators. It turns out that it is not the hardware or technology but the ability to properly use and apply it among systems and people—in other words, the "knowledgeware"—that is in critical supply.

With the advent of the 32-bit chip and AI-supplemented software systems, many of the most intricate computer-tied technologies that managers are buying and struggling with today will become "transparent." Things will simply work the way they are supposed to—like a bar code-reader works—with the complex technology behind all this activity being invisible. As technology continues to spread in the interim, what we do know is that, in most companies, it is not a single, official, jealous-of-its-turf, self-anointed priesthood (such as electronic data processing staffs) but a three-level mix of various "tech-knowledgeable" managers who are making the key decisions. What we further find, via reports from the field, is that in most concerns, before action is taken on new, interactive technology projects, there has to be a "climate of acceptance." That is, enough of the right people must reach a certain level of understanding and agreement, which permits a product or a project's proponents to "go for it." In effect, in areas of uncertainty where many are involved and the stakes are high—but decisions have to be made—it's a "group mind" that is at work.

One of the secrets of success for a seller of technology products or services lies in finding and developing champions or advocates within this group mind. A next step is that of helping these champions to establish that necessary climate of acceptance for a particular product or service. Meanwhile, Netmap International, a San Francisco-based, software development and consulting company, is generating corroborative studies of various corporate influence and decision nets. It does this via techniques for tracing out who talks to whom, with what frequency, and in what sequence, on different subjects in different companies.

A WIDE-SCREEN VIEW

What's happening here is that many tech decisions in medium- and large-size corporations are being diffused (and also slowed, by some accounts). What's going on that is causing these things to happen in the ways in which they are happening is that more and new groups of managers are becoming "tech-knowledgeable." As this happens, they are making themselves a part of the tech-systems decision pattern. The ramifications of these developments in U.S. and world corporations—if these trends continue—are fascinating and far-reaching. They point to new or altered forms of internal corporate organization of which, for now, we have only early signs. They also point to the fact that further, deeper researches on the matter are in order.

V SPECIAL-SECTOR STRATEGIES

13 SECURING THE FUTURE THROUGH TECHNOLOGY VENTURING

George Kozmetsky

Technology venturing as a newer form of economic development is vital to our nation's future. In today's hypercompetitive, protectionist-seeking global environment, technology venturing provides a newer approach to making and securing the U.S. future.

Technology, from an institutional development perspective, is a societal driver. It is a resource to be used for economic growth and diversification. Venturing involves a large and diverse number of institutions. Their multiplicity of programs, projects, regulations, policies, and other activities must be interlocked to successfully start firms, create jobs, educate and train sufficiently skilled and knowledgeable personnel, provide adequate capital, meet the communities' requirements, and at the same time, adjust to changing societal values and needs.

THE EMERGENCE OF TECHNOLOGY VENTURING

Technology venturing links science, technology, and management with an entrepreneurial spirit to accelerate the commercialization process and thus promote economic growth and diversification.

Prior to 1979, there was little evidence of technology venturing for economic development. What prevailed then was industrial relocation rather than the building of indigenous companies; separation of institutional relationships, especially between universities and corporations; adversarial roles between government and business; and policies—both national and industrial—that were reactive rather than proactive to international competition. The rules of the game seemed to be set in concrete, instead of being subject to the dynamics of an ever changing global environment and to an economy with changing values.

A short seven years ago, technology and its impacts were regarded more as threats than as opportunities with which to build a future; total, annual venture capital was less than the current one-day's loss of Amtrak operations; entrepreneurship was ignored as a force or driver; and technology transfer and diffusion were subjects of research, not mandates for commercialization of research and development. Six years ago, there was little doubt about U.S. leadership in high technology, particularly in electronics, with its industrial and scientific markets. There was no question but that high tech was a major contributor to the nation's trade balances. Layoffs, loss of earnings, and production curtailments were not part of management's major concerns in high-tech firms.

From the 1950s to the 1980s, it was generally assumed that scientific research would in one way or another transfer into developments or technologies and subsequently be commercialized. Little attention was paid to how science was transformed into technology and, in turn, commercialized and diffused among all industries, regionally and through international trade. The general paradigm was that basic research innovations would be utilized in applied R&Ds and that their embodiment in manufactures would naturally follow. Diffusion to other uses and industries would occur when R&D results were both economical and generally better understood. The utilization of technology as a resource was perceived as an individual institution's responsibility. Economic developments flowed from this process because of American ingenuity and entrepreneurial spirit.

Targeting industries for development may have been a Japanese national policy in this period; but in the United States, market opportunities at home and abroad seemed sufficient for economic growth and diversification. It was expected that all regions of the United States would in time enjoy the benefits of this paradigm in which new innovations from research were followed naturally by timely developments, commercialization, and diffusion.

CHANGING REALITIES

By the end of the 1970s, however, changing global realities forced us to question our traditional paradigm. These new realities revolved around shortages in materials and supplies, energy crises, loss of competitive advantages in U.S. basic industry, increasing unfavorable trade balances, high regional unemployment, strengthening of the dollar in international financial markets, and shifting investment patterns within the public and private sectors.

As the new realities emerged, hope for a quick fix to our problems through national income policies or monetary policies vanished, and our attention turned to new mechanisms that may secure our future through the commercialization of science and technology.

One way to identify these mechanisms is to review the allocation of resources to science and technology and to investigate the generally held paradigm of how research is transferred into commercially viable products and services.

The data available for this purpose are federal R&D obligations by source and performers; selected company-sponsored R&D by industry; traditional venture capital; emerging venture capital sources; and special funds for financial and organizational restructure.

The Sources and Performers of R&D

Up until 1980, the federal government and its agencies—primarily the Department of Defense (DOD)—were the major sources of R&D funds. Starting in 1980, the industry sector displaced the federal government as the largest source of funds. In 1985, the industry sector provided $54.0 billion, in contrast to $51.5 billion provided by the federal government. On the other hand, the major performers of R&D continue to be in the industry sector.

A closer analysis of the available data discloses important changes in both sources and performers of R&D:

1. The industry sector, between 1968 and 1977, decreased its R&D expenditures, on a constant 1972-dollar basis. This was the period when industry made heavy capital investments in environment, safety and health, and energy conservation. In 1980, industry

started to increase its rate of R&D growth by 3 to 4 percent annually. The National Science Foundation (NSF) forecasts that this rate will continue through the rest of the eighties. Consequently, a measurable increase in innovation, particularly in applied research, development, and commercialization, may be expected.

2. The industry-sector R&D growth produces a need for talent to sustain forthcoming innovations. Experienced scientific and engineering talent will be in short supply, as will marketing, financial, and managerial talent.

3. The government sector as a source, while relatively less substantial than industry, is still growing in absolute terms. We may also expect new centers of research, reflecting particular industries' R&D growth. In other words, not all the industry-sector R&D growth will be in Silicon Valley or on Route 128.

4. While the federal government is still the major source of funding for basic research (68 percent), and universities and colleges are still the main performers, a discernible shift in research expertise from engineering to physical sciences, math, computer sciences, social sciences, and psychology is occurring.

5. We are seeing the emergence of a number of very large-scale programs by the Departments of Defense and Energy and by NASA that are long-term (over ten years). The spin-off opportunities— lasers, computers, artificial intelligence, new materials, etc.—even if not of the same magnitude as chips and digital computers, will be major factors that will affect our lives economically, socially, and culturally.

6. R&D expenditure growth in both industry and government sectors affects institutional developments and particularly affects how the industry, government, and academic institutions are relating to one another and on the world trade.

Table 13-1 shows the present regional distribution of federal R&D obligation funds categorized by dominant states (that is, where over 50 percent of the funds are spent) and by major performers.

California leads all of the other dominant states in every category of performers except one. That is "federal intramural." The lead state in that category is Maryland. California's preeminence is based on a unique balance of performers, and in many respects, it has become a strong example of transformational leadership. More specifically, of the $8.4 billion of federal obligations spent in California, industrial

Table 13-1. Fiscal Year 1983 Distribution of Federal Obligations for R&D by Dominant States and by Performers.

State	Total Obligations (Billions of Dollars)	Federal Intramural	Industrial Firms[a]	Universities and Colleges[a]	Other Non-Profit[a]	State and Local Governments
First Tier						
California	$8.4	14%	61%	19%	6%	b
Second Tier						
Maryland	3.4	62	24	12	2	b
New York	2.5	3	65	27	4	1%
Virginia	2.3	32	61	4	3	b

[a]Includes federally funded R&D centers administered by indicated performer sector.
[b]Less than one-half of one percent.

Source: National Science Foundation, "Federal Funds for Research and Development Fiscal Years 1981, 1982, and 1983," *The Budget of the United States, Fiscal Year 1986*, vol. 31, pp. 82–326. Data compiled by IC² Institute.

firms received 61 percent, and federal intramural 14 percent; universities and colleges expended 19 percent, and nonprofit institutions received 6 percent of the funds.

When we look at the second tier of dominant states, we see that they individually received much less in federal expenditures compared to California.

Table 13-2 shows which government agencies are the major sources of funds for the dominant states. DOD dominates federal R&D obligations. Maryland has over 23 percent of the federal R&D obligations from the Department of Health and Human Services. In conclusion, each of the dominant states were and are able to have a broad spectrum of their institutional R&D performers compete successfully for federal funds, and at present, each has developed a large base of technology as well as R&D talent.

Selected Company-Sponsored R&D by Industry

The transformation of R&D from being federally funded to industry funded has occurred only since 1980. At present, the dominant industries, measured by R&D expenses, are those loosely defined as high-technology industries.

For the 1983–84 period, high-tech industry had 63 percent of the total R&D expenses; basic industry had 26 percent; "other manufacturing" had 10 percent; mining/metals and construction/building materials

Table 13-2.   Fiscal Year 1983 Distribution of Federal Obligations for R&D by Dominant States and by Agency.

State	Total Obligations (Billions of Dollars)	DOD	DOE	NASA	Department of Health and Human Services	All Other Agencies
First Tier						
California	8.4	17%	10%	26%	10%	37%
Second Tier						
Maryland	3.4	8	1	10	23	58
New York	2.5	7	7	1	11	74
Virginia	2.3	9	1	6	1	83
Agency Percent of Total Federal Obligations		61	12	7	12	8

Source: National Science Foundation, "Federal Funds for Research and Development Fiscal Years 1981, 1982, and 1983," in *The Budget of the United States, Fiscal Year 1986*, vol. 31, pp. 82–326. Data compiled by IC² Institute.

had the balance. High-technology industries' R&D expenses averaged over 5 percent of sales revenues during 1983–84. This was more than two-and-a-half times the R&D expenses to sales percentage for basic manufacturing industries.

What is important is not the specific ratio but the fact that all industries have been increasing their R&D expenses over the 1981–1984 time frame. This is an indication that the U.S. private sector is in a period of high innovation. R&D expenses do not generally bring immediate sales. By the time innovations are developed and tested for costs, quality, and market, the commercialization process spans at least five years. We can, however, expect a stream of innovative products from U.S. industries, unless unforeseen contingencies drastically reduce R&D expenses.

An analysis of dominance by industry and by individual firm discloses the dispersion and depth of R&D innovations. Two industries, automotive and fuel, out of the eleven, basic manufacturing categories, dominate in terms of R&D expenses. Four companies dominate these industries: General Motors in the automotive industry and Exxon, Chevron, and Mobil in the fuel industry.

Of the thirteen industries that comprise the high-technology group, three industries are dominant: information processing/computers, pharmaceuticals, and chemicals. These three industries are led by eleven companies. IBM and Digital Equipment dominate the information process/computer industry; in the pharmaceutical industry, six companies—Johnson & Johnson, Merck, Eli Lilly, Smith-Kline Beckman, Upjohn, and Pfizer—are the recognized front-runners. DuPont, Dow Chemical, and Monsanto head the chemical industry. These five dominant industries, accounting for the largest expenditures in R&D, are critical to the U.S. future in the global economy.

Traditional Venture Capital

The traditional capital-venture industry consists of private independent partnerships, corporate financial firms, corporate industrial firms, and small-business investment companies. This industry can provide a benchmark as to what technologies are fueling innovation as well as to which states are involved in innovative institutional transformations. Its main characteristics are listed below:

1. The traditional venture-capital industry, in terms of number of firms, has grown 89 percent during the 1980–86 period. In terms of professionals engaged in the process, it has grown 150 percent during the same six years. The data reflect the growth in innovation in the United States.
2. The industry raised approximately $12.7 billion between 1977 and 1984. In 1984, it raised $3.2 billion.
3. Traditional venture-capital pools have been formed outside the New York financial centers. The major, traditional venture-capital center is California, with 30 percent of all venture-capital funds in 1983.
4. The primary source of investors in these pools are pension funds and wealthy individuals.
5. The fastest growing sources of investors in the traditional venture-capital pools are foreign investors, including foreign capital-venture firms. In 1984, foreign investors provided 18 percent of the total, traditional capital-venture commitments, or $575 million.
6. Venture-capital firms are widely dispersed geographically; almost every state has its own traditional venture-capital firms.

In 1983, when $2.8 billion was disbursed, the dominant technologies were computer- (46 percent) and communication-related (13 percent). Investments were made in 1,002 firms, located mostly in California and Massachusetts.

These locations of dominance are directly linked to developments in industrial and university/college performers and attract venture capital independently from the location where the pools of capital are formed.

Emerging Venture Capital Sources

This category includes business development corporations (BDCs) and R&D partnerships. Both of these sources did not really take off until after 1981.

BDCs seem to be having a short life. Publicly held BDCs were the result of the Small Business Act of 1980. Until then, BDCs were defined as private companies with less than 100 shareholders, because of the Holding Company Act of 1940. They have become less important in new business growth since the passage of the Deficit Reduction Act of 1984, which taxed their distributions to shareholders as ordinary gains.

R&D limited partnerships between 1978 and August 1984 have raised at least $2.4 billion. During 1984, there was a decline in the number of partnerships but an increase in the total amount of funds per partnership. Indeed, R&D limited partnerships seem to be experiencing their own transformation from specifically designated projects to professionally managed, blind, and broadly designated pools. The dominant technologies around which R&D limited partnerships were formed are computer hardware, medical products, genetic engineering, and other electronics. These investments are made at an earlier stage of the innovation process than those made by the traditional venture-capital industry and provide a window on emerging technologies and their specific commercialization.

Special Funds for Financial and Organizational Restructure

These special funds consist of leveraged buy-outs (LBOs) and acquisitions and mergers.

Both the traditional venture-capital industry and emerging specialty funds are interested in having their investments become part of LBO and acquisition and merger activities. Many of their investees are also interested in becoming such candidates. Not all start-ups necessarily stay small or plan to become middle- or large-size companies engaging in global trade. Many innovators who build companies deliberately plan to "sell out." We are seeing dominant companies investing in the equity of independent growth companies: for example, IBM, AT&T, GM, Ford, GE, and Chevron. LBO investment, in principle, makes it possible to secure capital gains in less time than investments in start-up or mezzanine stages of growth companies. There was a dramatic change in 1984 in the magnitude of LBOs: four times the amount in 1983. There were over $18 billion of LBOs. Traditional venture capital firms invested over 12 percent of their 1984 funds in LBOs.

The explosive amount invested for acquisitions and mergers signals another major transformation. Today's acquisitions and mergers are, in many respects, different from past periods. In the past, they represented vertical or horizontal mergers for either manufacturing/market control purposes or financial purposes (conglomerates, for example). Today's mergers and acquisitions are more for capital gains, for increasing managerial effectiveness, or for providing investment opportunities that lead to increased liquidity. Because of the accelerated life cycles of newer products, processes, and services, many of today's acquisitions and mergers focus on innovations in terms of managerial effectiveness and in terms of telescoping the time to market.

Acquisitions and mergers have transformed the allocation of capital. In 1984, these special funds were over $105 billion, compared to $47 billion in 1983. In terms of dollar activity, the dominant industries were mining, oil and gas extraction, petroleum refining, retail trade, food and allied products, and banks and bank-holding companies. In terms of transactions, banks, bank-holding companies, and machinery (except electrical and electrical/electronic machinery) were the most active industries. Foreign buyers were involved with 182 acquisitions, out of a total of 2,946.

The dominant regions in which acquisitions and mergers take place are the Middle Atlantic, Midwest, and Pacific regions. The dominant states are California, New York, Texas, Illinois, Florida, Pennsylvania, and New Jersey.

With federal R&D obligations, traditional venture capital, and selected company R&D expenses being the major driving forces, the innovative developments are taking place in the seventeen dominant states and in the District of Columbia. They are listed and ranked in Table 13-3.

Table 13-3. Innovative State Rankings.

State	Dominant Federal R&D Obligations[a]	Dominant Selected Company R&D Expenses[b]	Traditional Venture Capital[c]
California	1	3	1
New York	3	1	2
New Jersey	8	3	10
Massachusetts	4	5	3
Maryland	2		6
Texas	7		8
Illinois			5
Virginia	5		
Florida	9		
New Mexico	6		
District of Columbia	10		
Michigan		2	
Pennsylvania		5	
Connecticut			4
Colorado			7
Minnesota			9
Delaware		5	
Ohio		5	

[a]For fiscal year 1983.
[b]For fiscal years 1983–84.
[c]For fiscal year 1984.

Source: National Science Foundation, "Federal Funds for Research and Development Fiscal Years 1981, 1982, and 1983," in *The Budget of the United States, Fiscal Year 1986*, vol. 31, pp. 82–326. Data compiled by IC² Institute.

It has become evident that the traditional paradigm—that science and technology naturally evolve into commercialization, which in turn secures a nation's future—is inadequate. Furthermore, the mechanism of allocating resources needs to focus more on companies' flexibility and adaptability than on efficiency and effectiveness. The traditional paradigm is undergoing transformation. Emerging institutional developments are leading to newer models of commercialization of science and technology within a compressed time frame and to a broader base of opportunities, generally called technology venturing.

TECHNOLOGY VENTURING—NEW INSTITUTIONAL DEVELOPMENTS

Technology venturing is a collaborative means for economic growth. New relationships among key institutions involved in economic growth and technological diversification are filling in some of the gaps existing in the traditional venture-capital and economic development processes.

The factors accounting for these institutional developments are: (1) increasing foreign competition; (2) shortages of highly trained scientists and engineers; (3) difficulty in keeping up-to-date with technological developments; (4) problems in technology transfer, particularly when it involves pulling together basic research from different disciplines; (5) problems of diffusion of technology among individual companies; (6) need for more basic research in universities; and (7) a desire to diffuse R&D activities across wider geographic areas.

Eight new institutional developments may be identified: industrial R&D joint ventures and consortia; academic-business collaboration; government-university-industry collaboration; incubators; industry-university research and engineering centers of excellence, small-business innovation research programs; state venture capital funds; and commercialization of university intellectual property.

These institutional developments share common elements:

1. They are generally unique collaborative efforts in the sense that each institution manages to maintain its own independence and specific objectives but effectively converges with the partners in providing timely, coherent, and synergistic inputs to shared goals.
2. The total funds involved are generally small when compared to the more traditional institutional efforts. For example, very few states provide as much as $20 million for seed funding for entrepreneurial endeavors. Corporations entering into cooperative technology ventures individually contribute annually in the low millions of dollars per year. Universities' cooperative efforts generally are funded with small amounts yearly. The largest biotechnology cooperative agreements we know of—between Harvard University and Hoechst—amounted to $70 million over a ten-year period. But others are much more modestly funded.
3. High leveraging is common. For example, universities are encouraged to establish centers of excellence, with either federal or state

governments offering small annual funding for three to five years, to be matched by much larger sums from the private sector. The public funds are used as catalysts of commercialization and diffusion processes.

4. Collaborating institutions are encouraged to utilize existing facilities and to share laboratory equipment.

5. Rights to patents and copyrights are used to produce future flows of research funding. For example, the federal government has given the rights to basic research breakthroughs funded under federal R&D obligations, to the performing universities and colleges. Besides the incentive to commercialization of scientific breakthroughs, the arrangements allow the creation of future research funds through fees and royalties.

Throughout America, states are moving to aid the growth of high technology and to foster technological commercialization. They, rather than the federal government, have taken a leadership role through the development of special policy initiatives, economic growth, organizations, and corporate-university partnerships. Since 1980, over 150 programs have been developed by states for high technology and economic development. The major source of R&D funds is still, for most states, the federal government. And there is a direct correlation between those states receiving the largest federal obligations for R&D and those taking the lead in initiating technology-venturing developments.

The result of these activities is the emergence of technopoleis where state government, local government, private corporations, universities, nonprofit foundations, and other organizations interact in a variety of technology-venturing initiatives that (1) encourage emerging industries, (2) provide seed capital for early and start-up entrepreneurial endeavors, and (3) create the necessary premises to U.S. economic preeminence in the global economy.

Encouraging Emerging Industries

The institutional relationships involved in encouraging emerging industries are academic and industrial collaborations and industrial R&D consortia. Because basic research is carried out mostly in universities and colleges, collaborative efforts between academia and industry accelerate the commercialization of basic research into emerging industries.

Also, since 1981, there have been a series of joint research efforts among private corporations. The pioneering institutions—such as Semiconductor Research Corporation (SRC), Council for Chemical Research (CCR), Center for Advanced Television Studies (CATS), and Microelectronic and Computer Technology Corporation (MCC)—are favored by the current administration and Congress. In the past, the obstacle to such consortia has been their ambiguous legal status, due to the risk of huge penalties under the antitrust laws. The passage of the Cooperative Research and Development Act in October 1984 has alleviated much of the legal concern and ushered in, perhaps, the proliferation of large-scale R&D consortia.

Already, a number of consortia are being considered. Under a military-software productivity consortium, TRW, Lockheed, Boeing, Rockwell, and seven other defense contractors are considering new ways to produce computer programs and other software techniques for military applications. Battelle is trying to put together a twenty-company consortium to develop components to tie together fiber-optic networks and high-speed communication systems. Allied Corporation, 3-M, and AMP, Inc. have already joined. Other consortia are being considered for the energy, steel, machine tools, airframe, and auto engines industries.

Although biotechnology is an important emerging industry, no U.S. R&D consortium has emerged to compete with the recently formed $100 million, seven-year Japanese consortium in this industrial sector. Most U.S. biotechnology research is being conducted by individual firms or through university-industry cooperative ventures. Some of the more recent start-up biotechnology companies have had as equity shareholders major firms in energy, drugs, and agriculture.

Newer institutional structures are emerging in the "megabuilding" business. Innovative financing is required to pull together banks, institutional investors, government financial export-credit agencies, and international development organizations, such as the World Bank and the International Monetary Fund. In addition, megabuilding institutions are required to make their own investments in the projects, carry on basic, generic, and engineering research, as well as keep up with technological advances in new materials, products, and processes. Their marketing strategy includes more than competitive winning of contracts. It involves the ability to do longer range planning and forecasting of markets, as well as the ability to generate new businesses based on commercial-size demonstration plants.

Providing Seed Capital

Some forms of institutional development such as incubators, Small Business Innovation Research programs, and state venture-capital funds, are providing seed capital for small and take-off companies.

A number of states are now developing special initiatives—such as tax incentives, enterprise zones, research and industrial parks, and direct financial assistance in the form of low-interest bank loans and loan guarantees—to meet the start-up capital needs of new technology firms.

One area of increasing interest is that of state support and implementation of private venture-capital sources for small technology firms. Given the high risk and generally long-term payback time of typical venture-capital investments, firms with less than $500,000 worth of "start-up needs" are not attractive investment targets for the private market.

A fine example of state involvement in this area is the Massachusetts Technology Development Corporation (MTDC). Operating as both a public agency and nonprofit corporation since 1979, the MTDC has invested $3.4 million of its own funds into twenty individual firms. More dramatically, it has used these investments to leverage more than $22 million in private-sector money to these same companies.

A creative approach was taken in 1982 by the Michigan legislature, which permitted the use of Michigan state retirement funds to be used as a venture-capital base for equity investment in Michigan high-technology firms. The estimated value of these venture funds is $350 million.

Incubators are another promising tool being employed to provide a suitable environment for "hatching" new spin-off applications of high-technology ventures. Funded by both public and private sources, there are now over 100 incubators across the country. The great majority have sprung up in the last eighteen months.

Finally, a number of states have established training and support programs for entrepreneurial development. The programs support the development of incubators and address one of the most critical areas in promoting technology commercialization.

U.S. Economic Preeminence

Most institutional developments are seeking to ensure U.S. economic preeminence in world markets. NSF centers of research and engineering excellence, government-business-university collaborative arrangements in technological areas, industrial R&D joint ventures and consortia, and NSF's sponsorship of industry-university cooperative research centers (IUCRs), are intended to provide a broad-based and multidisciplinary research program that would have been too large for any one company to undertake alone.

Much remains to be done in the new frontier of technology venturing. There is little question but that these newer institutional developments are acquiring their own momentum. How effective they will be is yet to be assessed. For now, we know that they are educating a newer group of entrepreneurs and have found newer means of allocating and using resources to meet the challenges of a hypercompetitive, protectionist-seeking marketplace.

There are still a number of critical questions that must be answered if technology venturing is to fulfill its promise:

1. What will be the impacts of new tax simplification regulation?
2. How will changes in the buying practices of DOD affect economic growth and technological diversification?
3. How will changes in the traditional peer-review process for basic research affect long-term development of science and technology brought about by private-sector support of proprietary research?
4. What will be the impact of changes in intellectual property rights on the commercialization process and on the nature of higher education?
5. How can entrepreneurial abilities be developed and enhanced over the long run? Is it possible to accelerate the learning and experiential processes?
6. How can we encourage more manufacturing activity among small and medium-sized domestic firms? Should flexible, full-scale manufacturing demonstration laboratories be publicly or privately sponsored?

Adequate answers make up the wisdom needed for guiding technology-venturing strategy in securing the future of the United States in the changing global environment.

BIBLIOGRAPHY

Dorsey, Helen Baca. 1986. ''Institutional Changes for Linking Public/Private Scientific Developments.'' Presented at the 1986 National Science Foundation Conference on Industrial Science and Technological Innovation, San Antonio, Texas, April.

Hisrich, Robert D. 1986. "Entrepreneurship and Intrapreneurship: Methods for Creating New Companies and Impacting the Economic Renaissance of an Area." In *Entrepreneurship,, Intrapreneurship, and Venture Capital: The Foundations of Economic Renaissance*, edited by Robert D. Hisrich, Lexington, Mass.: Lexington Books.

Konecci, Eugene. 1986. "National and International Technology Venturing." Presented at the American Association of Administrative Sciences 30th Annual Meeting of the Society for General Systems Research, May.

Konecci, Eugene B., and Robert L. Kuhn, eds. 1985. *Technology Venturing: American Innovation and Risk-Taking*. New York: Praeger Publishers.

Kozmetsky, George. 1986. "High Technology in Texas: The Current State of Affairs." IC2 Institute working paper, University of Texas at Austin (February).

———. 1985. "New Institutional Developments." Presented at the First International Technology Transfer Symposium, Salt Lake City, Utah, September.

———. 1985. *Technology Venturing: Institutional Developments for Economic Growth*, IC² Institute, University of Texas at Austin.

———. 1986. "Technology Based/High Growth Business Development." Presented to Utah Technology Finance Corporation Workshop, Salt Lake City, Utah, September 21.

———. 1986. "The Texas Future: What Will Texas Business and Economic Structure Be by 2036." Presented to the Texas Philosophical Society, Austin, Texas, December 6.

———, and Raymond W. Smilor. 1986. *Building Indigenous Companies: Public/Private Infrastructures for Economic Growth and Diversification*. IC² Institute monograph, University of Texas at Austin.

Mabry, Tom J. 1986. "How to Utilize University Research Professors for the Economic Betterment of the Austin-San Antonio Region by Developing the University-Industry Interface." Presented at the 1986 Economic Outlook Conference, San Antonio, Texas, January.

Petit, Michael J. 1987. "Industrial Research and Development Consortia: An Analysis of Survey Results." Professional report, University of Texas at Austin.

Smilor, Raymond W., and Michael D. Gill, Jr. 1986. *The New Business Incubator: Linking Talent, Technology, Capital and Know-How*, Lexington, Mass.: Lexington Books.

Smilor, Raymond W.; George Kozmetsky; and David V. Gibson. 1987. "The Austin/San Antonio Corridor: The Dynamics of a Developing Technopolis." IC2 Institute working paper, University of Texas at Austin (March).

Teece, David J. 1986. "Profiting from Technological Innovation: Implications for Integration, Collaboration, Licensing and Public Policy." Center for Research in Management working paper, University of California, Berkeley (June).

14 DEVELOPING NEW INDUSTRIES THROUGH NEW AND ESTABLISHED SMALL BUSINESSES

Robert D. Hisrich

Economic development involves more than just increasing per capita output and income; it involves initiating and constituting change in the structure of business and society. This change is accompanied by growth and increased output, which allows more to be divided among the various claimants. What facilitates the needed change and the subsequent development? One theory of economic growth depicts innovation as the key not only to the evolution of new products (or services) for the market but to stimulating investment in new industries, thereby expanding productive capacity. The new investment works on both the demand and supply sides of the growth equation: the new capital created expands the capacity for growth (supply side), and the new spending created utilizes the new capacity and output (demand side).

Yet, in spite of the importance of investment and innovation in creating new industries, an adequate understanding of the product evolution process—the process by which innovation develops and commercializes, creating new industries and stimulating economic growth—is still lacking (Hisrich 1986).

The product evolution process, indicated in Figure 14-1 as a cornucopia, the traditional symbol of abundance, begins with knowledge in science, thermodynamics, fluid mechanics, electronics, and technology and ends with products or services available for purchase in the marketplace (Tzu Li et al. 1980:27–30). The critical point in this process

197

Figure 14-1. Product Evolution.

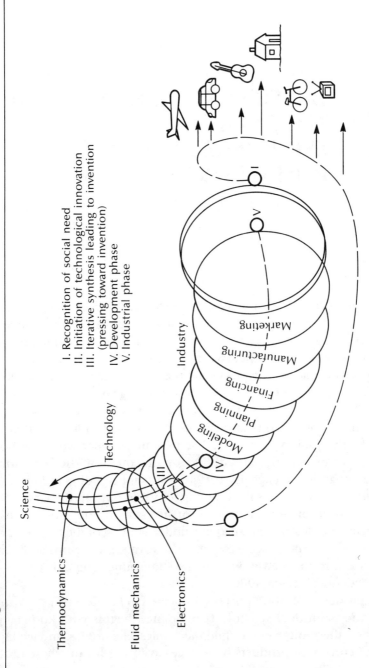

I. Recognition of social need
II. Initiation of technological innovation
III. Iterative synthesis leading to invention
    (pressing toward invention)
IV. Development phase
V. Industrial phase

Source: Yao Tzu Li David G. Jansson, and Ernest G. Cravelho, *Technological Innovation in Education and Industry* (New York: Von Nostrand Reinhold Company, 1980), p. 27.

is the intersection of knowledge and a recognized social need (iterative synthesis). It is here that the product development phase begins but frequently fails to produce a marketable innovation.

The innovation at this juncture can, of course, be of varying degrees of "uniqueness." As indicated in Figure 14-2, the largest number of innovations introduced on the market are ordinary ones, having little uniqueness or technology. These are followed by technological innovations and breakthrough innovations. How can these innovations be effectively commercialized, thereby bridging the gap between science and the marketplace and promoting the creation of new industries? It can be done by three mechanisms: government, existing businesses, and the formation of new businesses (Smilor 1986).

Figure 14-2. Types of Innovations.

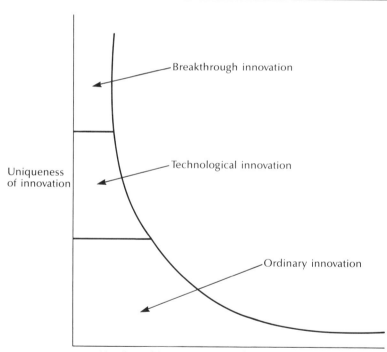

Source: Reprinted by permission of the publisher, from *Entrepreneurship, Intrapreneurship and Venture Capital* by Robert D. Hisrich (Lexington, Mass.: Lexington Books, D.C. Heath and Company, Copyright 1986, D.C. Heath and Company).

GOVERNMENT

The government is one method for commercializing the results of the interaction between a social need and technology. This method is often referred to as technology transfer and has been the focus of a significant amount of effort and research. Despite the effort, findings to date indicate that not enough inventions, from this otherwise sound scientific research, have reached the commercial market. Since much of this research has limited application to a social need, the by-products that do have such applications usually require significant modification to have market appeal. Though the government has the financial resources to successfully transfer a technology to the marketplace, it frequently lacks the necessary business skills, particularly in marketing and distribution. In addition, the bureaucracy and red tape often prohibit the new industry from being formed in the timely manner that is needed for success.

INTRAPRENEURSHIP—EXISTING BUSINESS

The second mechanism—existing business—can also bridge the gap between science and the marketplace. Established companies often have the existing financial resources, business skills, and usually the marketing and distribution systems to successfully commercialize a new invention and create a new industry. Yet, too frequently, the bureaucratic structure, the emphasis on short-term profits, and a highly structured organization inhibit creativity and prevent new products from being developed. Companies recognizing these inhibiting factors and the need for creativity and inventions have attempted to establish an intrapreneurial spirit in their organizations. What is this intrapreneurial spirit and intrapreneurship? It is entrepreneurship within an existing business structure.

How can intrapreneurship be established in an organization? Certain factors and leadership characteristics must be operant in the firm (Kanter 1983; Pinchot 1985).

First, an organization must encourage new ideas and be capable of operating on the frontiers of technology. Since research and development is a key source for successful new product ideas, this area must operate on the cutting edge of the technology relevant to the appropriate industry. New ideas must be supported and not discouraged, as frequently occurs in firms where rapid return on investment and high sales-volume requirements exist.

Second, experimentation—trial and error—must be encouraged. New products or services do not instantaneously appear. It took time and some product failures before the first marketable computer appeared. A company wanting to establish an intrapreneurial spirit has to promote an environment that allows or even encourages mistakes and failures. While this is in direct opposition to the established corporate career and promotion system, without the opportunity to fail, few, if any, corporate intrapreneurial ventures will be attempted.

Third, an organization should ensure that there are no initial opportunity parameters inhibiting free, creative problem solving. Frequently, "turfs" are protected, frustrating attempts by potential intrapreneurs to establish new industries. In one Fortune 500 company, the establishment of an intrapreneurial environment ran into problems and eventually failed when the potential intrapreneurs were informed that a proposed product was not possible because it was in the domain of another division.

Fourth, the resources of the firm must be available and easily accessible. As one intrapreneur states, "If my company really wants me to take the time, effort, and career risks to establish a new venture, then it needs to put money and people resources on the line." So often, insufficient funds are allocated to the task of creating something new; instead, resources are committed to solving problems that more immediately impact the bottom line. Also, even when the resources are available, the reporting requirements make it all too often so difficult to obtain them that frustration and dissatisfaction result.

Fifth, a multidiscipline teamwork approach needs to be encouraged. This open approach with participation by needed individuals, regardless of major area of expertise, is the antithesis of corporate organizational structure and theory. Yet, in successful cases of intrapreneurship, the success was often due to the existing "skunkworks" involving key people. Some companies can facilitate internal venturing by merely legitimizing and formalizing the "skunkworks" already occurring. Developing the needed teamwork is further complicated by the fact that team members' promotions and overall careers within the corporation are often related to their performance in their current position, rather than to their contribution to the new industry being created.

In addition to encouraging teamwork to start the venture, the corporate environment must establish a long-term horizon for evaluating the success of the overall program and the success of each individual venture. If a company is not willing to invest money with no expectation of return for five to ten years, then it should not attempt to create an intrapreneurial environment. This patient money in the corporate setting is no different than the investment-return time horizon used by venture capitalists and others in the risk capital market when investing in an entrepreneurial effort.

Sixth, the spirit of intrapreneurship cannot be forced on individuals; it must be on a volunteer basis. There is a difference between managerial thinking and intrapreneurial thinking, and individuals are closer to either one or the other side of this continuum. The majority of managers in a corporation are good at managerial thinking but are not capable of being intrapreneurs (Stevenson and Sahlman 1986). This self-selection of participants must be coupled with the freedom for each participant to carry a project started through to completion. Most corporate procedures for new product introduction involve different departments and individuals at each stage of the development process. An individual willing to spend the extra hours and effort to create a new venture must have the opportunity to nurture the project from start to finish. An intrapreneur usually falls in love with the venture he is promoting and will do almost anything to ensure that success results.

Seventh, the intrapreneur needs to be appropriately rewarded for the energy and effort expended in the creation of the new venture. Broad performance goals should be established, with the intrapreneur receiving rewards based on meeting these goals. An equity position in the new venture is the best reward for motivating the amount of activity and effort needed for success.

Eighth, a corporate environment favorable for intrapreneurship has sponsors and champions who not only support the creative activity and any failures but have the planning flexibility for establishing new objectives and directions. As one intrapreneur stated, "For a new business venture to succeed, the intrapreneur needs to be able to alter plans at will and not be concerned about how close they are to achieving the previously stated objectives." Corporate structures frequently reward managers on their ability to come in close to plan, regardless of the quality of performance related to this accomplishment.

Finally, and perhaps most importantly, the intrapreneurial activity must be wholeheartedly supported and embraced by top management. Top management must have a long-term horizon and must support the effort by physical presence as well as by making sure the personnel and financial resources are available. Without top management supporting the effort, a successful intrapreneurial environment cannot be created.

Within this overall company environment, certain leadership characteristics are needed. These include understanding the environment, being visionary and flexible, creating management options, encouraging teamwork while employing a multidisciplined approach, encouraging open discussion, building a coalition of supporters, and persisting.

In order to successfully establish a new business venture, creativity and broad understanding of the internal and external environment must be present. The person who is going to establish a successful new business venture must also be a visionary leader, a person who dreams great dreams. While there are many definitions of leadership, one best describes the needed intrapreneurial leadership: "A leader is like a gardener. When you want a potato, you take a seed, put it in fertile soil, and carefully water under tender care. You don't manufacture potatoes, you grow them." Martin Luther King, a great leader, said, "I have a dream," and thousands followed in spite of overwhelming obstacles. In order to establish a successful new business venture, the intrapreneurial leader must have a dream, must communicate it in such a way as to develop team commitment, and then must work against all obstacles for success to result.

The third characteristic is that the leader must be flexible and create management options. By challenging the beliefs and assumptions of the corporation, an intrapreneur has the opportunity of creating something new and of building a successful new industry.

The intrapreneur needs to encourage teamwork and the use of a multidisciplined approach. This violates the organizational practices—taught in most business schools—that are the basis for corporate structure. In every new industry formation, a broad range of business skills is needed, including engineering, production, marketing, and finance. Using these skills in forming a new industry usually requires crossing the established departmental structure and reporting systems. To minimize any disruption, the intrapreneur must also be a good diplomat.

In developing a good team for creating something new, open discussion must always be encouraged. Many corporate managers have forgotten the frank, open discussion and disagreements that were a part of their educational process and, instead, spend time building protective barriers in their corporate empire. A successful new industry can only be formed when the team involved feels the freedom to disagree and break down an idea until the best solution is reached. The degree of openness obtained is dependent, of course, on the degree of openness of the intrapreneur.

Openness is one factor leading to the establishment of a strong coalition of supporters and encouragers. The intrapreneur must encourage and affirm each team member, particularly during problem times. This encouragement is very important, as the usual motivators of career paths and job security are not operational. A good intrapreneur makes everyone a hero.

Finally, but not least important, is persistence. Several times throughout the establishment of the new business venture, frustration and obstacles will abound. Only by persistence on the part of the intrapreneur will successful commercialization result.

ENTREPRENEURSHIP—NEW BUSINESSES

The final method for bridging the gap between science and the marketplace—entrepreneurship—is the process of creating something different and valuable by devoting the necessary time and effort, assuming the accompanying financial, psychic, and social risks, and receiving the resulting rewards of monetary and personal satisfaction (Hisrich and Brush 1985:1–18).

Many entrepreneurs have difficulty bringing their innovations to the market, owing to lack of managerial skills, lack of finances, lack of knowledge of the product planning and development process, and lack of marketing skills, particularly in the area of distribution.

Yet, entrepreneurship and the accompanying entrepreneurial process has resulted in several million new businesses being formed throughout the world, even in controlled economies such as China, Hungary, and Poland. While no one knows the exact number, in the United States—leading the world in company formation—it has been estimated that from 900,000 to 1,850,000 new companies were formed in 1985.

Indeed, millions of company formations occur despite recession, inflation, high interest rates, lack of infrastructure, economic uncertainty, and the fear of failure. Each of these company formations is a very personal human process that, although unique, shares with the others some common characteristics. Like all processes, it entails a movement from a present lifestyle to forming a new enterprise.

The decision to leave a present career and lifestyle is indeed not an easy one. While individuals tend to start businesses in familiar areas, two work environments tend to be particularly good in spawning new enterprises: R&D and marketing. While working in technology R&D, individuals often develop new product ideas or processes and leave to form a new company when the new idea is not accepted by the present employer. Similarly, individuals in marketing become familiar with the market and with unanswered customers' wants and frequently start new enterprises to address those needs.

Perhaps even greater stimulation to leave a present lifestyle and create something new comes from a negative force—disruption. A significant number of company formations occur among people who have retired, whose spouse has moved, or who have been terminated by their employers. There is probably no greater force than personal dislocation to galvanize one into action. A study in one major city in the United States indicated that the number of new business listings in the yellow pages increased by 12 percent during a layoff period. Another cause of disruption, with resulting company formation is the completion of an educational degree, as in the case of a part-time student who does not receive a promotion upon completing an M.B.A. degree.

What causes this disruption to result in a new industry being formed, rather than something else occurring? An individual perception that starting a new company is both desirable and possible.

The perception of desirability is the result of an individual's culture, subculture, teachers, family, and peers. A culture that values the individual success of creating a new business will spawn more company formations than one that does not. For example, Americans place a high value on being one's own boss, on individualism, on being a success, and on making money. These are all dimensions of entrepreneurship. Therefore, it is not surprising to find a high rate of company formations in the United States.

But the entire culture is never totally for or against entrepreneurship. A strong educational support system is a prerequisite for entrepreneurial activity and new industry formation in an area. Peers are also important. Entrepreneurial pools and meeting places, where existing and potential entrepreneurs meet and discuss ideas, problems, and solutions, assist in spawning more new enterprises. Other factors—including government, individual background, marketing skills or assistance, role models, and financing—contribute to the creation of a new venture. Government provides the supporting infrastructure, including a favorable tax structure.

Individual background, consisting of knowledge from formal education and previous business experience, provides the potential entrepreneur with the confidence needed to form and manage a new enterprise. Individuals tend to start businesses in fields in which they have worked. Not only must a market of sufficient size be available for the new idea, but the marketing know-how involved in assembling the best total package of product, price, distribution, and promotion is needed for successful product launching. The most powerful influence in making company formation seem possible is that of role models. When someone else does something and succeeds, it makes it easier to picture oneself doing a similar activity. Finally, companies are formed when financial resources are readily available. While the majority of the start-up money for any new company comes from personal savings, credit, friends, and relatives, there is a need for seed capital, up to $100,000, to help spawn new companies. Each venture has need for risk capital. And when seed capital is readily available, more new companies form.

What are the types of start-ups formed from this entrepreneurial decision process? While many classifications exist, one most useful for industry development purposes divides start-ups into three categories: lifestyle firms, foundation companies, and high-potential ventures.

A lifestyle firm is privately held and usually achieves only modest growth owing to the nature of the business, the objectives of the entrepreneur, and the limited money devoted to R&D. This type of firm may grow after several years to between thirty and forty employees, with annual revenues of about $2 million. A lifestyle firm primarily exists to support the owners and has little opportunity for significant growth and expansion.

The second type of start-up, the foundation company, is created from R&D and lays the foundation for a new industry. This firm can grow in five to ten years to between 40 and 400 employees, and to $10–30 million in yearly revenues. Since this type of start-up rarely goes public, it draws the interest of private investors but not that of the venture-capital community.

The final type of start-up, the high-potential venture, is the one that receives the greatest investment interest and publicity. While the company may start out like a foundation company, its growth is more rapid. After five to ten years, the company could have around 500 employees, with $20–30 million in revenue. Given its growth and revenues, the high-potential start-up venture will frequently go public or be purchased by a larger company.

THE ENTREPRENEUR

While the concept of entrepreneurship is an evolving one, the term *entrepreneur*, derived from a French word meaning "between-taker" or "go-between," is used to differentiate the risk-taking and innovating function of the creator of a new business from that of merely supplying financial support to a new enterprise.

The profiles of the male and female entrepreneurs have been sketched. The male entrepreneur tends to be the oldest child in a family with financially independent parents. He is college-educated, married, self-confident, desires independence, and has a high tolerance for ambiguity and a high energy level. In his early thirties he usually starts his first significant venture in an area where he has previous experience.

While the percentage of businesses started and operated by women is less than that of businesses started by men, it is increasing at a rapid rate. The number of female sole proprietorships is 22 percent of all sole proprietorships, according to the IRS; but the Bureau of Labor statistics indicate that between 1974 and 1984 the number of self-employed women grew 74 percent, or six times faster than the number of self-employed men. Who is this female entrepreneur? She is the oldest child of middle-class parents and has a close relationship with her father. After obtaining an undergraduate and frequently a graduate degree in the liberal arts, she marries, has children, and starts her first entrepreneurial venture in the service area during her late thirties or early forties. Her biggest problems at start-up, and later in developing the new venture, reflect poor business training and lack of financial support.

One method for facilitating the formation of new industries and helping economic development is an enterprise development center. Such a center established at the University of Tulsa brings together state and city governments, engineering and business schools, businesses, venture capital firms, financial institutions, and potential inventors and entrepreneurs in the process of developing and forming new companies.

The center has four components addressing major aspects of enterprise development: the intrapreneurship center, the venture-capital exchange, the innovation center, and the incubation center.

The entrepreneurship center is involved in the process of researching the viability of new ideas and in helping established companies to create the needed "intrapreneurial" spirit and supportive internal environment that facilitates the formation of new industries.

The second component of the enterprise development center, the venture-capital exchange, facilitates the attainment of seed capital for a new company (Davis 1986; Wetzel 1986). The venture-capital exchange was funded through a grant from the Grace and Franklin Bernsen Foundation and assists entrepreneurs by identifying opportunities for risk-capital investment, identifying active informal investors, and providing a timely, confidential, and objective referral service for both investors and entrepreneurs.

The innovation center, the third arm of the enterprise development center, offers technical assistance to entrepreneurs and potential entrepreneurs in technological evaluation, entrepreneurial assessment, commercial feasibility, business planning, and product development and modification. This can result in the technology being licensed to an existing company or used in creating a new company.

The fourth dimension of the enterprise development center, the incubation center, provides a start-up company with a protective environment for survival and growth. Recently, this aspect of economic development has attracted widespread attention. While the more than 180 incubators throughout the United States vary in terms of objectives and services provided, in general each incubator is designed to assist entrepreneurs in developing business skills while operating in an environment that supports the growth of their companies. Most incubators provide services such as low cost office, laboratory, warehouse, and/or manufacturing space; secretarial support in word processing, typing, photocopying, filing, and other receptionist and clerical support; administrative assistance in mailing, accounting, equipment rental, billing, and contract administration; access to library and computer facilities; inexpensive graduate and undergraduate student assistance; consulting in management, marketing, loan packaging, accounting, and general financial and legal matters; and a network facilitating access to bankers, venture capitalists, technologists, and government officials. In this supportive environment, the entrepreneur can grow and nurture a company until he or she is ready to succeed in the general business environment.

In conclusion, bridging the gap between science and the marketplace requires a combination of deliberate policies, plans, and well established infrastructures, in an environment that encourages individuality, allows and condones errors, and rewards originality. The difficult and somewhat elusive balance among these apparently contradicting features is perhaps the ultimate challenge in developing new industries.

REFERENCES

Davis, Barry M. 1986. "Role of Venture Capital in the Economic Renaissance of an Area." In *Entrepreneurship, Intrapreneurship, and Venture Capital: The Foundations of Economic Renaissance*, edited by Robert D. Hisrich. Lexington, Mass.: Lexington Books.

Hisrich, Robert D., ed. 1986. *Entrepreneurship, Intrapreneurship, and Venture Capital: The Foundations of Economic Renaissance.* Lexington, Mass.: Lexington Books.

———, and Candida G. Brush. 1985. *The Woman Entrepreneur: Starting, Financing, and Managing a Successful New Business.* Lexington, Mass.: Lexington Books.

Kanter, Rosabeth Moss. 1983. *The Change Masters.* New York: Simon and Schuster.

Pinchot III, Gifford. 1985. *Intrapreneuring.* New York: Harper & Row.

Smilor, Raymond W. 1986. "Building Indigenous Companies: The Technology Venturing Approach." In *Entrepreneurship, Intrapreneurship, and Venture Capital: The Foundations of Economic Renaissance*, edited by Robert D. Hisrich. Lexington, Mass.: Lexington Books.

Stevenson, Howard H., and William A. Sahlman. 1986. "The Importance of Entrepreneurship in Economic Development." In *Entrepreneurship, Intrapreneurship, and Venture Capital: The Foundations of Economic Renaissance*, edited by Robert D. Hisrich. Lexington, Mass.: Lexington Books.

Tzu Li, Yao; David G. Jansson; and Ernest G. Cravelho. 1980. *Technological Innovation in Education and Industry.* New York: Van Nostrand Reinhold Company.

Wetzel, Jr., William E. 1986. "Entrepreneurship, Angels, and Economic Renaissance." In *Entrepreneurship, Intrapreneurship, and Venture Capital: The Foundations of Economic Renaissance*, edited by Robert D. Hisrich. Lexington, Mass.: Lexington Books.

15 "PROFITING" FROM TECHNOLOGY TRANSFER
A Novel Approach

E.J. Soderstrom, W.W. Carpenter, and H. Postma

In the past few years, interest in technology transfer from the public to the private sector revived in spite of persistent criticism of federal technology transfer initiatives (O'Brien and Franks 1981). It is our position that the limited success of past efforts is mostly due to the failure to recognize that technology transfer is not a unidirectional activity but rather is an exchange between two parties. In a capitalistic economy such as that of the United States, both parties must in some way benefit or "profit" from the exchange. A novel approach that utilizes this principle for inducing the transfer of technology at the federal facilities in Oak Ridge, Tennessee, is discussed in the pages that follow.

PAST EFFORTS TO ENCOURAGE TECHNOLOGY TRANSFER

One of the oldest technology transfer programs operated by the U.S. government is the Agriculture Extension Service Program. Established in 1914 by the Smith-Lever Act, the extension service has been very successful in promoting the utilization of agriculture research findings. Another program promoting the advantages and opportunities created by technology transfer was the National Aeronautics and Space Administration (NASA). The 1958 enabling legislation provided a clear technology transfer mandate, and NASA leadership saw technology spin-offs as a promising selling point for funding further space exploration (Doctors 1968).

Over the past twenty years, federal policymakers have continually acknowledged technology transfer as an important government activity and responsibility. This need was recognized in the creation of the National Science Foundation's Research Addressed to National Needs (RANN) project in the late 1960s and in policy statements by President Nixon in 1972 and President Carter in 1979. In addition, congressional initiatives have sought to facilitate and encourage federal technology transfer through passage of acts such as the State Technical Services Act of 1965 (P.L. 89–192), the National Science and Technology Policy Organization and Priorities Act of 1976 (P.L. 94–282), and the Stevenson-Wydler Technology Innovation Act of 1980 (P.L. 96–480).

Why Is Technology Transfer So Important?

The interest in obtaining a better return on federal R&D investments arises from a concern for the weakening of our industrial competitiveness in world markets and a consequent desire to improve productivity in industry and in government services. The U.S. Department of Commerce (1983) has identified two long term trends in the U.S. economy: the growing reliance on higher levels of technology and the worsening of our performance in coping with increasing foreign competition for products that utilize new technologies. Future economic productivity will be largely dependent on how well new technologies resulting from public and private investments in research and development are put to use in creating products, markets, and jobs (Mansfield 1968; Mansfield et al., 1982; Nelson 1982).

The primary intent of the legislation mentioned earlier was to encourage the inclusion of technology transfer in the mission requirements of every federal agency engaged in R&D activities. Even though the federal government is both a primary supporter and a major performer of R&D, only a small fraction of the results of this research finds its way into commercial applications. For example, only about 2.5 percent of the nearly 5,000 inventions reported by the federal government each year are licensed for commercial use (U.S. General Accounting Office 1985). The statistics reflect both the lack of commercial value of many government patents and the little effort made by government agencies to seek private-sector users for even their most important and commercially valuable inventions. In large part, this default by government researchers is the consequence of frustrations experienced in previous attempts to move technology into the private sector.

A strong case can be made that our eroding share of world markets is not necessarily the consequence of a loss of global leadership in technological innovations or of a deficiency in commercial development and marketing (Twentieth Century Fund 1984). Rather, the problem is related to the difficulties of coupling the nation's capabilities for generating scientific and technological innovations with its capabilities for undertaking commercial activities. This observation has motivated both Congress and the Reagan administration to reexamine the adequacy of our federal R&D efforts and the mechanisms used to support R&D (Hill 1985).

Even though some work is classified, there is broad agreement that with about $17 billion going in any one year to federal laboratories to employ about one-sixth of the nation's research workers, effective means of increasing the flow of technology from these laboratories to the private sector must be found (Congressional Budget Office 1984). A report by the White House Science Council, the so-called Packard Report, stated: "The National interest demands that the federal laboratories collaborate with universities and industry to ensure continued advances in scientific knowledge and its translation into useful technology. The federal laboratories must be more responsive to national needs" (Office of Science and Technology Policy 1983:11). A similar sentiment was espoused in a report by the National Governors' Association: "The fact remains that these national laboratories are far from having begun to realize their full potential as catalysts for close industry-university research cooperation or as collaborators in joint university/industry research" (National Governors' Association 1983:60).

Why Have Past Technology Transfer Efforts Been Ineffective?

It is our basic premise that the primary reason technology transfer efforts in the public sector have been, and continue to be, relatively ineffective is that policies governing the operation of such programs fail to recognize some of the fundamental tenets of a capitalistic economy. Technology transfer demands significant interactions between the parties involved in the transfer and requires large commitments of time and money. Without prospective profits, however broadly defined, the parties involved will not be motivated to participate in the exchanges.

Viewing technology transfer as an exchange is certainly not new in the private sector, but the application of this concept to the public sector has been overlooked. Pieces of hardware can be easily transferred from public to private ownership, but new technologies, typically, are partially tested ideas stored mostly in the heads of inventors. Therefore, government-funded inventions usually need considerable refinements and substantial investments of capital before they are ready for the marketplace. Only about 10 percent of the final cost of a new product development is claimed by the research that triggered the basic invention embodied in the product. The other 90 percent is expended in engineering design, production engineering, tooling-up, manufacturing start-up expenses, and marketing start-up expenses (Charpie et al. 1967). Private industry is willing to allocate corporate funds into developing ideas arising from government research only when there is a strong possibility of financial reward at the end of the development process. But both the originator of the technology and those responsible for its subsequent development and commercial exploitation must contribute to the innovation process if a technology is to enter the marketplace successfully.

The Hidden Cost of Technology Transfer

Successful technology transfer requires educating the recipients on the nature of the invention and assisting them in generating the information needed for its applications. These training and technical assistance functions, even when supported by a specific policy mandate, are a diversion from the major mission of a federal laboratory, which is to conduct long-term, high-risk R&D to further the goals of a sponsoring federal agency.

Providing training and technical assistance requires the laboratory to make an investment of resources much the same as industry would, and just as in industry, some form of tangible return is needed to kindle sufficient interest in undertaking the task. To date, the returns have been primarily in the form of accolades and acknowledgments that, while appreciated, are quickly forgotten.

In the past, policies appropriate to creating an environment in which technology transfers would return tangible benefits to both public and private parties did not exist. Recently this situation has begun to change dramatically.

NEW INITIATIVES TO ENHANCE THE TRANSFER OF TECHNOLOGY

One of the most often cited barriers to mutually beneficial technology exchanges is government patent policy. In the case of the Department of Energy (DOE), the report of the Multiprogram Laboratories Panel of the Energy Research Advisory Board concluded: "The Department's patent policy. . . . has been among the salient barriers to cooperative relationships with industry and to effective technology transfers" (Department of Energy 1982:22).

The traditional practice has been for the government to retain patent title to federally sponsored inventions, grant nonexclusive licenses to all interested U.S. companies, and widely disseminate the results of the research. The argument was that, if the public paid for the research, the public should retain rights to the results.

Most companies, however, are reluctant to invest the millions of dollars required to fine-tune inventions without the guarantee that a competitor would be precluded from receiving its own government license and copying the product by reverse engineering.

Patents are not the only factor in new product development, but they are certainly a critical one. When faced with a choice between investing in the exploitation of a government-held patent with significant commercial potential or in a privately held patent, even with less commercial potential in the private patent most companies decide against the government patent opportunity because of the lack of legal protection for intellectual property.

Since 1980, three major legislative changes in government patent policy have been enacted.

The first is the enactment of the Bayh-Dole Act (P.L. 96–517). This act allows nonprofit organizations and small-business government contractors to retain title in most cases to inventions conceived while under contract with the federal government. The Bayh-Dole Act also includes an initial effort to set up rules for exclusive, royalty-bearing licensing of federal inventions.

The experience from the first two years under the Bayh-Dole Act was positive enough to lead to the second major patent policy initiative. President Reagan issued an executive order on 18 February 1983 that includes all government contractors in the scope of P.L. 96–517, to the extent permitted by law. But since over twenty patent statutes and provisions are in effect for different agencies, a uniform federal patent policy could not be established by executive order alone.

The second change occurred on 9 November 1984, when President Reagan signed into law P.L. 98–620.

Specifically, Congress opened the door for most government-owned and contractor-operated (GOCO) research or production facilities, such as national laboratories, to directly obtain ownership of their patents if they fall within the definitions of the Bayh-Dole Act. Therefore, all nonprofit or university-type GOCO operations can now obtain the patent rights to technology developed through the activities of government-owned R&D facilities.

For-profit companies—such as Martin Marietta Energy Systems, Inc., operators of Oak Ridge National Laboratory (ORNL), and AT&T, operators of Sandia National Laboratory—were excluded from this legislation. In passing P.L. 98–620, however, Congress requested federal agencies to issue regulations as quickly as possible to provide for arms-length dealings between the contractors' subsidiaries running the government facilities and those developing commercial products. On 5 February 1985, Secretary of Energy Donald P. Hodel signed a new departmental patent policy that extends the provisions of the recent patent legislation to for-profit contractors.

A third major change was an amendment to the Stevenson-Wydler Act, entitled the Federal Technology Transfer Act of 1986 (P.L. 99–502). This act extends the same rights and priviledges given GOCO laboratories to the vast majority of federal laboratories, the government-owned, government-operated (GOGO) laboratories like the National Bureau of Standards. Thus, all government laboratories may maintain ownership of inventions arising from federally supported research conducted at the facilities.

Providing the Proper Appropriate Incentives

In order to participate effectively in technology transfer, the federal laboratories need to be endowed not only with enabling laws but with appropriate incentives for allowing staff and resources to be temporarily diverted and for rewarding staff and management who must cooperate in the transfer efforts.

DOE and Martin Marietta Energy Systems, Inc. have initiated an experimental program designed to enhance the flow of technologies from a national laboratory to the private sector. In the 1983 competition for the Oak Ridge facility's management contract, DOE asked the bidders to propose resourceful measures to accelerate the process of technology transfer. To provide the appropriate incentive, the technology transfer program was included as a factor in determining the amount of the management contract fee.

Martin Marietta proposed four primary measures:

1. Broaden the scope of existing technology transfer functions to include all operating facilities under the management contract and establish a central function, headed at the executive level, that would not just permit but indeed cause increased levels of technology transfer.
2. Put the title to all intellectual property of commercial value in the contractor's name under the terms of an advanced, blanket waiver.
3. Develop and implement an array of financial rewards and recognitions for the inventors.
4. Create supporting mechanisms to cause and encourage new business formation based on Oak Ridge-developed technologies.

These measures form the basis for a system of incentives that will reward the various organizational participants in the technology transfer process. Even though the blanket patent waiver initially requested has yet to be granted, Martin Marietta has received title on several, specifically requested pieces of intellectual property. Since receiving these rights in mid-1985, ORNL began offering licenses to interested client companies. In these instances, Martin Marietta acts as a representative of DOE in placing the technology in the commercial sector. As such, any royalties for these licenses do not become corporate income or profit but rather, are used to advance DOE's stated objectives regarding technology transfer. That is, the fund will be first used to pay investors their share of royalty income. Royalties will then be used to cover expenses incidental to patenting and licensing inventions. A portion of the remainder of the fund will be dedicated to fund selected technology maturation initiatives, and over a certain level, the balance of the monies will go directly to the U.S. Treasury.

As a first case of a company receiving a license directly from a national laboratory, Cummins Engine Company was granted an exclusive right to use a new superalloy, nickel aluminide, in heavy-duty diesel engines. In return for this license, Cummins agreed not only to pay an up-front licensing fee and running royalties, but also to commit to an aggressive, multimillion-dollar development program in cooperation with ORNL. The laboratory has subsequently negotiated a number of licenses with Armada Corporation, Armco, and Metallamics for the use of this material in other applications. Other technologies have been licensed to small and medium-sized firms. For example, a fiber-optics-based instrument capable of detecting small amounts of carcinogenic compounds on the skin or clothing of workers in industrial plants was licensed to a small, local company that supplies instrumentation for environmental monitoring. Another exclusive license was granted to a start-up company that will market an anaerobic bioreactor for municipal waste-water treatment. Finally, ORNL is negotiating with many firms to license other technologies for which the rights are being granted to Martin Marietta Energy Systems. Since the licensing capability has opened exclusive access to a technology, the volume of industrial inquiries has increased. As more technologies are placed under our management, this trend is likely to continue.

When innovations are to be generated, enhanced, and moved forward in an organization, several types of people must be involved. Roberts (1979) identifies five different key roles that must be fulfilled by (1) creative scientists or engineers, who are the source of new technological innovations; (2) entrepreneurs or product champions, who push technical ideas forward in the organization; (3) project managers, who focus on the specifics of the innovation, decide which aspects warrant further development, and coordinate the needed efforts; (4) sponsors, who protect scientists and entrepreneurs, ensuring that innovative ideas pass the initial development stages; and (5) gatekeepers, who bring essential technical and market information into the development process.

Although the above roles relate to the development of technological innovations in industry, analogous ones need to be fulfilled for the successful transfer of technologies developed at government laboratories. Each role describes a different person who needs to be recruited, managed, rewarded, and supervised with different types of measures and controls (Roberts, 1979). As one of the nation's largest R&D facilities, ORNL already employs many of these talents, albeit keeping them focused on satisfying traditional government R&D requirements. For some of them, such as project managers and information gatekeepers, the shift from the traditional roles can be easily accomplished. For others, a major change in the incentive system must be instituted.

ORNL has primarily emphasized the role of the creative scientist. Therefore, the laboratory possesses a vast reservoir of scientific and engineering talent. Although technically sophisticated and innovative, these individuals typically prefer to work on advanced problems rather than on industrial applications that exploit the commercial potential of their inventions. As scientists, they are rewarded proportionally to the quality and quantity of their work that finds its way into technical reports and journal articles. Therefore, ORNL scientists and engineers have had little incentive to submit patent disclosures; since patent disclosures delay professional publications, have onerous reporting requirements, and often lack obvious commercial applications, they are considered an unnecessary burden. Policies with respect to considering patents in conjunction with performance appraisals vary widely between divisions in federal laboratories. Some consider patents equal to a publication; others do not consider them at all.

In addition to ensuring the consideration of patents in annual performance appraisals, Martin Marietta offers the following additional incentives to induce reporting of inventions to the patent office: (1) an award of $100–1,000 per invention, depending on the level of technical merit and commercial value, to be granted at the time of patent application; (2) provision for the inventor to share in the royalties from licensed inventions, at the rate of 10 percent on the first $500,000 and 5 percent on the remainder, up to a limit of $100,000 per invention; (3) establishment of an "Inventor of the Year" award to recognize the inventor of the most significant new technology each year; (4) an annual patent award luncheon to recognize inventors receiving patents during the previous year; and (5) an internal "inventors' forum" open to employees holding patents and wishing to discuss issues of common concern.

The implementation of these measures has already produced results. For example, the number of invention disclosures in the first and second years were 15 percent higher than in the previous year. The change is particularly significant since it represents a reversal of a five-year trend of steadily declining disclosures and no increase in budget.

It was said earlier that successful technology transfer requires the presence of entrepreneurs who are able to recognize the commercial value of a scientist's latest discovery and aggressively promote the development of the technology with industry. The entrepreneur's ability to see commercial potential is often the result of a broad range of interests and activities, including private sector industrial experience and contacts. ORNL has begun to develop a cadre of entrepreneurial staff members interested in developing and maintaining closer ties with a wide range of industrial companies. Recognizing that most technology transfer occurs from one-on-one interactions, Martin Marietta allows and encourages individual consulting to firms outside normal work activities. Staff members are now encouraged to participate in trade shows, visit different companies' facilities, and maintain regular correspondence with scientists and engineers in industry to inform them of technical developments at ORNL. The executive-level Office of Technology Applications (OTA), headed by a vice president for technology applications, ensures the successful implementation of these initiatives.

OTA has developed and implemented new policies and procedures to coordinate and improve each step of the technology transfer process; it performs the important function of negotiating patent licenses with industry and manages special programs designed to promote technology transfer activities. One such program is the Technology Maturation Fund. The fund was established in 1984 when DOE gave $100,000 to ORNL, on a matching basis, to identify commercially promising technologies and bring them to a stage where industry can make a more accurate assessment of their potential. In the future, monies for the fund will come from royalties generated by patent licenses. Over the two years of the program's existence, eleven technologies have shared about $450,000 in support, and the program has produced about ten new patent applications. Five have won IR-100 awards—granted annually to the most commercially promising new technological developments—four have been licensed, two more are under negotiation, and one triggered a new business venture.

Another program, the Industry Technology Research Exchange Program, initiated in cooperation with DOE in 1985, supports visiting research appointments at ORNL for scientists and engineers currently working in industry. The intent of the program is to accelerate the understanding of new technologies and their adoption after the researcher returns to his or her company.

Decentralized patent licensing offers many advantages not available when the program is administered in Washington, D.C. First, ready access to the scientists and engineers who invented the technology provides a more accurate evaluation of its developmental status and a better understanding of its value to the private sector prior to and during the licensing negotiations. Also, the laboratory can offer, during the life of the license, access to further technical advances and assistance in developing a company's unique and proprietary applications.

Technology Transfer and Its Impact on Local Economic Development

The technology transfer program of ORNL, as it matures, will have a significant positive impact on the economic development of the region surrounding the laboratory, in the same manner that technology complexes such as the Silicon Valley, Boston's Route 128, North Carolina's Research Triangle, and Princeton's Forrestal Center evolved around major research universities and contributed to the economic welfare of the areas surrounding them.

As for the fear of a brain drain from our institutions of higher education, studies on the direct spin-offs from universities in the Boston, Ann Arbor, and Palo Alto areas indicate that the creation of new business is rarely associated with faculty giving up full-time positions to become their founders (Roberts 1969). Academicians, independently of their roles—from being the "driving force" to only giving advice—have usually kept a part-time commitment to commercialization ventures.

More specifically, as Martin Marietta continues to make technologies accessible to commercial firms, three developments resulting from the company's new policy will benefit the local economy.

First, established firms will desire more direct interactions with Martin Marietta staff and facilities in the form of collaborative R&D. This activity has already begun to expand. In the Metals and Ceramics Division, for example, there are major collaborative R&D agreements in place with Cabot Corporation, Cummins Engine Company, and Babcock & Wilcox. Other similar-scale projects are being developed with Atlantic Richfield Company and 3-M, among others. These activities provide additional resources in support of ORNL research programs, which in turn are growth generators for the local economy.

Secondly, established firms have more incentives for locating R&D facilities in the Oak Ridge region. Since successful transfers and further development of complex technologies involve close and frequent interactions with those responsible for the invention, commercial production facilities often need to be located in close proximity to the organization originally sponsoring the innovation. For example, Manufacturing Sciences Corporation chose an Oak Ridge location because of Martin Marietta's offer to access technologies important for rolling and forming depleted uranium. Their plant already employs thirty-five people and will continue to grow.

The third, local economic dividend from technology transfer is new business formation. Such technology-based small businesses are a leading source of both new jobs and important new technological innovations (Birch 1980; Gellman Research Associates 1982). Observers of the technological innovation process (Roberts 1968; Gilpin 1975; Heaton and Hollomon 1983) have argued repeatedly in favor of involving government laboratories in that process. Also, past entrepreneurship makes future entrepreneurship more likely (Cooper 1971; 1973; Shapero and Sokol 1982; Vesper 1983; Rothwell and Zegveld 1983), and the presence of successful entrepreneurs lends credibility to the actions of the inexperienced.

The need to improve technology transfer from the public to the private sector has been addressed numerous times by acts of Congress and presidential directives, but the programs that followed have been of uneven effectiveness. Industry and laboratory interactions will open up the possibility of future, additional joint technology development ventures. Collaboration between industry and government scientists permits cross-fertilization that results in the generation of new ideas and technologies that enhance the productivity of both organizations. Most importantly, these cooperative ventures with industry will help the federal laboratories to become more fully integrated into the nation's economy, and will help the nation to achieve the goal of enhanced economic productivity through technological innovation in a highly competitive global economy.

REFERENCES

Birch, D.L. 1980. "Who Creates Jobs?" *The Public Interest* (1980):3–14.
Charpie, R.A.; D.V. De Simone; L.S. Apsey; J.F. Costelloe; J.F. Dessauer; J.M. Fisher; A.J. Gellman; P.C. Goldmark; E.W. Kinter; M.S. Massel; R.S. Morse; P.G. Peterson; S.I. Roberts; J.C. Stedman; D.T. Smith; and W.R. Woodward. 1967. *Technological Innovation: Its Environment and Management.* Washington, D.C.: Government Printing Office.

Congressional Budget Office. 1984. *Federal Support for R&D and Innovation*. Washington, D.C.: Government Printing Office.

Cooper, A.C. 1971. "Spin-offs and Technical Entrepreneurship" *I.E.E.E. Transactions on Engineering Management* 28:2–6.

———. 1973. "Technical Entrepreneurship: What Do We Know?" *R&D Management* 3 (1973):59–64.

Doctors, S. 1968. *Role of Federal Agencies in Technology Transfer.* Cambridge, Mass.: MIT Press.

Gellman Research Associates, Inc. 1982. *The Relationship Between Industrial Concentration, Firm Size, and Technological Innovation*. Jenkintown, Penn.: Gellman Research Associates, Inc.

Gilpin, R. 1975. "Technology, Economic Growth, and International Competitiveness." Report to the Joint Economic Committee of the Congress of the United States. Washington, D.C.: Government Printing Office.

Heaton, Jr., G.R., and J.H. Hollomon. 1983. "Diffusing Technical Knowledge: A National Imperative." *Technology Review* (1983):12–14.

Hill, C.T. 1985. "Rethinking Our Approach to Science and Technology Policy" *Technology Review* (1985):11–15.

Mansfield, E. 1968. *The Economics of Technological Change*. New York: W.W. Norton.

Mansfield, E.; A. Romeo; M. Schwartz; D. Teece; S. Wagner; and P. Brach. 1982. *Technology Transfer, Productivity, and Economic Policy*. New York: W.W. Norton.

National Governors' Association. 1983. *Technology and Growth: State Initiatives in Technological Innovation*. Washington, D.C.: National Governors' Association.

Nelson, R.R., ed. 1982. *Government and Technical Progress*. New York: Pergammon Press.

O'Brien, T.C., and L.M. Franks. 1981. "Evaluation Framework for Federal Technology Transfer Initiatives" *Journal of Technology Transfer* 6, no. 1 (1981):73–86.

Office of Science and Technology Policy. 1983. *Report of the White House Science Council: Federal Laboratory Review Panel*. Washington, D.C.: Government Printing Office.

Roberts, E.B. 1968. "A Basic Study of Innovators; How to Keep and Capitalize on their Talents," *Research Management* 11 (1968):249–266.

———. 1969. "Entrepreneurship and Technology." In *Factors in the Transfer of Technology*, edited by W. Gruber and D. Marquis. Cambridge, Mass.: MIT Press.

———. 1979. "Stimulating Technological Innovation—Organizational Approaches." *Research Management* 22 (1979):26–30.

Rothwell, R., and W. Zegveld. 1983. *Innovation and the Small and Medium Sized Firm*. London: Frances Pinter Ltd.

Shapero, A., and L. Sokol. 1982. "The Social Dimensions of Entrepreneurship." In *Encyclopedia of Entrepreneurship*, edited by C.A. Kent, D.L. Sexton, and K.H. Vesper. Englewood Cliffs, N.J.: Prentice-Hall.

Twentieth Century Fund. 1984. *The Science Business.* New York: Priority Press.

U.S. Department of Commerce. 1983. *Information and Steps Necessary to Form Research and Development Limited Partnerships.* Washington, D.C.: Government Printing Office.

U.S. Department of Energy. 1982. *Report of the Multiprogram Laboratories Panel of the Energy Research Advisory Board.* Washington, D.C.: Government Printing Office.

U.S. General Accounting Office. 1985. *Federal Agencies' Policies and Practices Are in Accordance With Patent and Trademark Amendments of 1980.* Washington, D.C.: General Accounting Office.

Vesper, K. 1983. *Entrepreneurship and Public Policy.* Chicago: Heller Institute.

16 THE STRATEGIC DEFENSE INITIATIVE AND COMMERCIAL APPLICATIONS

Major General Donald L. Cromer, USAF

In 1983 President Reagan set forth the objectives for the Strategic Defense Initiative (SDI). He reaffirmed his support for strategic offensive modernization and arms control efforts and challenged the scientific community to determine the feasibility of developing systems capable of destroying ballistic missiles before reaching their target. Such a defense, he contended, could provide an alternative to reliance on offensive nuclear retaliation as the sole basis for strategic deterrence. In the long term, SDI could enhance the incentives for both the United States and the Soviet Union to safely agree to very deep reductions, even the elimination, of ballistic missiles and the nuclear weapons they carry.

SDI does not represent a major shift from the basic deterrent strategy of the United States. Rather, it represents a new approach: a means of enhancing deterrence. Our policy, in effect since the beginning of the nuclear era, has not changed in its fundamentals. Instead, our ability to deter has hinged upon differing military capabilities, ranging from a balanced nuclear bomber and air-defense capability in the fifties to almost total reliance on the threat of retaliation in the 1980s.

The shifts in the basis for deterrence have been forced by the development of various nuclear delivery systems and not by fundamental changes in policy. What has changed is the weapons and their effectiveness. Ballistic missiles are becoming more and more accurate. Hard

225

target kills are now possible from over 5,000 miles away. So, in order to maintain an effective deterrent force, we must seek corresponding improvements or alternate solutions.

While it need not be perfect, a defensive system must meet three important criteria: first, it must be effective, providing an acceptable leakage rate against a variety of attacks; second, it must be survivable, discouraging an attack as a prelude to an offensive strike, thereby decreasing, rather than increasing, crisis stability; and third, it must be affordable, that is, obtainable at a lower cost than continued offensive proliferation and countermeasures that attempt to overcome it. A cost-effective and survivable defense is the key challenge to SDI.

The Soviets currently have, located around Moscow, the world's only operational ballistic missile defense system. The system is for terminal defense, similar in many ways to the safeguard system that we had begun to deploy and then dismantled in the 1970s. The Soviets are presently modernizing their system.

In addition, they have developed a new antiballistic missile (ABM) that has potential for rapid deployment as a national ABM system. Of even greater concern, however, is their extensive development of technologies that have potential for advanced ballistic-missile defense applications.

They also have a directed-energy research and development site in the central Soviet Union, which could not only provide an antisatellite capability today, but is possibly a prototype for an ABM system to be deployed in the future. The Soviet's high-energy laser program, which dates from the mid-1960s, is much larger than the U.S. effort. The Soviets have built over a half-dozen major R&D facilities and test ranges, and they have over 10,000 scientists and engineers associated with laser development. Some of the advanced U.S. technology, especially in the area of particle beams, is derived from Soviet research reported in their technical literature several years ago.

As we look toward the future, effective strategic defense has the potential of decreasing the value of ballistic missiles as instruments of national strategy, thereby encouraging negotiated mutual reductions in those ballistic missiles. Negotiated reductions in offensive forces, in turn, will enhance the effectiveness of the defenses, hopefully creating a defensive spiral in which both parties would be more willing to negotiate further reductions.

To consider defense against ballistic missiles, one must first understand the character of a ballistic-missile attack. It starts in the boost phase, which can be characterized as an intensely bright plume that provides a very large infrared signature. The ballistic missile still has all its warheads attached. Hence, attack in this phase provides considerable defensive leverage. In the postboost phase, warheads and penetration aids are deployed in such a way as to attempt to confuse the defenses, still providing, however, a lucrative target, but with more targets to counter. This phase is followed by the longest phase, the midcourse phase, in which the warheads and penetration aids spread out and coast on a ballistic trajectory for several minutes on the way to their targets, presenting the greatest challenge owing to the discrimination problem. In the terminal phase, the warheads and the decoys reenter the atmosphere. Effective kill is essential here. Attacking ballistic missiles in all four of these phases is what is known as layered defense, a defense-in-depth approach.

Certain functions need to be accomplished in each of these phases for the ballistic missile to be effectively attacked: first, the sensor function, to accomplish surveillance, acquisition, discrimination, tracking, and kill assessment; second, the weapon function, to accomplish interception and destruction of the target; and third, the command and control function, to integrate the allocation of the weapons and sensors and place them under human oversight to accomplish battle management.

The ultimate scope of the SDI program can be described by identifying weapon system concepts for each function in each phase. The collection of technologies that will permit the realization of these concepts define the technical scope of the current program.

In the sensor area, we are looking at five, interleaved system concepts: a boost-phase surveillance and tracking system that would detect launches of ballistic missiles; a midcourse, space-based sensor system to provide the tracking from deployment to reentry; and a system to observe the reentry vehicle and decoy deployment and to be able to discriminate between the two. In the terminal phase, two systems are currently envisioned: an airborne optical system that would provide for long-range tracking and discrimination of the reentry vehicles and decoys; and a ground-based imaging radar. In the weapons area, both directed-energy and kinetic-energy concepts are under consideration.

Directed-energy weapons are being investigated primarily to attack ballistic missiles in either the boost or postboost phase. Options include chemically powered, space-based lasers, which might provide long-range, speed-of-light intercept and kill. Alternatively, ground-based

"Excimer," or free-electron, lasers could bounce their energy off space-based mirrors and thus be able to attack a large number of boosters without the need to put the laser device in space.

Space-based, neutral particle beams can penetrate deeply into the ballistic missile, causing catastrophic damage to internal components. Recent work on the mid-infrared advanced chemical laser (MIRACL) has demonstrated not only the highest power, but now also the highest brightness of any laser in the free world. This laser at the White Sands Missile Range will be a workhorse for SDI, allowing us to determine by actual testing the trade-offs between booster hardening and laser brightness.

Kinetic-energy weapons would provide for attack of ballistic missiles in all phases. In the boost phase, space-based projectiles propelled by chemical rockets or electromagnetic launcher systems would provide a capability for attacking boosters while they are still under power. These same systems would also be capable of attacking postboost vehicles and reentry vehicles during midcourse flight.

In the terminal and late midcourse area, ground-based interceptors would provide a non-nuclear, hit-to-kill capability to destroy reentry vehicles. The homing overlay experiment (HOE) conclusively demonstrated the technology for hit-to-kill intercept of reentry vehicles last year.

Beyond the military potential of SDI, there are some possible commercial applications. History has shown that new military technologies will inevitably have industrial and commercial applications that have produced a wide range of benefits that were totally unforeseen at the time. For instance, developments in military technology led to the fabrication of exotic materials like beryllium. Air-defense technology led to the first, large, commercial mainframe computers, which accelerated progress enormously in the advancement in commercial satellite communications.

The SDI pointing and tracking devices and technologies have direct application to commercial aircraft guidance and control and to ground-traffic monitoring, scheduling, and traffic flow. Ultraprecise sensing and measurement technology may lead to new, high-precision process control instrumentation.

Knowledge gained from understanding interactions between high-intensity radiation and materials may result in new manufacturing processes, new instrumentation, and new surface treatments and coatings.

The stringent requirements for precision mechanical structures for space applications may provide new materials for the construction industry, allowing lighter, cheaper, and stronger structures. New structural concepts being explored in SDI, such as fatigue resistant metal composites and ceramic matrix composites with high fracture resistance, have potential widespread applications in the automotive, maritime, and aerospace industries. For instance, the technology for cooling windows for terminal interceptor guidance could be of critical importance in the development of hypersonic commercial aircraft. Lasers of various types, including gamma-ray, will provide new and powerful techniques for probing and modifying materials.

Imaging techniques such as CAT scanners—using monochromatic radiation—will permit lower doses to patients, and higher resolution devices would allow discrimination between molecular species, not just density variations. Short-wavelength, coherent radiation holography would allow three-dimensional observations of the structures of molecules, crystals, proteins, and genes. From the developments in particle-beam generation will come new, safe, and more efficient concepts in medical diagnostic technology and treatment.

Nearly all elements of SDI require major advancements in space power. It is estimated that power and voltage levels in excess of four orders of magnitude above current space-based systems are needed. The technologies being pursued for these multimegawatt power sources should make power in space relatively plentiful for space manufacturing. The energy storage and high-power densities required for space applications could have direct benefit to public and private transportation concepts of the future.

Clearly, the potential for commercial space factories becomes a reality if SDI technologies are coupled with the space station. Low-cost mass-to-orbit weights are a major goal of the SDI program.

Specifically, at least a tenfold reduction in cost-per-pound-of-payload placed in orbit, based on current shuttle costs, is essential to achieve affordability of SDI deployments. Realization of this goal would translate into much more economical access to space for commercial applications.

The large number of space systems produced and launched in a fully deployed SDI would require a major change in the way we build and acquire space systems. We are beginning to address the subject even in this early stage of R&D. All of these things will have major impacts on the future of space industry. In that regard, the full and enthusiastic participation of contractors in SDI is going to place the basic capabilities I have been speaking of in our industrial base. They will be there for all to use.

It is important that the splendid opportunity to capitalize on results of SDI research and to apply it across all facets of our economy and society not be missed. For that reason, the Office of Educational and Civil Applications was created within the SDI organization. Among other things, its director will be responsible for developing and encouraging the widest possible civil uses of SDI-related technologies, consistent with security considerations, and for helping to identify potential and existing technology applications and techniques that have economic benefits for the nation.

Just a few months ago, the secretary of defense invited the participation of our allies in the SDI research program. We see this participation taking place in the forms of cooperative research programs between government laboratories, exchanges of scientists, and direct participation of foreign companies in U.S.-funded research, either through agreements with U.S. companies or by direct competition. It has been left up to each of our allies to propose the manner and extent of their participation.

This is the Strategic Defense Initiative, its scope and its possible commercial aspects. The goal of SDI has not changed since the President's March 1983 speech. Significant technical progress has been achieved. We believe that the goal is achievable.

It is important that everyone understand the Strategic Defense Initiative: what it is and what it is not. Its success or failure depends not only on the kind of technological advances that are made but, to a greater extent, on the public's acceptance of its value and its legacy for the future.

VI FOREIGN STRATEGIES

17 GLOBAL COMPETITION AND THE SPECIAL CHALLENGES OF DEVELOPING COUNTRIES
A U.S. Perspective

Kenneth McLennan

The international competitiveness of U.S. industry is currently a central issue on this nation's policy agenda. There is, however, no one best way to estimate the extent to which the competitiveness of U.S. industry has declined. From a U.S. perspective, restoring the competitiveness of many U.S. industries is essential for maintaining a high relative standard of living and for retaining a strong economic leadership position in the global economy. An increase in the aggregate competitiveness of the U.S. economy requires that the overall level of productivity be raised by moving resources to their most productive uses and by concentrating U.S. production in those industries whose comparative advantage is growing. The central challenge for policy officials, in both the public and private sectors, is to match or surpass the productivity growth rates of our international competitors in industrialized and developing countries.

THE EMERGENCE OF GLOBAL MARKETS

The growth of international trade over the past several decades has led to greater interdependence among the economies of the United States, other industrialized countries, and many developing nations. This has been mostly beneficial to the countries involved. Despite the decline in the U.S. share of world exports, from 14.6 percent in 1965 to 10.9 percent in 1984 (Office of U.S. Trade Representative 1986:22), the growth of global demand for goods and services has, at least until 1980, been sufficient to offset the negative employment effect of increased penetration of imports in U.S. markets and of the U.S. loss of share of the world market in traded goods and services (Lawrence I:1983).

During the 1970s, the United States was able to maintain an overall growth in manufacturing output and employment. There was, however, a loss of price competitiveness in U.S. manufacturing, due to the rapid increase of production costs relative to its foreign competitors. U.S. employment levels were maintained only through a significant depreciation of the U.S. dollar. Loss of competitiveness varied substantially among manufacturing industries, creating significant adjustment problems in many U.S. industrial sectors, especially those comprising basic industries such as steel, automobiles, textiles, and apparel.

Developing countries benefited significantly from the emergence of global markets. Among developing nations, the greatest beneficiaries have been those countries successfully creating manufacturing capability and transforming their export trade from an almost exclusive reliance on commodities to a more balanced mix of manufactured goods and commodities. Over the past two decades, newly industrializing countries (NICs)[1] increased their share of world exports of manufactures almost threefold and, by the end of the 1970s, accounted for about 8 percent of all trade in manufactured goods. Over the same period, the U.S. share of world exports of manufactures declined from over 17 percent to about 13.5 percent, while Japan's share more than doubled (OECD 1979:19).

By the mid-1970s, the NICs had captured over 10 percent of the OECD (Organization for Economic Cooperation and Development) market. The most significant penetrations occurred in textiles, clothing, wood manufactures, leather goods, and electrical machinery. The United States accounted for 42 percent of NIC exports to OECD countries (OECD 1979:10, 30).

In 1953, both Korea and Taiwan had virtually no exports of manufactures. By the end of the 1970s, however, the ratio of manufactures to total commodity exports was about 90 percent for both countries. This ratio also increased for Latin American NICs, but commodities still dominate their export trade (Maddison 1985:59).

The industrialized countries also benefited from the new pattern of world trade. Between 1963 and 1977, the proportion of exports from the OECD countries to the NICs increased from 7.6 percent to 9.2 percent, with the Asian NICs accounting for most of the proportionate increase. During the 1970s, OECD exports to non-oil-producing developing countries declined as the NICs increased their share of exports to these developing nations.

The success of the developing nations in shifting exports from an excessive reliance on commodities trade in manufactures is the result of high rates of saving and strategic investments in plants and equipment. Also, capital investments and loans from industrialized countries and the early 1970s', agreements—the Generalized System of Preferences (GSP) that gave exports from developing countries preferential treatment in OECD markets[2]—have contributed to the industrialization of developing countries.

SOURCES OF THE U.S. COMPETITIVENESS PROBLEM: CYCLICAL SOURCES OF U.S. LOSS OF COMPETITIVENESS

During the 1981–1983 recession, government action—aimed at eliminating double-digit rates of inflation—consisted of a mix of relatively loose fiscal policy and tight monetary policy. The results were relatively high interest rates, which, by attracting a substantial flow of capital to the United States, raised the value of the U.S. dollar, seriously damaging the competitive position of many U.S. export industries.

With expanded global markets and the increasing interdependence among world economies, the economic downturn taking hold in the United States and in other industrialized countries had serious adverse effects on the economies of developing nations. After 1980, the demand for imports from developing countries decreased while the rise in the value of the U.S. dollar increased the real cost of interest on the loans held by many Third World nations. This precipitated a third world debt crisis, partially attributable to the U.S. anti-inflationary policy and partially to the domestic policies of many of the debtor countries.[3]

Structural Sources of U.S. Loss of Competitiveness

The major factor in the loss of U.S. competitiveness over a period of at least two decades has been low productivity growth relative to its major foreign competitors. Countries such as Japan, West Germany,

South Korea, Taiwan, and Hong Kong have equalled or surpassed the productivity levels of many of our manufacturing industries (Baumol and McLennan 1985).

During the 1960s and early 1970s, labor-cost differentials did affect the competitive position of U.S. industries. But over the 1960–1973 period, higher rates of productivity growth among the U.S. major trading partners permitted rapid increases in their wage rates. This phenomenon, coupled with this country's moderate annual wage increases during the l960s and 1970s, substantially narrowed wage-level differentials among industrial nations. As shown in Table 17-1, by 1978, manufacturing compensation in West Germany was higher than in the United States; in Japan, average wages had risen from 48 percent of the U.S. rate in 1975 to 67 percent in 1978.

The labor-cost advantage of newly industrializing countries relative to the United States is narrowing, but remains extremely large. And those countries achieved outstanding growth rates during the past decade. For example, the average annual rate of growth of real GNP in both Taiwan and South Korea since 1975 was more than twice as great as that in most industrialized economies. Low compensation costs, combined with high levels of productivity in manufacturing, gave some developing countries a strong competitive advantage over the United States. As these countries acquire new technologies involving routine production processes, their lower compensation levels create a substantial competitive advantage.

Prior to 1978, the trend in exchange rates tended to offset the detrimental effect of low productivity growth and rising compensation costs on the competitiveness of U.S. production. After 1978, however, exchange-rate fluctuations had the opposite effect, making it more difficult for some U.S. industries to compete internationally.

For many industries, however, it is a mistake to assume that exchange-rate trends are the dominant, underlying reason for loss of competitiveness. In the long run, the more important determinants of competitiveness are comparative productivity levels and relative input costs.

U.S. RESPONSE TO LOSS OF COMPETITIVENESS: PRIVATE-SECTOR RESPONSIBILITIES

Since the United States relies heavily on the market system to allocate resources within the economy, much of the adjustment to a changing economic environment is expected to occur automatically, emerging

Table 17-1. Comparative Hourly Compensation Costs for Production Workers in All Manufacturing Industries and in Steel and Auto Industries for Selected Countries (Index: U.S. = 100).

Countries	1975			1978			1983		
	Manu-facturing	Iron and Steel[a]	Motor Vehicles and Equipment	Manu-facturing	Iron and Steel[a]	Motor Vehicles and Equipment	Manu-facturing	Iron and Steel[a]	Motor Vehicles and Equipment
United States	100	100	100	100	100	100	100	100	100
Major Trading Countries (on trade-weighted basis)									
Canada	96	73	80	93	74	79	93	71	72
Japan	48	51	38	67	69	54	51	49	42
Federal Republic of Germany	97	70	81	116	79	94	84	52	70
France	72	57	55	79	59	58	62	43	45
United Kingdom	51	38	42	52	39	39	53	36	39
Italy	73	58	55	73	54	50	62	42	42
Sweden	113	87[b]	79	116	85[b]	77	73	50[b]	48
Other Industrialized Nations									
Austria	64	48	—	75	53	—	56	38	—
Belgium	103	79	80	125	98	97	75	55	57
Netherlands	103	80	71	120	87	79	78	56	50
Ireland	47	—	—	47	—	38	45	—	33
Denmark	99	—	—	106	—	—	74[c]	—	—
Spain	41	—	—	47	—	—	43[c]	—	—
Newly Industrialized Countries									
Brazil	18	14	17	20	16	19	14	10	12
Korea	6	6[b]	5	10	11[b]	11	10	9	9
Taiwan	8	7[b]	7	10	9[b]	8	13	10[b]	9
Mexico	30	—	31	25	—	24	12	—	14[c]

Source: Compiled from unpublished data prepared by U.S. Department of Labor, Bureau of Labor Statistics, Office of Productivity and Technology, January 1984.

[a]Excludes foundries.
[b]Includes foundries.
[c]Figures for 1982.

from decisions made by business executives and from collective bargaining between labor and management.

There are five major adjustment techniques typically used by U.S. businessmen to respond to loss of competitiveness.

1. Industries affected by competition from developing countries, such as the textile and apparel industries and, more recently, the automobile and steel industries, have sought protection from foreign competition.

2. In response to changes in relative costs of production, U.S. businesses have relocated productive facilities in low-cost regions. Much of this relocation has occurred within the United States.

3. In some cases, however, productive facilities have moved offshore to industrialized and developing countries or have relied more heavily on foreign sourcing.

4. To protect the jobs of some workers, the gradual decline in the level of employment has been accepted as the price to pay for the loss of competitiveness.

5. More flexible compensation schemes, including absolute declines in wages, have been adopted as the desirable adjustment to maintain existing employment levels (Block and McLennan 1985).

Each technique has weaknesses even though it may be justified in specific circumstances. Protection is justified in response to ''dumping'' and unfair trade practices by foreign competitors. Domestic relocation of facilities is explained in the name of efficiency, as foreign sourcing is rationalized as integration of the world's economies. A gradual and permanent employment decline in an industry may be considered the result of structural adjustments, and variations in labor compensation may be expected to accompany the life cycle of the industry and the enterprise. But most of these options for responding to loss of competitiveness have serious disadvantages.

Trade protection may lead to retaliatory actions from other trading nations, harming both industrialized and developing countries. Apart from the adverse effects of a possible contraction in world trade, protection does not generate increased employment. It simply redistributes employment and income toward the less productive and frequently lower paid jobs and away from the more innovative and high-productivity sectors of the economy. Relocation of productive facilities imposes economic costs in the form of abandoned plants and equipment, incurring many social costs to the host communities. Failure to relate compensation levels to competitive market prices inevitably translates adjustments to loss of competitiveness into a loss of jobs among workers with low seniority.

The attainment of adequate increases in productivity growth is the only adjustment technique capable of minimizing the costs associated with loss of competitivenss. In the long run, the market system rewards firms that innovate, and it penalizes those that fail to adopt new productive techniques, improve quality, reduce unit costs of production, and pursue new markets. Management and labor bear the responsibility for adopting innovations and facilitating the movement of capital and labor resources to their most productive use. These are the only strategies that will maintain or restore the competitiveness of U.S. industry (CED 1984).

Public Policy Responsibilities

The government has major responsibilities for creating an economic environment favorable to restoring the competitiveness of U.S. industry. Many business executives and economists attribute the U.S. competitiveness problem to the rapid escalation in the value of the U.S. dollar since 1979 and argue that the goal of government policy should be to reverse that trend.[4]

During the period 1980–1984, the U.S. dollar was clearly overvalued, in part because of U.S. economic policies. Its recent rapid decline against the yen was appropriate. And the comparative productivity and inflation performances of Japan and the United States since the mid-1970s suggest further declines of the dollar against the yen. In my opinion, however, there is little evidence to suggest that the rise in value of the dollar was the major cause of declining competitiveness. As trade expanded in the 1970s, some increase in import penetration was to be expected. But one would not have predicted that imports would double, relative to domestic supplies, in such industries as industrial chemicals, phonograph and television equipment, semiconductors, photographic equipment, resistors for electronic applications, aircraft engines, and machine tools—rather than just in the automobile, steel, footwear, and apparel markets. This rapid penetration of relatively high-technology American markets occurred from 1973 to 1979—a period when the dollar depreciated substantially.

By 1981, Taiwan was the fourth largest supplier of imports to the United States and accounted for more imports than any European country, except West Germany. South Korea, Mexico, and Hong Kong each supplied more imports to this country than either France or Italy. While the Asian NICs continued to be major suppliers of textile mill and apparel products, countries such as Taiwan and South Korea became leading suppliers of fabricated metal products (third and fourth, respectively) and electrical machinery (second and fourth, repectively) (U.S. Labor Department 1983).

Government policy should improve the national economic environment so that business may compete more effectively, but budget balancing designed only to reduce the value of the dollar will negatively affect living standards. The devaluation of the dollar becomes the equivalent of a huge markdown on the sale price of U.S. export products, while forcing higher prices for imports. The consequence of this approach to the competitiveness problem is a reduction in relative income levels and the possible loss of economic leadership.

In making the difficult decisions of reducing federal expenditure, policymakers need to be selective. Expenditures for programs likely to increase productivity (such as funding of basic R&D) should be preserved or expanded, while income maintenance and subsidy programs for the nonpoor should be curtailed. Even the huge Social Security Retirement Income Program may not be exempt from budget cutting, since most of the beneficiaries of the program are not poor. In terms of after-tax income, and when in-kind subsidies are taken into account, the poverty rate among the elderly is, on the average, lower than that among the rest of the population. And middle- and upper-income elderly Americans may need to bear their share of pain in reducing the budget deficit.

Similarly, expenditures on national defense should not be immune from budget cuts. Those who believe that we need further real growth in defense expenditures need to be reminded that our future national security and continued political leadership position depends more on our superior economic performance than on the number of available weapons systems.

If we must raise taxes, the burden should fall far less heavily on saving than on consumption. Tax increases that discourage individual saving and reduce the ability of business to invest in new plants and equipment are counterproductive, since a major constraint on U.S. productivity performance has been a low rate of saving and investment. From the mid-1960s to the mid-1970s, Japan's rate of capital investment in manufacturing exceeded that of the United States by a factor of four, and that accounts for most of Japan's superior productivity performance over the past fifteen years. To match the investment performance of foreign competitors, government policies must induce Americans to allocate more income to saving and more savings to investment in new plants and equipment, even if it requires initial sacrifices in living standards.

RESPONSIBILITIES OF DEVELOPING COUNTRIES FOR PARTICIPATING IN GLOBAL COMPETITION

During the economic slowdown of industrialized economies, lesser developed nations had to face the consequences of a decline in demand for their exports and of the increased cost of debt servicing created by the strong U.S. dollar. The recent economic recovery of some of the leading economies and the sharp decline in the value of the U.S. dollar will help alleviate the problem. Yet, while it is in everyone's interest to facilitate debt servicing and economic growth among Third World countries, their governments cannot ignore the realities of global competition. Policies fostering heavy reliance on government controls rather than on the price mechanism, avoidance of monetary policy, and the use of rampant inflation for raising revenue and adjusting to shocks from international trade have not served them well, and in fact, since 1973, resulted in a poor record of economic growth, especially in Latin America (Maddison 1985: pt. 5:59).

Developing countries, particularly those with extraordinary records of economic expansion over the past two decades, have an important role to play in the new regime of global interdependence. A reform of the General Agreement on Tariffs and Trade (GATT) to reflect the changing composition and pattern of global commerce is needed to ensure the continuation of a relatively free international trade. Industrial sectors, such as agriculture and services, must be effectively included in the rules under the GATT. It is in the interests of both developed and developing countries to reduce non-tariff barriers—including subsidies to protect domestic industries and stimulate exports—and to recognize that unless intellectual property rights are protected under GATT and respected by all nations, the evolution of a global industrial structure will be retarded and many mutual advantages of trade for all countries will be lost.

There is no longer any justification for some NICs receiving special preferences under international trade arrangements. Many of them have rates of growth of per capita gross domestic product (GDP) that rival some of the industrialized countries and are larger exporters than some of the OECD countries participating fully under the rules of the GATT. All nations must work toward a procedure that gradually brings countries achieving sufficient economic development into full GATT membership (Frank 1979:290).

The future growth of global trade is also likely to be dependent on reforms of the international monetary system, which presently restricts the conditions under which countries can manage their exchange rates. For example, despite the claims of Taiwan and South Korea that they have abandoned fixed exchange rates, there has been little change in the value of their currencies for almost a decade. Given their superb performance in productivity and price stability, it is clear that they follow a policy of "managed floating" exchange rates to capture maximum short run advantage in export markets.

Both industrialized and developing countries must cooperate to assure the continued expansion of global markets. If individual nations in either group of countries fail to carry on their responsibilities under international trade arrangements, the benefits of global trade and economic interdependence will decline for all nations.

NOTES

1. These include several European countries (Spain, Portugal, Greece, Yugoslavia), three Latin American countries (Argentina, Brazil, Mexico) and several Asian countries (Hong Kong, Korea, Taiwan, Singapore).

2. In 1981, the GSP, which is based on a waiver of the "most favored nation" principle under the GATT, was extended for an additional ten years. For a review of the evolution of the GSP, and of previous preferential arrangements available to developing countries, see OECD 1983.

3. Many Third World countries, even those that had relied heavily on loans from industrialized countries to finance the restructuring of their economies toward manufacturing, have been successful in overcoming the debt crisis. The difference in response to the debt crisis between Asian and Latin American countries suggests that the external environment was only one factor in the problem facing developing countries in the 1980s. See Maddison 1985.

4. This argument is presented by many economists. See, for example, Bergsten, 1986. It is also a position supported by many U.S. business executives.

REFERENCES

Baumol, William J., and Kenneth McLennan, eds. 1985. Chapter 1 of *Productivity Growth and U.S. Competitiveness*. New York: Oxford University Press.

Bergsten, C. Fred. 1986. "The Dollar's Down, But Not Enough." *New York Times* (March 30).

Block, Richard N., and Kenneth McLennan. 1985. "Structural Economic Change and Industrial Relations in the United States' Manufacturing and Transportation Sectors: 1973–1983." In *Industrial Relations in a Decade of Change*, edited by Hervey Juris, Mark Thompson, and Wilbur Daniels. Madison, Wisconsin: Industrial Relations Research Association.

Committee for Economic Development. 1984. *Strategy for U.S. Industrial Competitiveness*. New York: CED.

Frank, Isaiah. 1979. "The Graduation Issue for LDCs." *Journal of World Trade* (July–August): 289–302.

Lawrence, Robert Z. I:1983. "Is Trade Deindustrializing America?: A Medium-Term Perspective." In *Brookings Papers on Economic Activity*, Issue 1, edited by William C. Brainard and George L. Perry, pp. 129–161. Washington, D.C.: The Brookings Institution.

Maddison, Angus. 1985. *Growth, Crisis and Interdependence, 1929#1938 and 1973#83*. Paris: OECD Development Center.

Office of the U.S. Trade Representative. 1986. *Twenty-Eighth Annual Report of the President on Trade Agreements Program*. Washington, D.C.: Government Printing Office.

Organization for Economic Cooperation and Development. 1979. *The Impact of the Newly Industrializing Countries*. Paris: OECD.

———. 1983. *The Generalized Systems of Preferences*. Paris: OECD.

U.S. Department of Labor. Bureau of Labor Statistics. Office of Productivity and Technology. 1983. *U.S. Imports and Related Output*. Washington, D.C.: Government Printing Office (November).

18 GLOBAL COMPETITION AND THE SPECIAL CHALLENGES OF DEVELOPING COUNTRIES
The Perspective of Developing Countries

Herminio Blanco

This chapter reviews the position of the developing countries and their perspective on the processes of international competition and cooperation.[1] Also, it focuses on some aspects of technology transfer from industrialized to developing nations. Most of these countries can be characterized as having low per capita income levels, very skewed income distributions, large disparities in the level of development among sectors (urban-rural, formal-informal), low education levels, fast population growth, and inadequate technology and public-services infrastructures. One of the main concerns of developing countries is to devise and apply labor-intensive techniques that would generate employment, while at the same time increasing productivity to maintain or achieve international competitiveness.

There was a general belief that some industries—characterized by causing environmental concerns, being labor- or energy-intensive manufacturers, or involving the processing of raw materials with high transportation costs—would be relocated from industrialized to developing countries. Recent technological developments most likely will inhibit the relocation of these industries. Additionally, the export-oriented strategy, successfully followed by some developing countries, no longer seems a good policy prescription. This assertion is based on the slow growth of the world economy, the decline in the terms of trade of the main exports of developing countries, increase in protectionism on the part of industrialized nations, and the fact that not all developing countries could adopt this strategy at the same time. The condition of the developing economies is further aggravated by their need to allocate a large share of resources to service their external debt and by the reduced flows of external capital. The lack of financial resources has important negative implications for the development of scientific and technological capabilities in developing countries.

The need for cooperation with the developing countries has been stressed in several forums. It may be illustrative to cite a statement on this topic by the U.S. National Academy of Science (1982):

> It has become evident that the industrialized nations of the world cannot conceivably engage in capital transfer to the developing nations on a scale sufficient to manage these huge (population-related) problems, even with great sacrifice. If, however, they wish to minimize the possibility that burgeoning populations elsewhere will generate irresistible pressures that will de-stabilize the world political situation, the industrialized nations must engage in extensive efforts to assist the developing nations. This means assistance in the development of adequate infrastructure, including educational systems as well as indigenous agriculture and industry. Particular emphasis should be given to the support of research and development. Some such technical assistance programs are in existence today, but their sum is far from adequate for the task. This circumstance constitutes a huge challenge to the scientific and technical communities of the industrialized world. It also requires the sympathetic understanding, the wisdom, and the courage of the peoples and governments of the nations of the already industrialized world (pp. 578–579).

By focusing on the technological aspects of the cooperation and competition exchanges in the global economy, it is the objective of this discussion to evaluate the likelihood that the recent unusual fast pace of technological progress will generate a widening gap between industrialized and developing countries. We will analyze first the process by which technology is generated and transferred to developing countries and the experiences of developing countries in acquiring it. Then, we will turn to the prospects for technological progress in industrialized countries and the implications for the future of developing countries. We will conclude with a discussion of possible strategies by developing countries for addressing technological progress and of the need for cooperation among developing countries, and between them and industrialized nations.

TECHNOLOGICAL PROGRESS AND TECHNOLOGY TRANSFER

As in other investments that have a high degree of uncertainty, firms will invest in high-technology-related projects only if they expect to receive an economic rent in excess of some normal, risk-free rate of return on the invested capital. Investments in the creation of new technology are usually rewarded by granting monopoly rights through some patent system. It has been argued, however, that granting monopoly rights may be suboptimal in terms of overall development. The argument is based on the fact that, in general, the cost of transferring technology is usually much lower than the cost of creating technology. The problem rests on devising a system that rewards the creators of technology and ensures that the knowledge is diffused at an optimal rate. Internationally, this problem has greater complexity, since developing countries need to maximize their access to technology in order to accelerate industrial development. Research and development has often been supported through procurement programs by the governments of industrialized countries. This support should grant some flexibility in the diffusion of technology, at least within a country, since the investment costs have been shared by the whole society. Internationally, the governments of industrialized countries may also have some ground for being generous in setting the terms for transferring technology to developing countries.

In spite of insufficient financial and human resources to adequately invest in technology, some developing countries have advanced on this front during the seventies and eighties. R&D expenditures in Latin America increased from about $250 million constant 1970 dollars in the mid-1960's to around $900 million in the mid-1970's, to nearly $1.6 billion in 1980. The number of researchers, laboratories, and research projects increased accordingly. Similar efforts have been made in the southern and southeast Asian countries. Yet, the Latin American share of the world R&D expenditures remained at about 1 percent through the 1970s and 1980s. This level of investment is still insufficient. For example, General Motors R&D expenditures are larger than the whole Mexican R&D budget! Also, Mexico invested only 0.54 percent of their gross domestic product (GDP) in 1982, while some countries (the United States, France, Japan, Russia) invested more than 2 percent. Furthermore, in the developing nations, 96 percent of the R&D funding was contributed by the public sector (Sagasti 1985).

The high cost of the equipment required for advanced research put most developing countries out of the technological race in some important fields (Kenney and Buttel 1984). The accelerating rate of obsolescence of research facilities, due to rapid scientific and technological advances and the increasing systemic nature of research requiring the fusion of different technologies, forces continuous investment injections that, when not forthcoming, substantially hinder the opportunity of technological progress in developing countries.

This fact, however, does not totally explain technological backwardness in some of these countries. Following the traditional industrialization route recommended in the fifties and sixties, many developing countries closed their economies to foreign competition and created industrial plants, without providing incentives for adequate investments in technology creation as a means to compete in the world market. On the other hand, it is partly true that, without protection, many firms would not have been established, and technology could not have been transferred.

Without technology-generating capabilities, less-developed countries are forced to import most technologies, even when they are "incompatible" with the labor-intensive production processes of such countries. Technologies are acquired not as substitutes for labor, but for use in manufacturing processes that are difficult to perform manually or for competing with new product quality enhancements. In fact, in discussing the incentives to transfer technology across countries, it may be useful to differentiate between technological progress that involves changes in products (quality, effectiveness, sophistication, etc.) and technological progress that consists of changes in production techniques (automation, efficiency through the application of CAD/CAM [computer-aid design/computer-aided manufacturing], laser controls, etc.).

For product technology, relative price differentials of productive inputs may induce firms to locate production sites in different countries. The same inducement is not present, however, for the transfer of production technology, since it is designed in accordance with the prices of inputs in industrialized countries. Other incentives to locate a production site in a developing country are created by logistic factors, such as transportation costs or strategic considerations, such as the host country's ability to offer to multinational or domestic firms substantial protection from potential competitors. It is important to remember that technological transfer is more than changing the geographical location of production processes, since it includes some technology-generating capability, that is, the capability of "copying" or adapting technology to the economic and environmental conditions of the host country.

Some authors have been debating whether the effective price paid for technology has been too high. The concept of effective price includes the cost of tie-in clauses, such as a prohibition against exporting or reselling the technology, as well as the obligation to buy machinery and equipment at above-market prices. There are serious problems to resolving this debate; it is difficult to clarify what one means by a "high" price, and measurement errors (payments through royalties and fees are only a part of the total price of technology) may occur.

Governments of developing countries have tried to strengthen the bargaining position of domestic firms, but it is not clear how successful they have been in changing the terms of technology transfer. The impact of the legislation governing technology transfer is substantially weakened by the investors' hard bargaining power and by the flexibility displayed by technology-acquiring parties.[2] The temporary application of stringent legislation in some countries of the Andean Common Market lead to a virtual stop in the transfer of technology. The United Nations has attempted—not very successfully—to change the legal framework of technology transfer in order to lower the price of technology paid by developing countries.[3] To effectively change the technology transfer framework, however, one must take into full consideration the profit-making nature of these transactions. It is highly unlikely that firms in industrialized countries would voluntarily sell technology at lower prices to developing countries. What is required is a framework that allows the cost of technology to be shared by the governments of industrialized and developing countries, thereby making the new technology more readily available to the countries involved.

RECENT TRENDS IN TECHNOLOGICAL PROGRESS AND THEIR IMPLICATIONS FOR DEVELOPING COUNTRIES

There have been substantial advances in the fields of microelectronics, computer science and information processing, automation and robotics, biotechnology, and new materials. There has also been rapid progress in methods of production. The introduction of flexible manufacturing systems (FMS), the CAD/CAM systems, and "production just-in-time"[4] have radically transformed production methods in manufacturing.

The recent fast pace of technological discoveries could lead to further obstacles to economic growth, or it could promote progress in developing countries. Most of these advances tend to save on the inputs that are abundant in many of these countries: labor (automation and robotics),[5] energy, and other raw materials (biotechnology and new materials). This phenomenon has been named "comparative advantage reversal." There is a definite danger that the new generation of robots will convert industries such as clothing, footwear, and assembling from being labor-intensive to being capital-intensive.

The cases of sugar cane and copper may be used as examples of the adverse impact of biotechnology on the exports of some developing countries. In 1981, the United States replaced 1.8 million tons, and Japan 400,000 tons, of sugar imports with HFCS (high-fructose corn syrup). This partially led to the drop in the world price of sugar and to the fact that, in the future, sugar cane production cannot be considered a safe source of foreign reserves. Sugar cane exports from Latin American countries to the United States decreased from over $1.3 billion in 1981 to $568 million in 1985, and only $344 million in exports has been estimated for 1986. The impact of biotechnology is also felt on mining, since 15 percent of U.S. copper production is now extracted from low-concentration deposits, using a specially designed bacteria (Kaplinsky 1984:65; Hoffman 1984).

Biomass technology could, in the near future, be a strong alternative to oil as a source of energy. This would benefit the majority of developing countries, even if at the expense of some oil-producing nations.

Will the patterns of technological progress in the industrialized countries lead to the economic annihilation of developing countries? In a neoclassical perspective, developing countries will have some comparative advantages and will be able to export, even in the face of these potentially adverse technological changes. But the relevant question is, What price will prevail for their abundant productive inputs? In particular, will the new "equilibrium" produce adequate wages for unskilled workers? It appears that technological progress has a labor-saving bias, originated by the high wages in the industrialized countries, and does not take into account the abundance of this productive factor in the developing countries. There are, however, some causes for optimism. First of all, there is some evidence that the production of high-technology capital goods is labor-intensive (Clair 1986). Additionally, the advances in microelectronics and biotechnology could lead to the attainment of some economic development objectives.

The added production flexibility in manufacturing processes implies that high production volumes are no longer needed for high productivity; developing countries are characterized by their inability to reach economies of scale, due to their small markets. The phenomenon of smaller scales of production is also present in biotechnology.[6] It is possible that some technological advances could help developing countries to initiate more autonomous manufacturing technologies that are energy saving and have small plant sizes.

Brazil is an example of the advances in biotechnology that are helping developing countries. Brazil was able to substitute an important part of its oil imports with alcohol refined from sugar cane. As energy production from biomasses and biogases become a feasible alternative, it may promote rural industrialization and, potentially, may shorten the gap between the rural and urban sectors in developing countries. Mexico has also experienced progress in the production of hormones and in the generation of improved seeds. In fact, genetic engineering is not far from separating the genes that support the different characteristics of plants. This will lead to the design of seeds appropriate to the conditions of most developing countries; then, self-sufficiency in food production may be attained by these countries.

Progress in telecommunications is having a positive impact on development by allowing access to education even in the most remote areas of developing countries.

For Mexico, the shift of production methods to production just-in-time has meant that many assembly plants that were located in the Far East have moved to the Mexican northern border, close to the U.S. Sun Belt and its dynamic manufacturing sector. The future of this important source of foreign exchange and employment depends upon the characteristics of the new generation of robots and on the reaction of U.S. unions.

In conclusion, it is quite difficult to evaluate the net outcome of the recent technological advances on developing countries. The future will be gloomy indeed if the negative impact on their terms of trade precludes them from buying and developing the technology that would be beneficial to them.

STRATEGY FOR TECHNOLOGICAL PROGRESS IN THE DEVELOPING COUNTRIES

The Third World has to develop technological capabilities in a time of diminished financial resources, increased social demands, and rapid advances in industrialized countries that are difficult to emulate. A three-pronged strategic approach has been proposed and consists of,

first, defensive measures to limit and contain the damages that technological advances could inflict upon the productive structure of developing economies; second, tactical moves to take advantage of the
opportunities offered by the rapid structural change in world industry;
and third, a long-term commitment to increase productive capacity
in selected fields through investments and cooperation agreements with
developing countries and appropriate institutions in the industrialized
nations (Sagasti 1985:193). It is absurd to expect that developing countries could become equal partners in the generation of advanced technology. But it is not unreasonable to hope that developing countries
become technologically competent in selected fields and that they adapt
to or imitate the technologies of industrialized countries.

Biotechnology is a promising specialization area for developing countries because of its high potential for country- or region-specific agricultural and medical developments, with small requirements of human
and financial resources.

Policies of commercial openness and the appropriate treatment of
direct foreign investment are important elements of strategies for facing
present and future advances in technology. By decreasing the protection
against foreign competition, a country promotes the technological
upgrading of its industrial facilities but also removes one of the main
incentives for technology transfer. Perhaps selective protection is a good
strategy for developing some technology capabilities—for example,
Brazil and its personal computer industry. The protectionism of industrial countries for not too technologically advanced sectors hurts the
economies of developing countries. The reaction of less-developed
countries must be that of promoting import rather than export
substitution.

In summary, developing countries should prepare for the future by
investing in education and R&D, promoting the interaction between
universities, industry, and agriculture, and promoting cooperation with
other developing and industrialized nations. It is also necessary to create
a legal framework that takes into account the profit-making nature of
technological progress and technology transfer.

CONCLUDING REMARKS

Given the present international environment, developing countries may
not expect the inflow of substantial financial resources. Yet, if they
do not make substantial investments in technological infrastructures,
they will not reap the benefits of the recent and expected scientific

discoveries and technological innovations. Actually, their relative position in the global economy would worsen as the terms of trade for their exports further deteriorate.

Overcoming the impasse requires actions from both developing and industrialized countries. But the mood prevailing in some industrialized nations is hardly one of cooperation. A recent OECD report (1981:79) warns against a possible "boomerang effect" when technology is transferred to developing countries and is possibly used to compete with the very country from which it originated. The report also indicates that industries such as textiles, clothing, leather, and footwear, or relatively more technologically advanced industries such as electrical equipment, optical products, petrochemicals, steel, and aluminum, are likely to face increased competition from the developing world.

NOTES

1. In this paper it will seem that the term developing countries refers to a homogeneous group of countries. Nothing, however, could be farther from reality. These countries differ greatly in the degree of industrialization and in many other aspects.
2. See Graham 1984, pp. 68–80, for a description of the experiences with regulating technology transfers in Mexico, Brazil, the Andean Common Market, and some other countries.
3. The legal framework used in different countries is fully analyzed and described in Delorme 1984.
4. This method was developed in the 1970s to offset the high costs of holding inventories, due to high real-interest rates.
5. Although the main intention could not have been that of saving the use of labor, the sophisticated nature of many of the new products requires intensive use of capital. See Chudnovsky 1984, p. 149, for some evidence on this topic.
6. See Sagasti 1985, pp. 39–41, for some interesting data on the diminished scales of production in biotechnology.
7. See Sigurdson 1983 for an evaluation of the trends in microelectronics and the virtual impossibility of developing countries becoming partners in this field.

REFERENCES

Chudnovsky, Daniel. 1984. "La Difusion de Tecnologias de Punta en la Argentina: el Caso de las Maquinas Herramientas de Control Numerico, los Robots y CAD/CAM." In *Revolucion Technologica y Empleo*, edited by Secretaria del Trabajo y Prevision Social y Secretaria de Comercio y Fomento Industrial. Mexico, D.F. (November).

Clair, Robert T. 1986. "The Labor-Intensive Nature of Manufacturing High Technology Capital Goods." *Economic Review* (Federal Reserve Bank of Dallas) (March):11–17.

Delorme, J. 1984. "The Changing Legal Framework for Technology Transfer: Some Implications." In *North/South Technology Transfer: The Adjustments Ahead*, by the Organization for Economic Cooperation and Development, pp. 55–85. Paris: OECD.

Graham, E.M. 1984. "The Terms of Transfer of Technology to the Developing Nations: A Survey of the Major Issues." In *North/South Technology Transfer: The Adjustments Ahead*, by the Organization for Economic Cooperation and Development, pp. 55–85. Paris: OECD.

Hoffman Kurt. 1984. "Clothing, Chips and Competitive Advantage: The Impact of Microelectronics on Trade and Production in the Garment Industry." Mimeo (July). Science Policy Research Unit, University of Sussex.

Kaplinsky, Raphael. 1984. *Automation: The Technology and Society*. Harlow, England: Longman Group.

Kenney, Martin, and Frederick H. Buttel. 1984. "Biotechnology: Prospects and Dilemmas for the Third World." Development and Change, March.

Organization for Economic Cooperation and Development. 1981. *North/South Technology Transfer: The Adjustments Ahead*, Paris: OECD.

Sagasti, Francisco R. 1985. "Crisis, Knowledge and Development: A Review of Long-term Perspectives on Science and Technology for Development." In *Workshop Mexico 2010: Views from Abroad*, edited by A. Alonso and G.O. Barney, Mexico, D.F.: Centro de Estudios Prospectivos, Fundacion Javier Barrios Sierra A.C. pp. 169–203.

Sigurdson, Jon. 1983. "Forces of Technology Change." In *Technological Trends and Challenges in Electronics*, edited by S. Jacobsson and J. Sigurdson. Lund, Sweden: Research Policy Institute, University of Lund.

U.S. National Academy of Sciences. 1982. *Outlook for Science and Technology: The Next Five Years*. San Francisco: W.H. Freeman and Company.

VII EPILOGUE

19 EMERGING POLICIES AND STRATEGIES

Antonio Furino and George Kozmetsky

The pressing economic problems of our times and the challenges they pose to this country are portrayed vividly in the previous eighteen chapters and in the appendix to this volume.

In addressing issues and outcomes of global competition, the authors' perceptions of threats and solutions are amazingly consistent with one another, in spite of the writers' differences in background and interests.

The realities of what Professor Rostow calls the Fourth Industrial Revolution set an unprecedented stage for the next act of the global drama. To make the performance more difficult, the characters are likely to play opposing roles. The United States must reverse trade flows and reduce a huge budget deficit. Developing countries, to honor large financial commitments, are likely to promote decreases in domestic demand and increases in exports. Other industrialized economies, to secure an uncertain future, may be expected to expand government spending and investments in human and physical capital. Demand-generation efforts may conflict with demand-reduction requirements.

The needed adjustments are of enormous proportions (Okita 1987) and development of the world economy is dependent upon reconciliation of diverse needs and strengths among three major groups of countries. One comprises the emerging economies, including the newly industrialized nations, and those countries, such as China, that have exhibited a remarkable economic performance. Many analysts suggest that these countries be progressively integrated into the international economic system to share advantages and obligations with the industrially advanced economies (Okita 1987; McLennan 1988). The second group includes the less-developed countries and those developing nations whose economic growth has been lacking. Their economic struggle is a global issue, and they represent the most important frontier of the world economy. The third group embraces the industrialized nations, whose competitive objectives must be reconciled with their need for cooperation.

For the United States to respond to these challenges it must regain its economic leadership within the international community. This view is not shared by everyone. But since the United States has a strategic influence on the stability of global markets, and cooperation among nations more easily prevails with a recognized leader, it may be in our best interest to be that leader (Jones and Teece 1988; Lawrence 1984).

A real average growth rate for the United States of 2.7 percent during 1985 and 1986, inflation down, and more recently, decreasing unemployment are seductive signs for an optimistic view of the future and a "business as usual" attitude. But troublesome clouds, clearly charted by the contributors to this book, forewarn of imminent problems. Unprecedented high dependence on foreign investors financing increasingly larger portions of budget deficits has kept interest rates uncomfortably high and has decreased the ability of traditional monetary and fiscal policies to deal with national economic issues, such as productivity increases, stimulation of investment and savings, or the avoidance of a recession. The condition is serious. Paying just the interest on $500 billion of U.S. foreign debt—forecasted by the Federal Reserve Bank of New York as likely to occur by 1990—will require a $40 billion-a-year trade surplus. A real challenge, since 1986 ended with a U.S. trade deficit of $169 billion (Senate Report 100-71:2-4; House Report 100-40:3-6).

A major piece of legislation, addressing some of the concerns presented in this volume, is now being discussed in Congress. It proposes major revisions of the Trade Act of 1974.[1] The purpose of the legislative effort is to establish a more effective national trade policy against foreign trade barriers and distortions, enhance the competitiveness of U.S. firms and workers, defend and expand intellectual property rights, and improve standards of living in the United States and ultimately throughout the globe (Senate Report 100-71; House Report 100-40).[2]

The proposed laws explicitly address the need for trade deficit reduction, require action by the president on multilateral trade agreements, and set specific goals and reporting mechanisms to monitor results.

The relationship of education to competitiveness, the low level of literacy of American children compared to their counterparts in other industrial nations, and the capacity of workers to function in a technologically advanced workplace are the bases for specific proposals to increase the authorization levels of existing programs and initiate new ones in technology training and international education (Senate Report 100–73; House Report 100–40:pt. 5).

Additional legislation has been submitted for enhancing technology transfer through new federal research priorities favoring manufacturing and commercialization—particularly through the National Bureau of Standards, through better cooperation between industry and the approximately 700 federal laboratories, and through the encouragement of new private research—by extending the intent of the National Cooperative Research Act of 1984 (P.L. 98–462) and providing seed money to promising or financially hard-pressed industry sectors (Senate Report 100–80).

To increase agricultural competitiveness, specific objectives with respect to agricultural trade are proposed for the upcoming round of multilateral trade negotiations concerning the General Agreement on Tariffs and Trade (GATT). Also, new agricultural trade initiatives and supporting programs are recommended (Senate Report 100–77; House Report 100–40:pt. 6).

Special provisions are proposed to curb alleged unfair trade practices by some U.S. trade partners that result in large trade surpluses with the United States. Their purpose is to obtain unrestricted access to foreign markets for telecommunications equipment, to subsidize special projects in new and advanced manufacturing technologies, to assess the extent of activities of foreign firms in the United States and in U.S. firms abroad, and to enforce reporting requirements on countertrade and offset arrangements (House Report 100–40:pts. 2, 4).

Since much of the proposed legislation includes authorizing retaliatory actions when negotiation fails to produce results favorable to the United States, it has ignited strong dissension, on the grounds that the protectionist nature of the legislation will destroy rather than create U.S. jobs (House Report 100–40:107–116; *Business Week* 1987:68).

It is clear that if the United States is to meet the competitiveness challenge, a global rather than a parochial view must be taken. This means broader and novel approaches to business management. An example is the selection of locations around the world that offer the best economic and political advantages for conducting R&D, manufacturing, marketing, and financial activities. Another example is viewing the whole globe, rather than its national and regional subdivisions, as the marketplace. In the new approach, competitiveness and cooperation are not conflicting goals but parts of effective strategies for commercializing new and innovating ideas. Scientific, technological, managerial, socioeconomic, cultural, and political considerations are integrated by the new managers into a plan of action that can withstand extreme time compression (Kozmetsky 1987). In the United States, this approach is fostered through new alliances and cooperative ventures among government, business, labor, and academia. To ensure successful continuation of these efforts, federal policy needs to support more basic R&D in nondefense areas; to focus on those disciplines, such as advance materials and human frontier sciences, that are essential to maintain scientific and economic preeminence; to ally with other nations when necessary to catch up or surpass present scientific knowledge; to promote incubators; to facilitate partnership between federal laboratories and entrepreneurs; to promote centers of excellence in integrated computer manufacturing and other enhancements of manufacturing processes; and finally, to support the education of a technology-wise work force gifted with multidisciplinary, multilingual, and problem-solving skills.

While the federal government might help in creating an environment that is conducive to technological progress and competitiveness, many of the preceding authors observed that it is the private sector's responsibility to rise to the challenges of the twenty-first century.

Among those challenges is coping with what has been called the "information economy," where the critical sectors are education, R&D, media and communications, and information services, while manufacturing is based on robotics, CAD/CAM, and numerical controls. More than just high technology, the information economy requires managers who are both creative and innovative and, therefore, successful in linking innovation with manufacturing centers.

Innovation centers like California's Silicon Valley and Massachusetts' Route 128 rely on universities and other institutions that foster R&D, on the existence of entrepreneurs, and on a favorable environment for building growth companies. Such centers have been organized in many U.S. regions and are characterized by a public-private infrastructure that supports high-technology development for cutting-edge products, usually designed through close customer interface.

A different mix of institutions and resources and different infrastructures is required for manufacturing centers capable of supporting the advanced manufacturing processes and production flexibility needed to bring technological innovations to domestic and foreign mass markets. Such centers are generally found in the Pacific Rim, namely, Japan, South Korea, Hong Kong, and Singapore.

Linking these two types of centers—innovation and manufacturing—may provide the economic growth and stability needed in the twenty-first century. It requires the fusion of the qualities of a creative manager—sensitive to new ideas and new modes of operation but still relying on individual judgment and performance—with those of an innovative manager, who is attuned to the realities of successful project implementation and teamwork but perhaps too absorbed in ensuring the efficiency of the process to sufficiently support basic research efforts. Traditional management decisionmaking is based on economic efficiency and cost-effectiveness. Creative and innovating management focuses on process flexibility and organizational adaptability to change.

In conclusion, the future can be bright if the United States and the rest of the world have the foresight and the inner strength to make the necessary adjustments. As the authors of this volume have suggested, the adjustments are neither small nor easy. Part of the difficulty is that, besides technical sophistication, adjustments entail a transformation of attitudes and beliefs. They require the individual wisdom of managers and entrepreneurs and the collective wisdom of governments. They imply a global view of long-term objectives inspired by enlightened self-interest. They demand a willingness to change, often radically, from deceivingly comfortable and misleadingly safe positions. Finally, they require sacrifices. A willingness to pay the price of change must prevail in the corporate boardrooms—where longer term growth strategies are to be preferred over glamorous, shorter term returns— in the public halls where realistic and unpopular policy adjustments are to be made, in the individual decisions to buy less and save more, and among the industrialized economies and the developing countries, whose destinies are inextricably entwined.

In the 1984 Economic Report of the President, the Council of Economic Advisors argued that the declining competitiveness of the United States and its merchandise trade deficits were not necessarily symptoms of weaknesses in our economic system but negative variables offset by positive ones such as broad economic choices, high standards of living, and surplus in services. The conclusion was that too much emphasis was being given to the topic (*Harvard Business Review* 1987a:9; 1987b). Since then, the debate on U.S. competitiveness has become a priority item in Washington circles and in the press. A recent survey of the approximately 4,000 readers of the *Harvard Business Review* (1987c) from all the fifty states and from thirty-four foreign countries indicates that some consensus exists on the following points:

- America's competitiveness is declining—largely because of the performance of U.S. managers—and it is up to them to respond to the challenge.
- While the government shares part of the blame, government-led remedies—particularly a national economic strategy—are not solutions to the problem.
- Basic U.S. values—such as the work ethic, pride in quality, and deferred gratification—have slipped and must be restored if the country is to get back on track (p. 8).

It is clear that agreement on problems and remedies among policy-makers in the public and private sectors is still wanting.

Professor Vogel indicated that the economic success of Japan was triggered by the need to rebuild a nation with practically no natural resources and almost total dependency on the outside world. Hopefully, the United States and its neighbors and partners are gifted with the wisdom to avoid the catastrophe considered inevitable by some economic analysts[3] and to act sensibly and expeditiously to build a safe bridge to the future.

NOTES

1. It also proposes revisions to later revisions such as the Trade Agreement Act of 1979, which implemented the results of the Tokyo Round of Unilateral Trade Negotiations.
2. For related legislation, see Senate Report 100–73, Senate Report 100–80, Senate Report 100–77, House Report 100–40, particularly part 2 (Committees on Energy and Commerce), part 4 (Banking, Finance, and Urban Affairs), part 5 (Education and Labor), and part 6 (Agriculture).

3. Among them, the best known is the controversial Southern Methodist University professor, Dr. Ravi Batra (1987). Other well-known economists, such as John Galbraith (1987) and Kenneth Boulding, without exhibiting the certainty of Dr. Batra, accept the idea that another serious depression can occur.

REFERENCES

Batra, Ravi. 1987. *The Great Depression of 1990: Why It's Got to Happen— How to Protect Yourself.* New York: Simon and Schuster.

"Can America Compete." 1987. *Business Week* (April 20).

"Competitiveness: 23 Leaders Speak Out." 1987b. *Harvard Business Review* (July–August): 106–123.

Economic Report of the President. Transmitted to the Congress together with the Annual Report of the Council of Economic Advisors. Washington, D.C.: U.S. Government Printing Office, 1984.

Galbraith, John Kenneth. 1987. "The 1929 Parallel." *Atlantic* (January).

Jones, Peter T., and David J. Teece. 1988. "Geopolitical Dimensions of Economic Decline." In Appendix to *Cooperation and Competition in the Global Economy*, edited by Antonio Furino. Cambridge, Mass.: Ballinger Publishing Company.

Kozmetsky, George. 1987. "The New Reality of U.S. Competitiveness." Testimony before the U.S. Senate Commerce Committee, January 20.

Lawrence, Robert Z. 1984. *Can America Compete?* Washington, D.C.: The Brookings Institution.

McLennan, Kenneth. 1988. "Global Competition and the Special Challenges of Developing Countries: A U.S. Perspective." In *Cooperation and Competition in the Global Economy*, edited by Antonio Furino. Cambridge, Mass.: Ballinger Publishing Company.

Okita, Saburo. 1987. "The Emerging Prospects for Development and the World Economy." Third Raul Predisch Lecture, Geneva, July 9.

"Probing Opinions—Do You Think There Is a Competitiveness Problem?" 1987a. *Harvard Business Review* (May–June).

"Probing Opinions—Competitiveness Survey: HBR Readers Respond." 1987c. *Harvard Business Review* (September–October).

U.S. Congress. Senate. Committee on Finance. *Omnibus Trade Act of 1987.* 100th Cong., 1st sess., 1987. Report 100–71 on S. Rept. 490.

U.S. Congress. House. Committee on Ways and Means. *Trade and International Economic Policy Reform Act of 1987.* 100th Cong., 1st sess., 1987. Report 100–40 on H. Rept. 3.

U.S. Congress. Senate. Committee on Labor and Human Resources. *The Education for a Competitive America Act.* 100th Cong., 1st sess., 1987. Report 100–73 on S. Rept. 406.

U.S. Congress. Senate. Committee on Commerce, Science, and Transportation. *Technology Competitiveness Act of 1987*. 100th Cong., 1st sess., 1987. Report 100–80 on S. Rept. 907.

U.S. Congress. Senate. Committee on Agriculture, Nutrition, and Forestry. *Agricultural Competitiveness and Trade Act of 1987*. 100th Cong., 1st sess. 1987. Report 100–77 on S. Rept. 512.

WHAT WE KNOW AND WHAT WE DON'T KNOW ABOUT COMPETITIVENESS

Peter T. Jones and David J. Teece

THE PRIVATE SECTOR: THE CORPORATION

The President's Commission on Industrial Competitiveness (1985:2) noted that "American ability to compete lies primarily within the private sector." Governments obviously cannot legislate success, though public policy both here and abroad does, of course, frame the environment in which firms compete. The important message from the President's commission has been drowned out in a panoply of requests for public policy "fixes." It is, therefore, instructive to see what can be done in the private sector. Recent history offers some tantalizing evidence.

One of the most promising aspects of U.S. economic performance is the emergence of highly competitive firms in industries once considered to be moribund (for example, Worthington Industry and Nucor Corporation in the steel industry) and the competitive revival of incumbent firms that had been battered by foreign competition (Xerox, for

Editor's Note: This appendix is an extension of Chapter 7, "The Research Agenda on Competitiveness," by the same authors. Here, the issues summarized at the beginning of that chapter are viewed as cognitive challenges that must be addressed to create a basis of theoretical and empirical knowledge sufficiently rich for guiding the complex choices this nation must make to progress or even survive in the global environment.

The four sections—"The Corporation," "The Industry," "State and Local Governments," and "The Federal Government"—are used to group the issues under the major institutional settings within which decisions that affect U.S. competitiveness are made.

instance, has stopped the advance of Japanese firms into the photo-copier market). The emergence of new competitors and the turnaround of incumbents demonstrate what is possible within the existing public-policy environment. The successful new entrants and the revitalized incumbents are not isolated instances. There are hundreds of examples, which include large firms as well as small firms. Often, but not always, it is the specialist firms that are emerging as the winners. It is very rarely the highly diversified conglomerates or their divisions that are the exemplars of the new competitiveness.[1] Big firms such as Chrysler and Shell, however, must often be counted among the successes. So must many medium-sized firms. The industry-by-industry, sector-by-sector evidence is undeniable, from textiles to autos, from semiconductors to computers and biotech, from banking to health care. New competitors using new ways of doing business are showing the way.

Not all of the successes of these firms can be attributed to luck. Many have rethought virtually every facet of their business. Often it is top management that is making the difference. Whatever the causes, the fundamental conclusion, however, must be that significant opportunities exist for firms to improve performance without the help of government.

In some cases, it has been takeover or the threat of takeover that has been the instrument of change. While takeovers have often had the unfortunate consequence of causing management to focus on the here and now, and while the quest for investment banking fees may have caused Wall Street to "put into play" some companies that were already engaged in restructuring, takeovers have clearly had beneficial effects in some cases (TWA, for example). What these outcomes demonstrate is that opportunities for significantly greater efficiencies do exist within American companies. The challenge is to find the most efficacious instruments for unlocking those efficiencies. The preferred approach is for management and labor to initiate the process through internal consensus, rather than through external threat.

It is important to recognize that government policy and national institutions provide the structures within which firms build the base of the capabilities from which they compete domestically and internationally. The evident performance differences among firms, however, even within the same industries and markets, underscore the fact that opportunities for superior performance are generally available to the participants of those organizations, no matter what the policy environment within which they operate. In what follows, we identify important organizational, technological, and strategic areas where we believe additional research could shed light and provide the basis for action.

INNOVATION AND MANUFACTURING

Technological Innovation, Imitation, and Postinnovation Performance. Technological innovation has long been viewed as the engine of the capitalist system. In the world economy today, however, it is not always the case that those firms and nations that generate the innovation are the ones that capture the largest proportion of the benefits flowing from it. For instance, the British company EMI, which developed and was first to commercialize the body scanner, was by no means as successful in the marketplace as was GE, which had a derivative model that drew heavily on the EMI technology. Similarly, though Ampex invented and commercialized the videocassette recorder for the broadcast market, it captured almost no market value from subsequent versions engineered for the home market. Sony, Matsushita, and others markedly enhanced the product to achieve superior performance, compactness, and manufacturability, thereby opening up a mass market that they then successfully exploited. Likewise, in the microcomputer industry, Xerox has pioneered many of the key technologies; yet it has still to reap any profit in the line of business to which it has contributed so very much. Imitators and enhancers (for instance, Apple with its MacIntosh) have proved the marketability of important hardware and software innovations made at Xerox's Palo Alto Research Center, such as the "mouse" and "icon" constructs for user-friendly interface.

There are, on the other hand, many cases where innovators have been able to parlay an innovation into an extremely profitable, worldwide market position. G.D. Searles' success with aspertame (Nutrasweet) is a case in point. Polaroid, with instant photography, is another well-known success story.

We need to develop a better understanding of the factors that systematically differentiate innovators who succeed in the international marketplace after product introduction from those who fail. Prior research (Teece 1987) has indicated the importance of speed and the criticalness to the innovator of certain cospecialized assets that the innovation requires for successful commercialization. These considerations are especially important when intellectual property is not easily protected by the standard legal devices. Cospecialized assets may consist of complementary technologies, dedicated manufacturing, specialized distribution, and after-sales support. If a firm lacks these assets or competitive access to them, it will be seriously disadvantaged in the commercialization process and may well lose out to imitators better positioned with respect to these key complementaries. In this regard, what *Business Week* refers to as the "hollow corporation" may be especially disadvantaged. In many instances, manufacturing matters (Cohen and Zysman 1987).

A program of research is needed that can test the complementary-cospecialized assets thesis. Systematic study of postcommercialization successes and failures is needed to explore issues such as:

1. The implications of different appropriability regimes (Teece 1986) for business strategy. In particular, when imitation is easy, to what extent do winning market entry strategies require speed and control over cospecialized assets?
2. Whether manufacturing production equipment in-house, rather than relying on outside vendors, is a necessary prerequisite for success in an industry where intellectual property law affords little protection for new products.[2]
3. The extent to which having competitive offshore manufacturing is a substitute for competitive onshore manufacturing. What trade-offs are associated with taking manufacturing offshore? Is subsequent product improvement hampered? Do manufacturing skills deteriorate within an organization if research and development departments are not forced to confront the challenge of engineering for low-cost manufacturing?
4. When a firm is missing complementary capabilities—whether it is in manufacturing, marketing, or related technologies—are collaborative arrangements with competitors or potential competitors an effective way of pulling together all the pieces needed for a successful commercialization? In particular, it would be useful to understand:
    a. the type of governance structures, such as joint ventures, coproduction, and codevelopment, that are appropriate for particular technologies;
    b. the hazards associated with engaging in codevelopment activities with competitors and potential competitors;

    c.   the legal and organizational structures, processes, and strategies that best guard against technology misappropriation by strategic partners; and

    d.   the nature of the savings in cost and time that collaboration can yield.

5.   The conditions under which the economic profits associated with innovation at home can be captured by foreign firms in their own markets if access to these markets is regulated by government. When technologies are easily imitated, it may be that importing countries can alter the allocation of the profits from innovation in favor of the imitator and away from innovators by temporarily restricting the entry of the innovators' products and/or investments. If this is the case, then barriers created against U.S. high-technology exports and investments will have a far more pernicious effect on U.S. welfare than barriers erected against commodities—such as foodstuffs or raw materials—that are not exposed to imitation. Both theoretical and empirical analysis of these issues is required if a deeper understanding of them is to evolve and have operational utility.

Collaborative Agreements and U.S. Competitiveness.   Over the past decade, the frequency with which U.S. firms in high-technology industries have engaged in international collaborative arrangements has markedly increased. These include technology licensing and know-how agreements, joint ventures, distribution, coproduction, and codevelopment agreements. For instance, AT&T has an arrangement with Olivetti whereby Olivetti manufactures the AT&T 6300 personal computer. Hewlett-Packard has an arrangement with Canon whereby Hewlett-Packard sells the Canon LBP-CX laser printer in the United States under Hewlett-Packard's label.

Firms engaging in collaborative agreements see them as important competitive devices. Some competitors have discovered, however, that the result is a gradual giveaway of U.S. technology and an erosion of the skill base, particularly in manufacturing. With respect to U.S.–Japanese joint ventures, Reich and Mankin (1986) have warned:

> Before this trend becomes an irrevocable destiny, U.S. business and government leaders need to review the facts carefully and decide if they should follow a different course. Two questions, in particular, frame the issue: What skills and abilities should be the basis for America's future competitive performance? And how does the current strategy of Japanese investments and joint ventures affect those skills and abilities? (p. 79)

Reich's own view is that, through these coalitions, foreign workers gain valuable experience in applications engineering, fabrication, and complex manufacturing. U.S. workers, in contrast, occupy the two "perimeters of production." A few get experience in research, and many get experience in assembly and marketing. In short, Reich and others believe that participation in collaborative arrangements, more often than not, results in the transfer of skills from the U.S. firms to their competitors.

These allegations would appear to warrant further investigation. Private-enterprise firms are not renowned for knowingly "giving away" their intellectual property. If imitation results from their activities, it must be owing to systemic or institutional factors over which firms do not have good control. While strategic errors at the firm level do occur, a persistent pattern of such errors without correction is unlikely.

Hence, it will be useful to examine more deeply the kind of collaborative agreements that lead to technology leakage and to ferret out why firms engage in collaboration that is ultimately injurious to their health. It will be necessary to examine whether the time horizon of firms affects outcomes. Are managers facing short-run performance rewards more prone to license technology and to contract-out manufacturing?

It will also be useful to examine the strategic alternatives to collaboration that innovating firms may have possessed at the time they entered into these agreements. Perhaps there was some other realistic way to enter particular markets. For instance, if a particular market is closed to foreign firms, joint venturing may be the only path open. In other cases, in-house facilities may have been inefficient, and the financial capital to build new facilities unavailable. In any event, it will be instructive to examine situations in which American firms knowingly or unknowingly create their own competitors. What is it that compels capitalists, as Lenin once remarked, to sell someone the rope that is used to hang them? At the same time, it will be equally important to identify and understand the nature of those collaborative arrangements between U.S. and foreign firms that are positive sum solutions of sufficient value to both firms and their respective national interests to merit emulation.

Besides exploring collaboration between U.S. and foreign firms, a deeper understanding is needed of the benefits and managerial challenges associated with cooperative R&D. With this kind of arrangement, firms agree to share the costs and fruits of a research project before they undertake it. Cooperation of this kind is far more common outside the United States than within. Cooperative research, which was perceived by many to be illegal in the United States until the signing of the National Collaborative Research Act in 1984, has several benefits, at least theoretically (Katz 1986). By allowing firms to share their research output, cooperative R&D increases the efficiency of R&D efforts and eliminates wasteful duplication. Second, cost sharing provisions restore at least some of the incentives to conduct R&D. In short, a cooperation arrangement, appropriately structured, ought to be able to internalize many of the spillovers.

Whether cooperation of this kind is best achieved through contracts—for example, codevelopment agreements through joint ventures, confederations, or directorates—warrants further attention. Ouchi and Bolton (Forthcoming) have demonstrated that useful insights can come from case studies, and further research along these lines is needed. In addition, a systematic explanation of the governance mechanism and managerial processes that match different kinds of technological endeavors warrants further study.

Manufacturing: Productivity, Quality, and Process Technology.   A statement, damning in its simplicity, was found recently in *Consumer Reports* (1984:333): "No domestic car approaches the high quality and reliability of most Japanese imports." The United States has apparently lost its reputation as an efficient manufacturer of quality products. Product standardization, process innovation, high-quality production, and incremental improvements are all Japanese strengths.

The available evidence seems to be unambiguous: while the United States may still command some lead in product innovation, it is failing in the area of process technology. This contrast in performance—relative success in product innovation and relative failure at process innovation—is itself intriguing and begs for an explanation. Several hypotheses exist that need to be explored:

1. Is it simply that U.S. firms are unable or unwilling to invest in new plants and equipment? In other words, since most new technology is embedded in new capital goods, is it simply low rates of investment that explain low productivity and slow process innovation in the United States?
2. Is the slow rate of process innovation linked to failures in industrial engineering and business education? In particular, is the low status of manufacturing management a cause or an effect of business school curricula, which commonly neglect manufacturing management?

3. Is the failure in process innovation linked to management styles that suffocate shop-floor initiative and experimentation?
4. Is the failure due to the fragmented structure of many U.S. high-technology industries? Does fragmentation eliminate opportunities for scale economies and related process innovations?

What is striking about the U.S. experience is the enormous variation in manufacturing productivity across firms operating in the United States. Some firms, such as IBM, Nucor Steel, Lincoln Electric, and Maytag, have manufacturing performance levels that far exceed those of other companies in the same lines of business. We doubt that all we need to know has been learned from such instances of compelling success. In particular, we need to know whether better human-resource management is the critical factor. If it is, then an enormously important finding will have been made, with strong implications for management and public policy.

We suspect that careful analysis will show that the new-style American competitors have much flatter managerial hierarchies, screen new employees much more carefully, often offer stock ownership to employees, and/or include profit and productivity sharing as part of the compensation package. Careful empirical research should provide more certain answers to these critical questions.

The Utilization of the World's Stock of Nonproprietary Knowledge. Many consider that the United States contributes proportionally more to the world's stock of nonproprietary knowledge than it is able to extract from it. Not only is most of the basic research performed in the United States open to the world scientific community through publications and visits, but the United States also continues to educate engineering students from abroad in large numbers. In 1984, for instance, foreign students accounted for about 56 percent of all doctoral degrees in engineering awarded in the United States and about 38 percent of all doctoral degrees in computer sciences (NSF 1985:208). Many of these graduates remain in the United States, but most return home. Very few U.S. students receive science and technology education abroad, and very few U.S. doctoral recipients study abroad. In 1983, only 1.08 percent of all engineering doctorates were studying abroad (NSF 1985:210). Moreover, "in recent years the number of new U.S. science and engineering doctorate recipients who have pursued post-doctoral study abroad has decreased substantially. During a period when science outside the U.S. has advanced rapidly, the use of this channel for the transfer of knowledge back to the U.S. has diminished'' (NSF 1985:26).

Recent scientific and technological developments have accentuated the importance of foreign countries as a source of know-how. Timely access to foreign, particularly Japanese, research is of great importance. It is widely recognized, however, that an obstacle to early access is the ''dearth of technologically sophisticated Americans with research experience in Japan and with Japanese-language capabilities'' (Coleman and Samuels 1986:206).

Studies need to be done that can assess the relative efficiency and efficacy of the various channels by which the results of nonproprietary basic research performed abroad impact basic science in the United States. An assessment of the tacit dimension (Teece 1981; Mansfield et al. 1982) of technology transfer is needed. In particular, the potential effectiveness of new forms of information transfer need to be examined.

An assessment is also needed of the openness of basic research abroad. If the largest contribution to science in Japan occurs in the private sector—rather than in the universities, as it does in the United States—then the efficacy of academic exchanges is seriously brought into question. If there are substantial similarities in the institutional locus of basic research in the two economies, then like-for-like exchanges can be expected to be mutually profitable as long as each party can access the other's language and culture with similar facility, a matter largely within the control of the parties involved in the exchange.

More generally, it is apparent that a set of interesting questions relating to the acquisition of science and technology abroad, and hence, to the feasibility and efficiency of various channels of access, warrants closer study. The objective ought to be to identify mechanisms and structures to preserve and enhance the openness of the system while simultaneously taking steps to reduce asymmetric free riding.

HUMAN-RESOURCE MANAGEMENT, ORGANIZATIONAL BEHAVIOR, AND INDUSTRIAL RELATIONS

The Performance of Japanese Manufacturing Operations in the United States.   In the past decade there have been numerous books and articles exploring, explicating, extolling, or condemning Japanese management practices (for example, Abegglen and Stalk 1985; Cole 1979; Keys and Miller 1984; Ouchi 1983; Sethi 1985; Vogel 1985).[3]

A central theme often addressed by these authors concerns the applicability of various management approaches adopted by Japanese firms to non-Japanese cultures. Arguments have been made for both positions. For instance, Ouchi (1983) has observed that many successful U.S. corporations have management practices that are similar to those of Japanese firms. Others have claimed that much of what we see as Japanese management may be a unique aspect of Japanese history and culture that is fundamentally inappropriate for American values and beliefs (for example, Sethi 1985). Which argument, if any, is correct?

While academics and practitioners engage in these often abstract debates, the real answer to the applicability of Japanese human resource practices to non-Japanese settings is already being quietly but convincingly answered, not through debate but through practice. Japanese direct investment in the United States is accelerating with the fall in the value of the dollar, resulting in increasing numbers of firms being operated by Japanese managers (for example, Burstein 1986). Already there are over 500 enterprises in the United States run by Japanese firms, accounting for over 80,000 employees.

Studying these 500 + Japanese-managed enterprises in the United States should, therefore, be made a priority. The generally successful management of U.S. workers by Japanese firms—such as Sony, Honda, New United Motors Manufacturing Inc. (NUMMI), Nissan, Nippon Electric Limited (NEC), and others—offers the chance to investigate how Japanese approaches can be modified and used successfully with American workers. In addition, research into this issue will provide important insights into Japanese practices more generally. The Japanese success is particularly interesting inasmuch as:

1. Japanese companies have used very different strategies in the United States. Some (like Toyota) have embraced unionized work forces. Others (like Nissan) have located in nonunion areas, such as Tennessee.
2. At least one of these companies, NEC, has deep American roots. (NEC was established in 1899 and reorganized into a joint-stock company with a 200,000-yen capitalization, half of which was provided by the Western Electric Company of Illinois (WECO), until recently the manufacturing arm of the Bell System.) NEC closely studied and replicated Western Electric's advanced systems of management and production control. (These included such novelties as time clocks.) NEC's Mita plant, which it began to construct in 1925, was patterned after WECO's Hawthorne Works (NEC 1984).

3. The productivity advantage of Japanese-managed enterprises in the United States is very significant. The NUMMI plant in Fremont, California, for instance, is believed to have as much as twice the labor productivity of that averaged by the U.S. auto industry, despite the fact that the capital equipment employed is quite standard.

It would seem that there is more relevance to U.S. business from understanding how Japanese management works in America than from understanding how it works in Japan. Surprisingly, little systematic study of this topic has been done to date, despite its obvious importance.

We need to know how Japanese successes have been achieved. Why, for instance, has NUMMI, the Toyota–GM joint venture in Fremont, California, been able to achieve a two-percent absenteeism rate and virtually no grievances, when the average GM absenteeism and grievance rates are four or more times higher? Recall that NUMMI workers are UAW members, the majority of whom worked for GM when the absenteeism rate exceeded 18 percent. What accounts for the ability of Japanese-managed firms to succeed with U.S. work forces, many of whom worked in the same plants under American management, but with far lower rates of productivity and quality?

Useful research ought not, therefore, to assert that Japanese human-resource practices either are or are not appropriate for non-Japanese settings. Instead of focusing on the various policies, research is needed to explicate the psychology underlying a set of management approaches used by Japanese firms in Japan, the United States, and Europe. The focus ought to be on understanding why certain approaches to human-resource management are likely to be successful in generating high levels of motivation and commitment from employees. Does the general approach followed by Japanese firms in selecting, orienting, and managing workers promote the psychological identification of the worker with the firm and act to legitimate high levels of teamwork and performance? To what extent do the underpinnings of Japanese human-resource systems, both at home and abroad, rely on the construction of strong social control systems generated through psychological mechanisms such as: (1) systems of participation and incremental commitment that encourage choice and result in feelings of personal responsibility; (2) the development of strong work group norms that maintain social control of the work group and promote cooperation; (3) the effective use of symbolic management to focus on sanctioned goals and enhance managerial credibility; and (4) incentive systems using approval and recognition to promote psychological attachment to the organization (for example, O'Reilly 1983; Pascale 1985).

The evidence suggests that the general approach adopted by Japanese firms may rely on these psychological mechanisms to foster identification of the individual with the firm. Research can reveal whether these policies are applicable in the management of both Japanese and non-Japanese work forces and whether they contribute to our understanding of the management of both Japanese and "strong culture" U.S. and European firms.

Employee Compensation and Ownership.   Over 10 million American workers, participating in some 8,000 plans, are now share-owners. ESOP programs and profit-sharing plans are proliferating, with important consequences in many cases. We know very little, however, about the efficacy of employee ownership and compensation plans, about what makes them successful in some cases and ineffectual in others.

Potential hypotheses to be explored include the following:

1. Must the level of total employee stock-ownership pass some initial threshold for incentive effects to be manifest?
2. Does the class of stock (that is, voting versus nonvoting) make a difference?
3. Does the efficacy of ESOPs depend critically on other policies (for example, putting into place institutional mechanics that invoke some form of participative management)?
4. Are there compensation structures and delivery systems (like bonus plans) that are more effective than others in generating financing flexibility for the firm and a greater sense of ownership and shared responsibility among employees?

Profit sharing and other approaches must similarly be studied where there are preliminary indications that such approaches create significant performance improvements.

Managerial and Union Barriers to Change.   Recent history indicates that, in some cases, progress towards more competitive organizational structures and work practices is hindered by the existence of interest groups within firms that block change because they would be harmed by it. This is a constant refrain of the corporate "raiders," and it is by no means clear that it is a position without foundation. What kind of incentives and threats, short of corporate takeovers, can be employed to bring about such change? What role does the executive team and the board of directors have in managing the transition? To what extent can managers and other interested parties be relied upon to abolish their own jobs? To what extent is corporate raiding, or the threat of it, the principal instrument in use today to bring about such change?

Leadership.   When change is required, corporate leaders can give direction and imbue enthusiasm for a new set of goals. Since the 1920s, the upper echelons of American management have become increasingly populated by managers who are rationalists, who are predictable, but who may not be so good at leading. American business, however, has not been without great leaders, like Watson at IBM, Durant at GM, Olsen at Digital Equipment, Packard at Hewlett-Packard, Treybig at Tandem, and Iacocca at Chrysler.

It may be, however, that management education and business practice, through excessive emphasis on analytic techniques, is downplaying the significance of the leadership factor in good management practice, particularly in turnaround situations. An analysis of successful turnarounds and start-ups—both important to corporate performance—that focused on the leadership role of the CEO would help shed light on the importance of leadership and on the manner in which corporate leaders are developed (Bower 1983). Besides exploring the role of individual leaders, the role of the top management team can also be investigated.[4]

Implementing Participative Management.   Dean Raymond Miles of the UC-Berkeley business school was recently quoted in *Fortune* (1986:58) as saying, ''The problem with participative management is that it works.'' Despite strong evidence that participative management can cause dramatic improvements in productivity, the consensus is that the concept has run into difficulties because of resistance from upper, middle, and lower management, who are threatened by loss of power. Moreover, the skills required for participative management—communication, motivation, and idea championing—are not always well-developed in industrial managers.

Further study is needed to identify the factors that block the implementation of participative management. What role, for instance, does the CEO play in the implementation process? Is implementation easier when plant closings are in sight? There are now sufficient instances of success and failure to permit a study that could discriminate between the successes and failures, thereby generating useful guidelines for management and labor.

MARKETING

No matter how successful firms are in innovation and manufacturing, marketplace success will escape them, except in rare instances, if the product is not supported by appropriate sales, marketing, and distribution activities. Moreover, Japan's postwar success appears to have been associated with the skillful formulation and execution of competitive market strategies. Japanese businesses seem more adept than U.S. businesses at information gathering and opportunity identification. Perhaps our competitors are more meticulous and strategic in their product, pricing, distribution, and promotion strategy.

According to one study of the Japanese entry into the U.S. automobile market, "Japanese marketers spent their time continuously refining their marketing strategy. They emphasized market segmentation and targeting; product quality and innovation; pricing according to perceived value; careful dealer selection and motivation; focused and heavy advertising" (Kotler, Fahey, and Jatuscripitak 1985:57).

Clearly, more attention needs to be given to market-entry strategies and market-maintenance strategies. There are many questions that remain unanswered:

1. Do global marketing strategies work? Some analysts claim that tastes and attitudes are becoming so universal that the same product can be marketed in the same way everywhere. We doubt that this is correct. Indeed, U.S. success stories are often associated with adaptations to local tastes. For example, Ford successfully made small cars in Europe to meet European-market requirements. Pizza Hut offers jalapeno toppings in Mexico, squid in Japan, and bacon in Canada. Levi-Strauss products are fitted differently for different markets, and Levi's commercials are modified to appeal to different nationalities.

2. Is U.S. competitive performance substantially impaired by inadequate market intelligence? If so, what kinds of programs might overcome these problems? Can industrywide cooperation be forged

to enable U.S. firms to obtain economies with respect to the acquisition of unfamiliar or foreign markets? Can trade associations play a role in this process?

3. Are distribution agreements with foreign firms an adequate substitute for building a direct sales network? There is a tendency for American companies to sell wholesale when distribution appears difficult. One consequence is that certain customer information may not become available to the manufacturer, thereby crippling the manufacturer's ability to respond to customer needs. In short, the low-cost strategies may permanently impair the firm's ability to compete effectively.

4. What market-entry strategies are most appropriate to blunt the opportunities of imitators and/or emulators? In particular, what level of capacity and competence do innovators need to have in manufacturing and marketing in order to succeed at innovation? Are small, science-based entrepreneurial firms disadvantaged in today's business environment?

Additional issues relating to international marketing and sales are considered under the section below entitled, "International Business Skills and Organizations." It is important to bear in mind that domestic marketing practices also impact competitiveness inasmuch as most domestically produced and distributed products face international competition in the U.S. market. In short, marketing practices and policies at home, as well as abroad, affect U.S. competitiveness.

ACCOUNTING

The accounting system is the major quantitative information system in almost every organization. Managerial accounting supports routine planning and control, as well as special projects. Financial accounting, on the other hand, is much more involved with the historical and stewardship aspects of external reporting. Financial accounting issues are discussed in the section below entitled, "Securities and Disclosure."

American industry has in the main been well served by the managerial accounting systems that have been put in place.[5] In large organizations, there is often the problem, however, that the mere generation and presentation of data may cause managers to focus on what can be measured to the neglect of that which cannot, even if it is more important. Standard accounting procedures, for instance, generally ignore the intangible benefits associated with a new investment, such as improved quality, greater flexibility, and possible lower inventories. Given that new projects typically permit quality upgrades, nearsighted application of standard techniques can cause otherwise profitable new investments to be passed over, possibly in favor of less meritorious ones.

Research is needed to ascertain whether cost accounting information is systematically misused in evaluating new technologies. In particular, it will be instructive to see whether different types of innovations, particularly those which have been called "systemic" (Teece 1984) or "architectural" (Clark 1987), are often the victims of the misapplication of cost accounting procedures. Accounting and organizational responses to identified problems also need to be developed. Clearly, major investments that change the whole strategic positioning of the firm are not easily evaluated using standard techniques; approaches that enable qualitative and quantitative information to be balanced and synthesized need to be explicated. This can be assisted through methodologies that rely on the analysis of best practice among leading U.S. and foreign firms.

Finance

The American financial markets are the most complex and sophisticated in the world. There are more different kinds of financial markets in the United States than in any other nation. Academic research in business schools over the last two decades has helped immeasurably in the understanding of how financial assets are valued. Sophisticated theories have been developed to explain how stocks, bonds, and options are priced. These theories have worked well when put to the test, but there are still many unsolved problems in finance. Following Brealey and Myers (1984), we examine several that have particular significance for competitiveness.

Integrating Corporate Strategy and Capital Budgeting.   Major strategic decisions about where to move the business enterprise over the long term can be thought of as "capital budgeting on a grand scale" (Brealey and Myers 1984:786). Strategic decisions are resource-allocation decisions par excellence, but it is hard to calculate their net present value. Moreover, there are important irreversibilities at work, and strategic decisions in one period constrain decision opportunities in the next. This is not only because certain irreversible capital investments may be made, but also because technological development and skill accumulation typically follow a certain trajectory, affording minimal opportunities for major strategic shifts.

A significant challenge remains: to integrate the "bottom-up" approach of capital budgeting with the more "top-down" perspective of corporate strategy. It is impossible to estimate and sum the net present values of all future investment projects that a given strategy decision would imply, but it is just such an exercise that capital budgeting methodologies would require. Given the difficulties associated with assembling the relevant accounting data (see the section above entitled, "Accounting"), new procedures may be needed for applying project evaluation techniques. Research that would explore alternative decision criteria, including those used abroad (see the section below entitled, "International Comparisons in the Institutions of Capitalism"), ought to result in superior decisionmaking procedures that would overcome the disabilities associated with existing techniques.

Relatedly, textbooks in managerial finance and capital budgeting contain very specific guidance on how to evaluate different income streams, but are remarkably silent on how to develop and protect from international competition a given income stream. Once again, this is the essence of corporate strategy. Research that integrates the two approaches is likely to yield procedures that avoid the pitfalls associated with naive applications of either approach.

Capital Structure. "We still don't have an accepted, coherent theory of capital structure" (Brealey and Myers 1984:789). This is a troublesome admission, and it represents a failure to couple institutional and theoretical finance. The recent increase in "junk-bond" financing, as well as the recognition that capital structure impacts competitive strategy, makes it all the more urgent that we understand the managerial and public-policy implications of the capital structure of the business enterprise.

Explaining Merger Waves. Despite serious efforts from scholars in the fields of both industrial organization and finance, we do not understand in any kind of systematic way the phenomenon of merger waves. Overall, stock market asset values, as well as antitrust policy and enforcement, are undoubtedly important factors. More is at work, however, than can be understood by employing notions of wealth maximizing behavior. Evidence suggests that stockholders of ''acquiring'' firms on average do not benefit from merger behavior. If significant gains do not exist for the firms instigating merger activity, a broader set of merger motives, including ''managerial,''[6] must be explored.

Mergers and acquisitions clearly matter, but we know very little about their long-run implications for competitiveness. A program of research that assesses the effects of mergers and acquisitions, using multiple performance indicators, is required. Research cannot stop with the identification of the impact on the market valuation of the acquired or acquiring firm's securities. This is because the valuation of a firm's security does not in any way capture the total economic impact of the deal, especially when labor markets and the market for know-how are riddled with imperfections. For instance, we need to know whether the large amounts of debt used to finance takeovers and buy-outs diverted capital from more productive uses and impaired the *long-run* performance of the target firms and the industries they occupy. We also need to know under what circumstances the threat of hostile takeover spurs greater efficiency, and under what circumstances it does the opposite, by spurring managers to damage the profitability and strategic value of the firms they manage.

INTERNATIONAL BUSINESS SKILLS AND ORGANIZATIONS

Though there are many important exceptions, U.S. firms often seem inept in the international marketplace. Language skills are often absent, sensitivity to foreign cultures is not high, and few CEOs have been posted abroad for significant periods of time. Our foreign competitors seem to do a better job of understanding U.S. firms and the U.S. market than we do of understanding theirs.

The nature of the institutions that American firms bring to bear upon the problem is also relevant. The trading-company construct is one that seems to have assisted the Japanese and Koreans. Known in Japan as the *sogo shosha*, the trading companies coordinate product systems that can be larger and more complex than the systems of almost any integrated firms. Obviously rivals in size and complexity are the global systems of the major international oil and auto companies, but the present diversity of the *sogo shosha* is very much broader than that of the latter (Yoshino and Lifson 1986). The *sogo shosha* use information systems strategically and keep track of changing market opportunities on a worldwide basis; yet their profile is low, and few Americans know and understand them well. Most businessmen, however, acknowledge them as a powerful force.

The United States passed the Export Trading Company Act of 1982; but there was no dramatic rise of large and profitable American-style *sogo shosha*, and some high-profile ventures, such as Sears World Trade, have suffered large and embarrassing losses. Important research questions have been addressed only fleetingly, such as:

1. Would American export performance be enhanced by *sogo shosha*-type organizations?
2. What are the reasons for the failure of U.S. export trading companies? Can one separate the relative contributions to failure stemming from law, personnel, structure, and incentives?
3. Do antitrust barriers prevent the kind of deep and sustained cooperation needed to have a successful trading company?

Business and Public Policy

There are many ways in which firms must be more effective in dealing with government if competitive performance is to be enhanced. An extensive literature now exists that indicates how firms might manage public and regulatory issues. Getting similarly sophisticated on an international level is where attention must now focus. Scholarship, particularly that which involves area specialists, can help unlock the mysteries of dealing with foreign governments. The experience of the Semiconductor Industry Association—the only U.S. manufacturing-based trade association represented in Japan—has considerable utility, which warrants documentation and dissemination.

The area where the greatest efforts ought to be focused, however, is in exploring ways for business to attain consensus on important national, state, or local issues affecting competitiveness. Interest-group politics must be tempered, even within the business community, so that legislation beneficial to competitiveness will become enacted. Mechanisms to achieve this must be found. Important insights can come from comparative research, as Ouchi (1984) has demonstrated. In addition, domestic successes and failures need to be explored. Obviously, such analysis will require the skills of the political scientist, and possibly those of the historian.

Designing a Competitiveness Audit

Performance audits of one kind or another are commonly executed in well-managed firms. It is rare, however, that such audits are accomplished with an eye towards the international competitiveness of the firm being audited.

We propose researching and testing the feasibility and desirability of two kinds of audits: one in which the auditor would have access only to publicly available information, and one that would assume access to proprietary data. With respect to the former, attention would be given to the desirability of expanding publicly available information to include data on capacity utilization, plant-level productivity, employee turnover and absenteeism, quality control, and investment in R&D and employee training. (See the section below entitled, "Securities and Disclosure Law.") With respect to the audits with access to proprietary data, a standard format that would not necessarily lead to a quantitative score would need to be investigated. At a minimum, such a process might flag matters that would deserve greater managerial attention, such as foreign markets that had not even been explored. The process might even involve the making of comparisons between the audited firm and the industry's best-managed firm, either domestic or foreign. Results ought to be instructive. The audit would need to be as standardized as possible so that its execution by third-party observers would be possible.

THE PRIVATE SECTOR: THE INDUSTRY

Strategic Industries

The debate on competitiveness often makes reference to the concept of a "strategic" industry. Indeed, whether industries can be classified meaningfully as strategic is the source of considerable discussion. Mainstream economic theory maintains that the importance of an industry can be measured only by the quantity of its output valued at market prices. To claim that some industries are more important than others is to assert implicitly some unspecified distortion in market prices.

Yet the concept of strategic industries forms part of the parlance of economic historians, development economists, and long-range planners in the private sector. A priority research issue is to explore the kind of market failures that may be at work and the potential implications for strategic management and public policy.

At least three definitions of a strategic industry can be developed, and all warrant exploration. Briefly:

1. An obvious definition of strategic industry is industry that has military significance, inasmuch as the capabilities at issue cannot be stockpiled and the output of the industry is an important determinant of the performance of modern weapons systems. Semiconductors and machine tools are two such industries.
2. Another definition of strategic industry is industry that is research intensive, like drugs and aircraft. Such an industry can be identified by its high R&D-sales ratio.
3. A third concept of strategic industry, one closely related to the second, is industry operating in situations where there are considerable technological and market-demand spillovers from one industry to another that are not fully reflected in price. By nature, spillovers are often difficult to specify. They could include the supply of key components that enable manufacturers of products containing the new components to obtain competitive advantage because of early knowledge about performance and standards.

Each of these three concepts of strategic industry needs to be explored, both theoretically and empirically. In addition, product-level analogues—so-called technology-driver products—also need to be investigated. The aim of the research ought to be to ascertain the nature of possible market failures that could lead an industry to generate pervasive advantages for others. In particular, the geographic nature of possible spillovers would need to be evaluated and the social context of information exchange explored. An investigation of this issue would require the merger of a number of disciplines, including engineering, economics, organizational behavior, corporate strategy, geography, and sociology.

Industry Studies.   Whether or not they turn out to be strategic as defined above, there are several industries of such importance to the economy that their economic and strategic significance to U.S. competitiveness warrants priority attention. Three leading-candidate industries are telecommunications, semiconductors, and energy.

Telecommunications.   Economic historians currently recognize that the expanding infrastructure of the economy—in particular, the railroad and the telegraph—played a critical role in the development of the American economy in the nineteenth century. It is possible to hypothesize that a critical factor in the infrastructure of the economy in the twenty-first century, as well as in the closing decades of the twentieth, is the availability of state-of-the-art telecommunications technology. Cheaper, more reliable, and more varied services will provide a cost advantage (for example, low-cost teleconferencing substituting for business travel) to firms with access to technologies (like high-speed data communication) that can enhance decisionmaking and control. These *could* turn out to be decisive advantages. Whether telecommunications will be the "railroad" of the future will depend upon researchable issues, such as:

1. Potential cost reductions and service enhancement likely in the future
2. Speed of agreement on domestic and international telecommunications standards.
3. Degree to which new technologies will be rapidly diffused internationally (and accordingly, are less likely to be the basis of a competitive advantage)

Semiconductors.   Historically, the semiconductor industry has grown rapidly. New uses of semiconductors and advances that have lowered their costs have combined to produce average annual growth of 20 percent in nominal sales. While European countries have not substantially participated in this industry, except for captive domestic demand, Japan's share of the world market has steadily increased, so that it now exceeds that of the United States.

Semiconductors remain, however, critical components in many other industries, ranging from supercomputers to home appliances and automobiles. Semiconductor chips are at the heart of the digital telecommunications revolution. They are also important to energy conservation, being found in fuel-injection systems and controls. New products in the service economy, such as cash management systems, depend upon computers that have products of the semiconductor industry at their core.

An important issue is whether the sociological and technological networks that couple the semiconductor industry to various original-equipment manufacturers (OEM) in other industries would in any sense be impaired by the loss of the U.S. semiconductor industry. What benefits, if any, do various user industries, such as computers, capture by virtue of social and geographical proximity to the U.S. semiconductor industry? Clearly, the design cycle of various semiconductor-using products can be shortened through easy access to development information from semiconductor suppliers, but if foreign producers are vertically integrated into competing application technologies, could U.S. OEMs expect no impairment to the product development process if they had to source from East Asian-based semiconductor manufacturers? Relatedly, will U.S. OEM manufacturers and users be willing to pay a premium to source from nonintegrated (domestic) suppliers, and will such a premium suffice to eliminate possible market failures? To what extent does antitrust law stand in the way of beneficial exclusive supply contracts between users and suppliers?

These issues require a detailed analysis of customer-supplier relationships, both upstream and downstream, as well as antitrust law. There is very little research that examines the various linkages and relationships and the tangible-intangible costs and benefits associated with them. Work in this area is likely to elucidate the fine-grained structure of industry, and is work where the industrial-organization economist, the sociologist, the design engineer, and the antitrust specialist could fruitfully collaborate.

Energy.   Through much of its economic development, the low-cost availability of energy has been a major factor assisting U.S. competitiveness. This has been particularly true in energy-intensive industries such as aluminum, steel, and petrochemicals. As U.S. reserves of oil and gas go into decline, with nuclear power in a policy malaise, and with regulations that have shifted costs onto industrial and commercial users and away from residential users, a traditional source of cost advantage has been eroded.

Energy policy in the United States has rarely been tempered by competitiveness considerations; yet energy policy undoubtedly has had important impacts on U.S. competitiveness. To help ascertain these impacts, it would be useful to document the cross-subsidies and taxes embodied in our current energy system, assess the merits of existing structures, and explore ramifications for competitiveness and economic growth. Results are unlikely to be homogeneous across states because of differences in state regulatory commissions, or across industries because of differences in their energy-intensiveness.

Studies should not be confined to oil and gas, although important policy issues exist around natural gas price regulation and the export ban on Alaskan North Slope crude oil. With respect to natural gas regulation, one critical issue is the cross-subsidization of residential rates by industrial and commercial users. In some states—California, for instance—this may be the source of considerable cost penalty on industry and, consequently, may be a highly distortionary way of distributing wealth (Russo and Teece 1987). The magnitude of the cross-subsidies needs to be calculated, and the distortions, particularly on international trading patterns, need to be measured.

Policies that govern the generation of electricity need to be similarly assessed. Entry conditions, even for self-supply, are heavily regulated because many utilities have been given airtight franchises. Should exemption be granted if the firm in question is producing entirely for export markets? This and other questions are routinely considered by regulators abroad but rarely in the United States. It is time to look at the international ramifications of "domestic" energy regulation, a topic more fully developed below.

Services.   Needless to say, one way to understand the importance, or unimportance, of "key" industries is to compare them to industries that, at face value, might not appear so important. In this regard, it would be valuable to conduct studies of various service industries and of the service sector in general. The quantitative importance of this sector is beyond dispute. What needs to be examined are the links to manufacturing industries—for example, the relationship between computers and financial services—and the importance or otherwise of locating interdependent industries within the same economy. What institutional factors, if any, cause service industries to benefit from access to domestic product innovation? What evidence exists, if any, of the failure of market prices to register all of the critical factors? These are subtle issues that need to be addressed from an interdisciplinary perspective. The literature in development economics (for example, Hirschman 1958) recognizes a whole set of issues with respect to backward and forward linkages. The relevance of these arguments to developed economics is a matter that needs close and immediate attention.

Strategic Alliances and Related Interfirm Issues

The large enterprise in America evolved, as Alfred Chandler has explained, in response to expanding markets opened up by the railroads.

It was facilitated by a telecommunications revolution that enabled coordination among business units over long distances. The large, vertically integrated enterprise thus emerged in America to help capture and support scale economies in manufacturing and distribution. Hierarchies thus came to displace markets as coordination mechanisms.

Defining the domain of the corporation in the 1980s, however, is no longer simple. The inside structure has a more complex and varied set of rules. The distinctions and boundaries between organization and environment is blurred. There are now a variety of ways to join forces with a variety of external actors. The concept of industry is no longer clear in many cases, such as biotechnology. The boundaries of the firm are equally blurred. New paths are now available for achieving meaningful strategic success. A different set of linkages connecting a diverse array of firms, universities, government agencies, and a whole group of support industries, including financial, consulting, and information services, has emerged in the United States and elsewhere. Research is needed to understand the full import of these structures and their implications for competitiveness. Has the nature of the corporation so changed that major revisions in classical thinking about management are necessary?

Linkages amongst the corporation and external institutions such as universities raise a number of important research issues. One must determine not only the desirability of such linkages (see the section above entitled, ''Technological Innovation, Imitation, and Postinnovation Performance''), but also the type of linkage, the identity of collaborators, the time frame for the endeavor, and the management systems to support them. The answers to the questions may well differ according to the functional activity (research, manufacturing, marketing) being supported under these arrangements.

The Entrepreneurial Firm

There is little doubt that a source of great dynamism in the American economy in the postwar years was the emergence of small entrepreneurial firms in industries such as semiconductors, electronics, minicomputers, and microcomputers. The important movers for change in these industries were individuals who built very distinctive corporations around themselves.

The important point is that modern innovation in electronics and biotechnology has proceeded rather differently from the models outlined by Galbraith, Schumpeter, and Chandler. Early-stage innovation can clearly be fostered in an environment away from the large corporation. It is of interest to note, however, that these firms now face a group of foreign competitors that often outdistance them in size and financial resources. These firms were not able to play a significant role in the early evolution of the industry; but now that these industries are reaching maturity, the distinctive capabilities of foreign competitors are becoming more apparent. Perhaps there is too much entrepreneurialism and too much fragmentation for today's competitive environment?

Does this situation indicate the need for private initiatives to radically transform industry structures in the U.S. semiconductor industry? Should Silicon Valley "cartelize," as one U.S. executive (Sporck of National Semiconductor) has suggested? What set of factors has triggered such a suggestion, and what alternative remedies are available to the industry?

Are new forms of horizontal and vertical collaboration necessary?

In particular, do the high levels of labor mobility that characterize American high-technology industries cause technology to "leak out" to competitors, thereby causing innovating firms to underinvest in R&D?[7] Or is the informal flow of technology sufficiently symmetrical that gains and losses "wash out"? What are the implications when U.S. firms and foreign firms with differing employment policies and practices confront each other in the international market?

Supplier Relationships

American firms have historically been vertically integrated, particularly in steel, automobiles, aluminum, and chemicals. Those that did not, often had multiple suppliers that were played off against each other.

In recent years, both vertical integration and antagonistic supplier relations have come to be seen, in some instances, as competitive liabilities. The outsourcing phenomenon has taken on new characteristics, and many companies are experimenting with fewer suppliers. Xerox, for instance, has pared its vendors from 5000 to 300.

In analyzing vertical disintegration trends, it is important to distinguish outsourcing driven by the inability of a domestic subsidiary to compete because of integration diseconomies from outsourcing driven by inability to compete because of the declining competitiveness of the U.S. economy. Research is needed to isolate the competitive disabilities of organizational structure from other factors. Likewise, the move to pare the number of suppliers raises important issues about sole-source management and about managing supplier-assembly relations under conditions of extreme dependence (Williamson 1985). This topic merits deeper study and will tend to merge with the exploration of just-in-time delivery systems. Finally, just-in-time delivery systems must be investigated to determine how they would work in the U.S. environment, and what opportunities there would be for additional cost saving if such methods were more widely adopted.

THE PUBLIC SECTOR

Federal Government International Trade and Investment Policy

Relationship Between the Exchange Rate and U.S. Exports and Imports.   An important issue affecting the formulation of strategies for promoting industrial competition at the federal government level is the responsiveness of U.S. exports and imports to the exchange rate.[8] In particular, it is important to understand whether markets lost when the dollar was priced high will be regained as the dollar falls, and if so, when.

This issue is of great policy significance. If the U.S. trade situation will be restored by modest dollar devaluation (compared to earlier highs) and interest-rate reductions, policymakers and managers do not need to stay awake past midnight. This is probably the prevailing view in the economics profession. But if firms operating in the United States remain uncompetitive in world markets even though the dollar has fallen dramatically, the structural nature of declining U.S. competitiveness will be evident to all.

In addressing this question, it will be necessary to examine:

- The effect of the high value of the dollar and high interest rates on specific industries
- The response of specific industries to the high dollar
- The impacts on these industries now that the value of the dollar has declined and interest rates have fallen

A first step will be to understand how specific industries were affected historically in terms of both sales and employment by the appreciation of the dollar and by unprecedented high real-interest rates. A second step will be to examine how affected industries responded to these macroeconomic changes in terms of their own marketing, production, and other strategic decisions. This requires examining real-world experience in specific industries. Such information is important for predicting how these industries will respond to future changes in macroeconomic conditions. For example, if an industry responded to the high value of the dollar by changing its product line, adopting new technologies, or training workers for new types of assignments, it might be well positioned to respond to an improved macroeconomic environment. On the other hand, if an industry simply cut back production, reduced its work force, and failed to make further changes aimed at improving productivity and marketing, it might or might not be well positioned to respond to improved macroeconomic changes. (An industry with a unique product or one not readily available elsewhere might not need to do more than await the return of pent-up demand.)

The key to selecting specific industries for deeper analysis of how they are likely to respond to macroeconomic changes is to distinguish among different kinds of industries. Industries differ in types of products and types of competition that they face. Industries that produce commodity-type products (for example, pulp and paper) must be competitive. On the other hand, industries that produce more differentiated products (for example, customized microchips) compete more on quality than on price. Few industries have unique, nonreplaceable products, although some minerals, such as diamonds and cobalt, tend to be that way. When faced with major changes in exchange rates, these different types of industries can be expected to respond differently. The research should distinguish among the different types of industries in developing an overall analytic framework for understanding the impact of exchange rates and interest rates on specific industries.

Understanding these impacts and the ways they differ by industry type is important for moving toward policy prescriptions. The current debate on U.S. industrial competitiveness contrasts two conflicting points of view about the likely effects of a decline in the value of the dollar and a decline in real-interest rates on the position of U.S. industry in the world economy. The macroeconomic point of view—reflected, for example, in the work of Robert Lawrence (1984) and the Committee for Economic Development (1984)—suggests that macroeconomic changes alone will be sufficient to restore U.S. competitiveness. On the other hand, the report of the President's Commission on Industrial Competitiveness (1985) and some contributors to Rosenberg and Landau

1986 maintain that a series of specific, often structural, actions need to be taken to promote productivity growth, to enhance technological innovation, to train a skilled work force, to improve management techniques, and to reduce the cost of capital. The President's Commission report explicitly maintains that although a reduction in the value of the dollar can be expected to improve the U.S. trade balance, it will not address the overall, long-term problem of declining competitiveness, which is rooted in slow productivity growth.

The way to resolve the debate between these alternative viewpoints is to examine industries at a disaggregated level to determine the relative importance of macroeconomic factors and other factors, such as productivity growth, the cost and quality of labor and management, and pricing behavior for the performance of different types of industries. In this way, specific strategies for competitiveness may be designed that are more appropriate to the needs for particular industries.

Export Competitiveness of U.S.-Based Multinationals and the Export Competitiveness of the U.S. Economy.   The pervasive presence of multinational corporations is largely ignored in analyses of international competitiveness and national development strategies and policies. Yet, the available data indicate that in the last two decades or so, U.S.-based multinationals have overcome some of the relative decline in the competitiveness of the United States as a production location by shifting their production to export platforms abroad, from which they can more effectively exploit their intangible, difficult-to-market assets. Between 1957 and 1977 (the last date for which comparable data is available at the time of this writing), exports of manufactured goods from the United States fell from 21.3 percent to 14.4 percent of world totals, whereas the exports of U.S. firms, including majority-owned affiliates, fell from 25.8 percent to 23.5 percent (Lipsey and Kravis 1985). Over the period 1966–1976, the U.S. share of world exports fell (from 16.4 percent to 12.3 percent), while exports by U.S. multinationals, including majority-owned affiliates, actually rose slightly.

The data seem to indicate a large shift in the geographical origins of exports by U.S. firms. This shift reflects a relative diminution in the advantage of the United States as a location for manufacturing. It also suggests that the U.S. advantage in developing and exploiting difficult-to-market assets, such as know-how, has been maintained relatively well. Put differently, U.S.-based multinationals appear to have developed firm-specific comparative advantages separate from those of the U.S.

economy. Hence, in fashioning U.S. policy, it is important to recognize that some policies that contribute to the export competitiveness of U.S. firms, such as certain R&D policies that assist in knowledge generation, may not contribute so strongly to the export competitiveness of the U.S. economy as to the export competitiveness of U.S. multinationals. The latter is likely to be more sensitive to policies that impact manufacturing productivity rather than just R&D.

It is important to explore further the relationship between the competitiveness of U.S.-based multinationals and the competitiveness of the U.S. economy. The superior competitiveness of U.S. multinationals as compared to the U.S. economy signals that U.S. management and technology are competitive, while the basic infrastructure of the U.S. economy,together with other U.S. factors of production, is lagging. Clearly, the phenomenon at issue is an intriguing and important one; yet we know very little about it.

Import Protection and Adjustment at the Plant Level. Various studies have been completed that attempt to assess the impacts of import restrictions. We have fairly good estimates of the impact on prices and features, but we have less knowledge of the impact on the manufacturers and their suppliers. Have the voluntary restrictive arrangements (VRAs) made transition easier by providing a necessary cushion, or has the primary effect been simply to stave off necessary adjustment?

One way that we propose to examine this is to look at the kind of adjustment obtained when plants actually close for some substantial period and then reopen, versus that which has been obtained when operations have been ongoing. Such an investigation would provide a useful "micro" test of the thesis that economies atrophy as they age because interest groups form coalitions that eventually cause political gridlock. It can be argued that it takes a decisive event, such as war or a national disaster, to end the gridlock and enable the crafting of a legislative framework that supports economic progress. Such a phenomenon may also be applicable to units smaller than nation states, regions, or cities. The business corporation certainly has interest-group characteristics, and it may be difficult to shake apart the status quo in the absence of plant closings.

Possible case studies include the automobile industry, motorcycles, and shoes. An excellent test site would be a company some of whose plants have remained open and some of which have closed and reopened. These studies would help shed light on the potential payoff from "green fields" experiments, such as GM's Saturn project in Tennessee. In particular, the contribution to productivity and competitiveness stemming from new technology versus that stemming simply from different organizational techniques can be gauged from these kinds of studies.

Patterns of Foreign Investment in the United States.   In recent years, there has been a marked increase in foreign investment in the United States. While still quite small, the levels are growing rapidly, partly in response to the U.S. trade deficit and the Japanese and German surpluses.

In the postwar period, U.S. multinationals invested large sums abroad, particularly in Europe. There was a pattern attached to such investment that was distinctive—U.S. firms relied on local suppliers where possible, and in fact, engaged in extensive technology transfer to suppliers when their capacities were inadequate.

It will be of interest to compare the nature of U.S. investment in Europe with foreign investment in the United States. In particular, are there differences between the supplier-assembler relationships? What is the relationship between financial-institution and manufacturing-assembly enterprises? An examination of these differences might shed light on the spillover benefits that U.S. factors of production can expect to enjoy from foreign investment in the United States.

Creating Advantage, Technology Gaps, and Competitiveness.   It is now widely recognized that a large and growing share of world trade is not explainable in terms of traditional theories of comparative advantage; nor is it amenable to the assumptions of perfect competition and international differences in technology. Such assumptions are not realistic, nor do they provide the foundations of a theory that is able to predict competitive advantages.

One class of evolving views on comparative advantage, best represented by researchers at the University of California at Berkeley Roundtable on the International Economy (BRIE) (for example, Zysman and Tyson 1984; Tyson 1986), holds as its central tenet that comparative advantage is not locked into a nation's inherited endowments, but that such endowments are shaped, if not created, by the actions of both firms and governments. According to this view, which seems eminently sensible, a significant if not *the* significant portion of world trade reflects arbitrary or temporary advantage resulting from static or dynamic economies of scale, shifting positions in technological leadership, product differentiation, and other factors.

The "new trade theory" has latched on to some of these ideas and has now convincingly demonstrated theoretically what many observers have always suspected: that national policies to promote or protect domestic producers in international competition can sometimes improve national welfare. An opportunity exists to synthesize findings from the recent literature and to explore their policy implications, if any. Do the administrative mechanisms exist to enable astute application of the findings of the new theories to international commercial policy? Are there implications for corporate strategy as well as national strategy?

A related and possibly more important set of ideas surrounds the role that differences in technological capabilities and competencies may have on trade flows and trade patterns. Neoclassical trade theory ignores the significance of the superiority of techniques between nations by assuming that technology, once produced, is available for zero-cost imitation and transfer. While imitation is easy in many instances, transfer is rarely costless (Teece 1977). The cumulative nature of innovation, its learning-by-doing character, and the fact that technological development often follows a certain trajectory, imply that the relative advantage of a nation may well stem not from original endowments, but from differential technological knowledge and experience, which tend to self-generate and become further articulated alongside production activities. This is the foundation for a potential absolute advantage of a nation in the world trading system (Dosi and Soete 1985). The protection of intellectual property, either by legal instruments or business strategy, is obviously required to make a nation's absolute advantage economically meaningful. Comparative advantage and export performance then stem from absolute advantages coupled with relative production costs and the relative appropriability capacities of different nations.

The evident failure of mainstream trade theory to adequately explain the commodity composition of trade, and belated efforts to shore it up, present business school faculty with an opportunity to build upon knowledge of competitive strategy at the firm level to develop an understanding of national strategy. In particular, the way in which science and technology policy—and the openness or otherwise of the research establishment—impacts trade patterns could be explored. This would help shape theorizing about international trade and might suggest how trade policy and science and technology policy ought to be linked to best serve national and international interests.

Macroeconomic Policy Issues

Savings and Investment.   Most economists agree that for a nation to grow faster it must increase its level of investment. By effectively augmenting the nation's capital equipment to which labor has access, labor productivity can be enhanced and GNP per capita along with it.

Savings.   To support investment, our economy must have access to savings, domestic or foreign. Accepting that the stock of foreign savings is exogenous, the only way to increase investment in the long run is to increase domestic savings, private or governmental; for this increase is what will reduce the cost of capital and stimulate investment. Put differently, capital formation in an advanced economy such as the U.S. one must ultimately be financed by domestic saving rather than by imported capital. For the type of long-run issues discussed herein, investment can usefully be considered as constrained by the supply of domestic savings.[9]

Research is needed to identify ways in which this can be achieved. One school of thought implies that savings are determined primarily by the rate of interest; another maintains that individuals save for purposes of attaining a fixed goal, such as purchasing a car, buying a house, or retirement. The efficacy of IRAs, KEOGHs, and 401K plans as a stimulus to net savings plans is, at best, imperfectly understood. Many efforts to increase savings via tax incentives often appear simply to substitute one form of savings for another. For instance, IRAs may simply displace after-tax savings; to the extent that they extend government deficits, IRAs may increase government dissaving without a corresponding increase in private savings, for a net decrease in total savings.

Other mechanisms for engendering savings perhaps need deeper investigation. The famed Japanese savings rate appears to depend not so much on the innate thriftiness of the Japanese as on the structure of Japanese credit markets and on the absence of a comprehensive social security program. Institutional factors that impact savings are candidates for deeper investigation, particularly as tax changes in the United States have modified many tax-associated savings plans.

Investment.   In the short run—and especially in our economy, which has open capital markets—investment levels can rise or fall independent of the private savings rate and possibly independent of the economy's total savings rate as well. Investment tax credits and depreciation rules are important factors. While both of these mechanisms have been closely studied, the role of other factors, such as regulatory policy, macroeconomic policy, and trade policy, as well as uncertainties with respect to the above, all matter.

One aspect of investment stimulation that especially warrants deeper investigation is the inter- and intraindustry implications of tax credits. Investment tax credits reward putting new physical capital into place, but not new human capital. When a company hires a new engineer, its investment is just as important to the economy as when it hires a new robot. Historically, the latter has been singled out for special treatment, while the former has not. We need to address the differential incentives that past policies have created, examine whether they are effective, and if not, what, if anything, needs to be done.

The Cost of Capital.   The willingness and ability of firms to make the long-term investment needed to support competitiveness depends critically on the cost of capital. Whether there are differences among countries in the cost of capital and whether these differences are a significant explanatory factor in determining competitiveness are hotly debated issues. (Hatsopoulos 1983; Flaherty and Itami 1984; Ando and Auerbach 1985). The reason that the issues have not been settled stems in part from various difficulties associated with determining the cost of capital. Not only does capital take many forms, such as either debt or equity, but its cost also depends on real, not nominal, borrowing costs, as well as other factors.

The cost of capital for a firm equals the weighted average of its cost of debt and equity, with each source weighted in proportion to its share of the firm's total capitalization. The cost of debt is generally less than that of equity, owing to the tax deductibility of interest payments. If risk could be ignored, increases in the firm's ratio of debt to equity would lower its weighted average cost of capital. Increased financial leverage, however, raises the probability of bankruptcy, as well as the risk premium that must be paid to investors. This means that, beyond a certain point, increases in leverage cause the firm's average cost of capital to rise.

Consider the costs of debt capital. Corporate bond rates are a measure of the cost of debt; however, interest payments are deductible from income before determination of taxes, so that part of the cost of debt is shared by taxpayers, the amount depending on the corporation's level of profits and other tax deductions. Because real bond rates have varied markedly in different periods, the cost of debt varies from company to company, depending on the structure of their debt obligations.

The cost of equity is even more difficult to ascertain. As the valuation placed by the market on shares rises, the cost of equity capital falls, and vice versa. Volatility in the market obviously complicates the calculation of the cost of equity. Calculation of international differences in the cost of capital is further complicated by different institutional structures that permit and support different debt-equity ratios.

Attempts to quantify international differences in the cost of capital have been severely criticized. One problem appears to be that there is no representative, economywide number that can represent the cost of capital. Because of differences in the incidence of taxes across industries, and possibly across firms, according to size and diversity, a meaningful comparison of international differences in the cost of capital needs to include several countries and needs to disaggregate the economy into sectors, if not into individual industries. We propose such studies, as they will help settle the debate about the existence of differences in the cost of capital. One school of thought maintains that there cannot be differences inasmuch as capital markets are now predominantly "open." Furthermore, a comprehensive study of differences in the cost of capital could help ascertain how differences in taxes and institutions impact competitiveness. Landau and Hatsopoulos (1986:602) maintain, for instance, that the lower cost of capital in Japan means that, over a long enough period of time, less efficient Japanese firms can drive more efficient U.S. firms out of business. If this phenomenon is occurring, it may be deleterious to both nations; and if differences in the cost of capital are responsible for the phenomenon, some important policy implications follow.

Tax Policy.   Even a high rate of savings and investment may not help the economy if capital is invested unwisely. Policies that divert resources away from their most efficient uses will dampen growth and hurt competitiveness.

There is absolutely no doubt that tax policy has an enormous impact on competitiveness; it affects the total amount of capital resources available for investment, as well as the allocation of those resources to different uses. For instance, there is no doubt that changes in the tax laws in 1978 and 1981, which reduced the effective capital-gains tax to a maximum of 20 percent, provided a tremendous spurt to new-enterprise development. State and federal tax policies distort investment in favor of some industries and away from others.

We anticipate that the enactment of tax legislation in 1986 will raise a whole new set of issues that will need to be analyzed. While proposed changes will eliminate various distinctions, such as the favorable treatment of commercial real estate, the equalization of income and capital-gains rates will eliminate one of the few remaining tax incentives favoring long-term investment.

The philosophy behind the 1986 legislation is that the tax law should be neutral as to long-term versus short-term capital gains. If one's principal economic competitors have more favorable gains rates, however, it could well be that distortions are created rather than eliminated by the taxation of capital gains at income tax rates.

What is needed is an evaluation of our tax system from the perspective of promoting economic growth and competitiveness. Most observers agree that on balance U.S. tax law favors consumption rather than investment (the investment tax credits were the significant exception), and it could well be that competitiveness goals are best served by the phased abolition of the corporate income and its replacement by a value-added tax. This is one issue that needs to be explored. Others include the effects of the R&D tax credit and the tax credit for corporate sponsorship of basic university research.

Infrastructure Issues

Banking, Finance, and Capital Markets.   It is commonly agreed that the nation whose currency is the dominant medium of exchange in international commerce has certain advantages as well as responsibilities. This was a role once enjoyed by sterling; but in the second half of this century, sterling was eclipsed by the dollar, which is now being eclipsed by the yen. The dominance of sterling and then the dollar was based on the importance of the British and then the U.S. economies to international trade, coupled with the contribution of each economy to the world's stock of savings.

Since the United States is now a net dissaver, the role of U.S. financial institutions in international commerce can be expected to change. Indeed, Tokyo now appears to be a more significant financial center than New York. Such transformations appear to warrant scrutiny with respect to the implications for U.S. wealth, competitiveness, and international commerce. What spillover costs and benefits, if any, did London and then New York enjoy from their prior status? Relatedly, how has the internationalization of U.S. banking affected access to capital by U.S.-based firms? These are undoubtedly difficult issues to research, but there is little doubt that the policies and practices of banks, despite common regulation, vary according to ownership and management. These differences have not, to our knowledge, been systematically explored.

On the domestic issues, there seem to be several aspects of the functioning of U.S. public capital markets that warrant special attention. It is almost conventional wisdom in certain quarters that public capital markets deflect management attention and corporate investment policy from the long run to the short run. Once public, corporations must "manage" quarterly earnings to support stock values. Otherwise, the market will lower its valuation of the corporation's stock and expose it to the risk of takeover.

This allegation is easier to make than it is to prove. It can be argued that if firms are behaving so as to neglect long-term performance, there are opportunities to buy up such enterprises, restore a policy of focusing on long-run performance, and capture enhanced values. If the market, however, is in fact causing investment horizons to be foreshortened, far-reaching implications would seem to follow.

There appear to be a number of studies that business school researchers could perform that would shed light on these issues:

- There could be studies of public companies that have gone private, with the purpose of ascertaining how investment and compensation policy has been impacted.
- There could be studies of start-up enterprises, differentiating between those that have gone public early in their development and those that have gone public only after attaining significant sales and profitability. The proposed studies would investigate whether going public—and having the attendant focus on meeting the expectations of security analysts—would impair subsequent performance.

Such studies would go some way towards answering very fundamental questions about the way U.S. capital markets are organized and the way assets are managed.

Industry Regulation and Deregulation.   Among developed economies, the United States is unique in its reliance on private enterprise in the provision of infrastructure services—communications, energy distribution, transportation, and financial services.[10] With the exception of postal services and some electric utilities, these services are provided by private corporations operating under a grant of—and continuing supervision by—public authority. In Europe and Japan, these industries have traditionally been nationalized, but with much the same effect: strict requirements on the provision of services to all consumers at published tariffs (the "universal service" or "common carrier" obligation). The chief difference in the two forms of organization lies in the use of public funds versus private investment capital.

Over the last decade, we have observed a marked shift in public policies toward these industries—from outright deregulation of securities brokers, airlines, and telecommunications equipment to partial deregulation of trucking, railroads, financial depository services, and long-distance telecommunications services. Nor is it likely that this movement has run its course. Liberalization of industry regulations is continuing, if not accelerating, in the United States, paralleled by "privatization" in France, Japan, and the United Kingdom.

The deregulation movement has been motivated by an increasing emphasis on economic efficiency in public policy-making and by an ideological shift toward "free" markets as the basic, industry organizing principle. If and as industry deregulation improves economic efficiency through increased reliance on competition, those benefits will accrue to both consumers and other industries in the form of lower prices, greater diversity in services, and increased responsiveness to customers' needs.

What is surprising, if not shocking, about the public debate over industry regulation in the United States is the utter lack of concern over the international implications of domestic policies. Consider, for example, the decision to deregulate telephone equipment, prohibiting telephone operating companies from manufacturing telephones or switching equipment. What has transpired was virtually assured by our disregard of international trade effects: exports of telephone equipment have grown modestly in the past four years, while imports have exploded. The balance of trade in telecommunications has shifted dramatically from a sizable surplus to a huge deficit, and not because U.S. firms are not, or could not be, competitive with foreign producers.

A priority research issue is the study of the effects of domestic regulatory policies on international competition and U.S. competitiveness. The best industries to study are those with significant regulation or deregulation, which would include energy, financial services, medical products, biotechnology, telecommunications, and transportation.

Domestic industry-specific regulatory policies in the United States, Japan, and Western Europe need to be compared. Research ought to have three main objectives:

1. Analysis of the effects of existing and alternative U.S. regulatory (and deregulatory) policies on international competition
2. Analysis of the effects of European and Japanese industry policies on international competition
3. Devising of industry regulatory policies that would improve U.S. competitiveness in world markets

Research projects could first review empirical studies of the effects of recent changes in regulation—particularly in transportation, where deregulation appeared early. The evidence suggests that deregulation causes significant reductions in operating costs, owing to more efficient use of resources and to falling wage rates. With lower costs and major shifts in rate structures, large, intensive users of transportation are paying considerably less (in real, if not nominal, prices) for transportation services. The research would attempt to quantify these effects and draw lessons that might be applicable to deregulation in other industries.

In each of the traditionally regulated industries, regulators restrict entry to one or a few firms. In part, entry is limited to sustain cross-subsidization across user classes (for example, large-business customers' rates exceed costs in order to subsidize residential telephone, electricity, and natural gas). These distorted rate structures provide economic incentives for large-volume users to bypass the public utility or common carrier, often by providing these services for their own use (for example, privately operated trucking fleets, telephone systems, or cogenerated electricity). Researchers could analyze the incidence and consequences of private or self-supply of infrastructures, with particular attention to the effects on international competition in the related equipment industries.

With respect to telecommunications, the forced divestiture by AT&T of its operating companies marks a watershed, the international implications of which need to be explored. In particular, pursuit of the following research issues would appear essential:

• As long as U.S. operating companies are prohibited from manufacturing, where are they likely to turn for switching and transmission equipment? Have U.S. markets been opened to foreign suppliers while the procurement policies of national PTTs (post, telegraph, and telephone) effectively foreclose foreign markets to U.S. equipment makers?

- As long as U.S. operating companies are prohibited from offering enhanced services, who are the likely entrants into these markets? Is it likely that U.S. firms will be allowed entry into enhanced information-services markets in other countries?
- Whereas the U.S. policymakers typically dichotomize the choice of structural regulation to "no entry" or "free entry," both Japan and the United Kingdom are pursuing policies of "liberalized but controlled" entry. What is the differential effect of free entry and limited entry, especially in terms of the transition from a highly regulated market to a competitive market?

At both the federal and state levels, firms in regulated U.S. industries are restricted from other lines of business, participating in joint ventures, developing long-term strategic alliances, and other aspects of corporate structure. In comparison, the linkages between national PTTs and other domestic enterprises are quite strong (witness the references to the PTT "family" of companies). What effects will these restrictions on U.S. regulated firms have on their ability to compete in global markets? What effects will nationalistic intercorporate relations have on the ability of U.S. firms to compete in foreign markets?

The Educational Challenge. As Raymond Vernon (1986:20) has remarked, "The ability of the United States economy to maintain a high living standard relative to other countries will depend on its being able to develop a literate and flexible labor force." Historians usually explain that the spectacular rise of Germany and Japan and the relative decline of the United Kingdom are due in part to their respective systems of education. The nature of the problems with our own schools is well known. What is needed is the political will to address them. This must come from parents, the schools themselves, and government at all levels.

Education is obviously a critical factor in U.S. competitiveness. It must be addressed if enhanced performance is to be attained. But the only aspects of education that we propose to address in this proposal are:

- Employee training: What is its significance to productivity enhancement? Observers have noted that Japanese firms invest as readily in human capital as they do in physical capital. Before opening its truck plant in Smyrna, Tennessee, Nissan apparently spent $63 million in training its first-line people in the plant, for an average cost of $15,000 per employee!

- Business school education: An interesting question here is whether the schools should provide what the market demands or whether the schools should take a leadership role in shaping the set of talents that students bring to managerial tasks. While it is doubtful that this issue can be solved by empirical research, it is essential that the issues be explored, that the requirements of the global environment be assessed, and that the implications for managerial education be articulated.

Weapons Procurement and Science and Technology Policy. It is widely held that market economies will generally lead to an underprovision of investment in science and technology. Recent research, however, has indicated that this problem may be more severe for some technologies than for others, depending on the relevant "appropriability regime," the forms of business conduct that the firm can undertake, and the prior positioning of the innovator with respect to certain cospecialized assets (Teece 1986). A role for government as stimulator of innovation is thus commonly recognized.

There is no doubt that a wide range of government policies has defined the climate of, influenced incentives for, and imposed constraints on industrial R&D. Some of these policies have been very successful; others have been unsuccessful. The legacy is a diverse one, with the nature of innovation policies ranging greatly from sector to sector.

What is needed is a comprehensive, analytic review of the historical experience of government involvement in technical change in the United States. This history must be brought up to the present and must include the arms buildup of the Reagan years. If previous research is any guide, we can expect very different findings in different industries (Nelson 1982).

Policies that either retard or stimulate innovation need to be examined. With respect to the latter, mechanisms include supporting basic research, supporting generic research, directing weapons procurement with an eye towards stimulating innovation, and simply attempting to "pick winners," such as the SST aircraft (Horwitch 1982).

Substantial research has already been done in science and technology policy, but there are certain areas where further fruitful research is needed:

1. An imaginative attempt could be made to unlock the age-old puzzle of the quantitative impact of DOD defense spending on civilian technology. To what extent does the impact depend on the kinds

of research being sponsored and on the relative technological positioning of civilian and military markets? Do generalizations useful to policymakers exist?

2. A question about the role of national laboratories in international competitiveness is, to what extent have they overcome commercialization hurdles? How might the governance structure of the laboratories be changed to facilitate the coupling of technology to user needs? What strategies must be employed to ensure that the fruits of U.S.-funded research accrue primarily to U.S. interests?

3. Nelson (1982) and his collaborators have made an excellent beginning at assembling evidence on the effect of federal policies on a variety of industries, and this work needs to be updated and made more comprehensive.

4. What are the relative merits of allocating R&D funds to incremental research versus "megaprojects," such as the superconducting collider project, the breeder reactor, and the proposal to map the human genetic code?

Legal Issues

American rules of law and regulatory regimes have been developed in the context of domestic markets and relative insularity. As globalization of the economy takes place, it is important to step back and reassess our laws with an eye toward determining what laws may impede America's ability to compete fully and aggressively in a world economy. Of course, laws may serve goals other than competitiveness, but by focusing on competitiveness explicitly, the trade-offs and costs associated with present legal regimes will become clearer.

The areas of law most in need of reassessment from a competitiveness perspective include antitrust, regulation, intellectual property, labor law, and tort law. The following paragraphs will sketch the kinds of issues and questions that merit serious scholarship and public attention.

Antitrust, Mergers and Acquisitions, and Dynamic Competitiveness.[11] Despite recent legislative, judicial, and administrative changes that have served to inject economic analysis into antitrust policy, it may well be that certain U.S. antitrust laws, fashioned in a political and economic environment markedly different from today's, are anachronisms that no longer serve the public interest and impede international competitiveness.[12] The paradigms employed have tended to focus on mature oligopolistic industries competing in domestic markets and experiencing little in the way of technological change and/or learning.

It has always been the case—though it may be more evident today than in earlier periods—that innovation is the most powerful source of competition in a market economy. As Schumpeter (1942:85) noted almost half a century ago:

> In capitalist reality, as distinguished from its textbook picture—the kind of competition that counts—comes from the new commodity, the new technology, the new source of supply. . . . This kind of competition is as much more effective than the other as bombardment is in comparison with forcing a door, and so much more important that it becomes a matter of comparative indifference whether competition in the ordinary sense functions more or less promptly.

Yet it is competition in the ordinary sense that much of the antitrust law seeks to foster. In so doing, it would be surprising if dynamic competition were not injured occasionally, if not systematically. Accordingly, attention should be paid to the role of innovation in the economy and to whether current antitrust laws may operate to stifle innovation by not permitting market structures or private contracting arrangements that allow and encourage innovating firms to appropriate the returns of innovation.

A program of empirical research is proposed that would critically evaluate the antitrust laws from the perspective of dynamic competition. Such a program would seek to ascertain whether in promoting competition in the static sense (for example, more price competition, less cooperative or "collusive" activities, lower industrial concentration), innovative activity might not have been impaired. For instance:

- Whatever the merits and demerits of the AT&T divestiture, it is remarkable how small a role considerations about the impact of divestiture on R&D at Bell Labs played in the delineation of the consent decree. This was despite the fact that Bell Labs had accounted for a major share of the total innovation in telecommunications and electronics over the past half-century.
- It is quite remarkable that in the FTC deliberations over the NUMMI joint venture between GM and Toyota, so much of the discussion and analysis of the competitive impact of the arrangement centered

around the impact on market concentration rather than around the impetus to dynamic competition that the injection of new management techniques and managerial styles promised to offer.[13]

At a minimum, the "efficiencies" defense that is now an integral part of antitrust reasoning[14] needs to be broadened to include dynamic as well as static efficiencies. The whole canvas of antitrust policy, including policy towards mergers and acquisitions, is likely to change if such an exercise is successfully concluded. It is possible, for instance, that such an investigation might reveal that:

1. Certain mergers and acquisitions that violate Section 7 of the Clayton Act are procompetitive, while others that do not violate it are anticompetitive, in Schumpeter's sense.
2. Collusion and the cartelization of declining industries promote efficient adjustment and renewed competition by allowing the least efficient capacity in an industry to be abandoned first. Empirical studies have shown that in the normal competitive regime, efficient capacity sometimes gets shut down first!
3. Below-cost pricing to build market share for new product introduction is a mechanism to support innovation by enabling innovators to keep imitators at bay. This is despite the fact that it might violate predatory pricing rules in received antitrust dogma.

Intellectual Property Law. Patent, copyright, and trade secret laws should be examined to determine whether they effectively reward and induce innovation.[15] Inadequate domestic and international protection of intellectual property may permit foreign competitors to appropriate the rewards of domestic innovation, resulting in lost profits and decline in domestic economic welfare.

Antitrust and intellectual property law are sometimes seen to be in conflict, at least by those who perceive competition in static terms. Intellectual property protection serves the goal of dynamic competition; antitrust, when it has economic goals, more often than not serves the goal of static efficiency. In general, therefore, it is probably the case that innovators need to be allowed to fend off imitative competitors who are using forms of business conduct that might currently be considered anticompetitive. Intellectual property protection is no more anticompetitive than is the protection of any other forms of property. When, because of the nature of the technology, intellectual property protection is inadequate to protect the rent stream generated by creative activities, then business conduct that might otherwise be considered anticompetitive ought to be considered procompetitive if it has the purpose of permitting an innovator to capture a greater share of the returns that the new product or process generates.

Research is needed to identify the kinds of business conduct that help innovating firms shore up marketplace positions. Research is also needed to explore the feasibility and implications of broadening the scope of intellectual property protection, particularly in new areas such as biotechnology. Relatedly, it would be helpful to investigate whether agreements to convey rights to use technology can under any circumstances be anticompetitive. The results of this research would provide the basis to determine whether "rule of reason" antitrust standards are desirable for forms of business conduct that are currently considered anticompetitive.

Labor Law.   Lack of flexibility in the workplace hobbles American competitiveness. Labor laws that once protected workers by transferring power to unions may now be responsible for the loss of American jobs to foreign producers. Comparatively high wage rates and excessively detailed and stifling work rules naturally drive producers out of the country. At the same time, lack of worker security and adequately funded pension plans may cause a substantial loss in worker loyalty and productivity. These issues need to be examined from a fresh perspective, to assess whether legal changes are necessary to increase labor productivity.

Securities and Disclosure.   Research in economics and finance has shown that the importance of large and efficient capital markets to the allocation of resources in an economy and to its progress cannot be overestimated.[16] Indeed, a successful economy is almost always correlated with an efficiently functioning capital market.

Capital-market efficiency is predicated, among other things, on a continuous flow of reliable, timely information on the operations and financial condition of corporations. Serious misallocation of resources results from shortcomings in the quality and/or quantity of such information. Among the most serious consequences of inadequate financial information is investors' inability to monitor and discipline lax and inefficient managements through stock price decreases (affecting management's compensation), proxy fights, etc.

One area in which financial statement information is particularly deficient is productivity information. In this area there has been virtually no progress in measurement and reporting since the early days of accounting. For example, current financial statements are devoid of any information on capacity utilization (such as, load factor for airlines), labor and capital productivity changes, employee turnover and absenteeism, average plant size (to evaluate economies of scale), investments in human capital (on-the-job-training, for instance), quality of the product (percentage of defects), customer satisfaction, number of successful R&D projects, and economic depreciation (obsolescence).

Obviously, without such information, capital markets are unable to directly evaluate management's performance—hence the undue emphasis on quarterly earnings. Research is needed that is aimed at identifying and defining quantifiable efficiency measures and at analyzing both the capital and the real market consequences of the public disclosure of such productivity measures.

The aim ought to be to integrate into accounting the economic models and empirical findings dealing with productivity, R&D, innovation, and survival-of-business-entities. Of course, the consequences of such research extend well beyond external financial reporting. It might even fill a gap in managerial internal information systems.

Research should consider not only the feasibility but also the costs of such a system, and the reasons why private markets would not supply such information in the absence of mandatory disclosure.[17] To what extent, for instance, does nondisclosure protect incumbent management? Is it the case that managerial malfeasance would be more assuredly exposed? Would such information need to be available on foreign competitors to be most valuable? Would disclosure of competitive cost structures and performance opportunities facilitate anticompetitive behavior? Should such data be available only to an industry trade association, which would then disclose rankings only? What, if anything, can be learned from the FTC's experimentation with the data of business reporting?

Bankruptcy Law.   An economy that is experiencing significant change in competitive conditions, because of enhanced international competition, deregulation, or technological change, must be able to adjust and redeploy assets in a timely and efficient way. In capitalist societies, bankruptcy laws shape the institutional context in which adjustment takes place under adversity. The bankruptcy code is thus of great importance to competitiveness.

In 1978, the U.S. Congress overhauled the nation's bankruptcy laws for the first time since the Depression. In general, corporations received an expanded right to federal protection from creditors. Managers of troubled companies are empowered to reorganize finances while debts are frozen under Chapter 11 of the bankruptcy code.[18] Chapter 11 protection has subsequently become a management tool to rescue companies and help them adjust while they still have significant operating flexibility. Many corporations, including large ones such as LTV, Mansville, Continental Airlines, A.H. Robbins, and Texaco, have used the bankruptcy courts for a variety of purposes, including the management of lawsuits (Texaco, Mansville, and Robbins), the renegotiation of labor contracts (Continental, LTV), and the shedding of massive, unfunded pension liabilities (LTV).

It is time to assess the effectiveness of the bankruptcy institutions since the 1978 revisions. To what extent have firms been able to achieve greater efficiency under the new code, and with what costs and benefits to society? How do U.S. institutions compare to foreign bankruptcy institutions in efficiency and effectiveness? Would it make sense to grant firms antitrust immunity if they are in bankruptcy and face significant international competition? These and other provocative questions are rarely asked, yet the answers would be of some importance to evaluating the fitness of U.S. institutions to the realities of the world economy.

STATE AND LOCAL GOVERNMENT

State and local government policies obviously shape a firm's business environment. While monetary policy is exclusively in the domain of the federal government, on fiscal matters as well as most regulatory matters the states also have a very significant policy impact. Available research issues include everything from education to tort law.

Education and Infrastructure

Practically all of the federal issues identified above in the section entitled, "Infrastructure Issues" have a state-level analogue. This is particularly true of education—where state and local government is even more deeply involved than is the federal government—and of regulation. Rather than reiterate these issues here, we refer the reader to that section.

Capital Formation and Technological Development

Various states have from time to time engaged in policies that directly impact such important competitive factors as capital availability and technological development. For instance, state regulations can reduce the availability of capital to entrepreneurs by imposing interest ceilings on business loans and by restricting the availability of funds to high-risk start-up companies. On the other hand, some states have invested directly or indirectly in new ventures. Others have gone out of their way to attract foreign investment.

A program of research is needed to examine the efficiency of such programs. In particular, it is necessary to ascertain the domain within which state government can be more effective than the federal government by virtue of closer proximity to the actors. It will also be instructive to examine the extent to which certain policies, such as incentives for foreign investment, have de facto "beggar-thy-neighboring-state" attributes.

The identification of successful and unsuccessful state-level programs may well be extremely instructive not only to other states, but also to the federal government. Inasmuch as certain states, such as Massachusetts, have adopted competitiveness goals, a review of the performance implications of these policies would be most useful.

Inward Foreign Investment, Plant Location Decisions, and the Unitary Tax

Inward, direct foreign investment has increased significantly in recent years, spurred in part by the depreciating dollar and in part by state policies that encourage firms to locate plants in a particular state. Inasmuch as states compete against each other for foreign investors, a greater share of the benefits flows to the investor rather than to the states. Accordingly, it may well be time to explore the possibility of setting up mechanisms to coordinate competitive state incentive programs when it is clear that a foreign investor has strong incentives to locate somewhere in the United States.

In addition, research needs to be performed to understand the implications of unitary taxes on corporations with activities in particular states.[19] These taxes impact both U.S.-based and foreign firms and have consequences for competitiveness that are poorly understood and, therefore, warrant further research.

Tort Law

America has the world's most liberal tort law. Legal standards governing negligence and strict product liability impose substantial costs on American business (whether these costs are insured or covered directly). Viewed from a perspective of competitiveness, this legal regime may be too generous, too distortionary, and in need of major revision. Alternatives, and possible national legislation, should be explored.

In theory at least, a tort law system is supposed to promote efficiency by causing manufacturers and others to pay attention to the hidden costs associated with using their products. A well-functioning tort system aligns costs and benefits and can be the source of competitive advantage.

In the United States, however, the system appears to have become administratively inefficient. The "joint and several" nature of product liability is motivated by perceived equity for the injured and has no connection to economic efficiency; that is, it does not put the penalties on those most capable of correcting the situation at least cost. In addition, corporations face absurdly large judgments in product- and director-liability cases. That Texaco would need to file for Chapter 11 in order to shield itself from Penzoil's legal claims would be completely unfathomable in any other nation, and especially among America's principal economic rivals. Additional research is needed, however, to establish:

1. the impact of tort law, and especially product-liability law, on international trade (While both foreign firms and U.S. firms operating in the United States are exposed to the same tort standards, it may well be that U.S. firms are disadvantaged abroad because of the fragmentation of international markets that U.S. law creates);
2. whether placing a ceiling on liability or sharing its burden is the most efficient way to deal with the crisis;
3. that more efficient mechanisms for organizing a liability system exist and can be implemented in the American context; and
4. whether the existence of a legal system that pays attention to intent as well as to results "fouls up" the R&D process by causing costly activities to be performed to establish good form as protection against potential litigation hazards.

THE NATION: HISTORY AND INSTITUTIONS

Business and Economic History

Competitiveness issues raise several key questions about long-run economic and organizational change.

Must the United States Experience Relative Decline?   The economic historian Charles Kindleberger (1973) over a decade ago, warned of "a dynamic failure of the economy to produce new exports to replace those now being eroded by the product life cycle." He questioned whether the decline in U.S. export competitiveness might lie in "a slowing down of American economic vitality and elan—a climacteric in the life of the economy and perhaps society, such as Britain experienced (after 1870) when it was overtaken by Germany and the United States as we are now being overtaken by Japan." This fundamental question caused Moses Abramovitz (1981:10) to ask, in a presidential address to the American Economic Association in 1980, whether "the United States can mount a more energetic and successful response to the newly rising foreign competition after 1970 than Britain did after 1870."

These questions remain unanswered. There is undoubtedly more to be learned from the historical record. The earlier studies on the British decline need to be reread and extended. No more than a handful of scholars have made significant contributions to this analysis. What is needed is a cross-disciplinary investigation that focuses not just on the economic conditions of the time, but also on structural analysis, including political, cultural, and managerial factors. Our understanding of these issues may well be advanced significantly by a renewed research emphasis on these questions. Of equal importance, positive spillover effects will occur if the current competitiveness debate can be informed by current as well as new insights from the historical experience of Britain and other European countries.

Are Structural Problems to Blame?   An additional and critical advantage of structural analysis of this kind is that it should help untangle the relative role of macroeconomic policy effects from secular factors. Lawrence Summers (1983:82), among others, questions the "undocumented premise—the existence of industrial problems which go beyond those that could be expected to result from current macroeconomic policies." In other words, Summers and many of his colleagues believe that competitiveness problems would evaporate if the United States could only adopt the right monetary and fiscal policies.

Institutionalists and historians are likely to take issue with the Summers point of view. His hypothesis, however, is difficult to *either* support or refute, as we have never had, and are unlikely ever to have, a clear test of the theory. But a thorough historical and anthropological analysis of the British decline, in the light of the recent macroenvironment in the United States, may well yield important insights into the mainstream economic premise that our current industrial problems are purely the result of flawed macroeconomic policies. Such a research agenda would be very Schumpeterian, for Joseph Schumpeter saw the limits of capitalism not in its economic shortcomings, but in its political weaknesses, caused by its very success. Schumpeter argued that this success would create a political environment likely to undermine capitalist values and, ultimately, capitalist policies. It may well be, of course, that competition from Japan and the NIC will so rock the foundations of the U.S. economy that it will again adopt the prodevelopment policies of the past.

Is Adjustment Today Occurring With Greater Facility and at Lower Cost Than in an Earlier Period?   Federal and state governments, in recent decades, have put into place numerous governmental programs that are designed to facilitate adjustment. These include trade adjustment assistance, unemployment benefits, training programs, and the like. Some corporations and unions have added their own programs to facilitate adjustments. These programs are designed to impact workforce adaptability and mobility. Labor-force mobility is, however, only one element of the adjustment process. Capital is another. It is problematic whether labor *and* capital are redeployed with greater or less facility today than they were in an earlier era. To the extent that adjustment to changing economic conditions occurred with greater facility earlier, what is it about U.S. institutions that impedes the process? Are there lessons from history that have been overlooked? If adjustment is in fact more rapid and effective today than earlier, what are the reasons, and can adjustment be speeded further?

Geopolitical Dimensions of Economic Decline

In order to ascertain the stakes associated with declining U.S. competitiveness, it is necessary to explore not only the attendant domestic economies and the political and psychological consequences, but also the geopolitical costs and benefits associated with U.S. hegemony. One view, espoused by Brookings economist Robert Z. Lawrence (1984), is that the relative economic position of the United States is of little consequence—what matter are the absolute levels of living enjoyed by Americans. If citizens abroad are living better, or if the output of their economies is greater, it is of no negative consequence. Indeed, by creating larger markets for U.S. exports, the growth of foreign economies is a marked positive for U.S. welfare.

The Lawrence argument stems directly from textbook trade theory. As such, however, it pays no attention to the governance mechanism of the world economy or to the advantages and/or disadvantages to the United States and the rest of the free world associated with the United States being the hegemon. Alliances are more easily maintained if a hegemon exists, and the hegemon is certainly able to give political direction to alliances.

In short, the stakes involved may be political and geopolitical. If the United States wants to preserve and enhance its economic and political interests, values, and ideals on an international scale, it is essential to understand and achieve the economic performance necessary to buttress the requisite amount of global influence to do the job.

Hence, a broad-based program of research on competitiveness must analyze both the domestic and the international stakes involved. It is doubtful that these can be perceived accurately without developing a detailed understanding of the basis for U.S. hegeomony and of the major consequences of this hegemony eroding and passing to a different hegemon, whose national history and goals would most certainly be different from those of the United States.

International Comparisons in the Institutions of Capitalism

According to one of the nation's leading Japanologists, Chalmers Johnson (1985:7–8):

> All of the social sciences have tended to be blind to the implications of different institutions performing the same or similar functions for different but similar societies. . . . As a result, all of the social sciences have taken too long to realize that although Japan is an advanced capitalist democracy, the institutions of capitalism that it has built through its industrial policies differ fundamentally from those encountered in American capitalism—we are only beginning to recognize that Japan has invented and put together

the institutions of capitalism in new ways, ways that neither Adam Smith nor many others would recognize or understand. . . . Common capitalist and democratic theory is realized in Japan through different institutions from those in the West—and with markedly different tradeoffs.

Institutions such as "labor unions," "joint-stock companies," and the "banking system" may have similar names in Japanese and in English, but they nonetheless function in quite different ways and with very different results. Japanese unions are company unions, and organized labor in Japan has no role or voice in politics. Joint-stock companies may be "owned" by shareholders, but at least 70 percent of the shares of Japan's most important companies are owned by competing companies and are never traded, regardless of price. Japan's banking system is the primary means whereby the Japanese transfer savings to industry instead of using capital markets, and the largest "bank" in Japan is the postal savings system, which is government-owned and -operated.

There is little doubt that our lack of adequate understanding of such foreign institutions has inhibited our ability to address an important set of managerial and policy issues. A coherent set of comparative studies of the institutional forms of capitalism prevailing in several of our key trading partners would be most useful. It would also help dispel the theory that such institutions are to be explained by culture. In the case of Japan, this is often "an ideological way of avoiding the competitive implications of Japan's institutional innovation" (Johnson 1985:9).

Focusing on Japan, but with a set of similar researchable issues available for other key economies, candidates for study would include the following issues:

Japanese Management.   Aoki (1985:3) has argued that there is nothing mysterious about Japanese management. "Imperfections" in the labor market and the capital market are the twin prerequisites for, as well as consequences of, the development of Japanese management. As these markets change, Aoki argues, there will be a gradual transformation of the way in which the Japanese firm operates.

Specifically, according to this view, "Japanese management"—which recognizes employees along with shareholders as stakeholders—is a postwar phenomenon rooted in institutional changes wrought in part by "reforms" imposed by the Occupation Army. In order for Japanese firms to behave the way they do, they must be shielded from unfriendly takeovers, and there must be an ideology supporting the recognition of the employee as a legitimate stakeholder.

The United States was a catalytic force by compelling the dissolution of the *zaibatsu* and by giving priority to employees and local residents in the purchase of liquidated shares. In addition, no single individual was allowed to acquire more than one percent of any liquidated company. Bank holdings of stocks steadily increased during the postwar years, however, so that by 1968, financial institutions held 30.3 percent of total stocks outstanding, thereby effectively insulating management from takeover threats (Aoki 1985:19). The management of member firms in the industrial groups is subject instead to reciprocal monitoring.

These factors and others help explain why the Japanese system is viable. By deepening understanding of the institutional context in which the Japanese firm operates, scholars can help management realize why Japanese firms behave the way they do and discover what, if anything, about Japanese management practice is transferable to the United States.[20] Research along these lines can also help determine how to shape the institutional context so as to generate different corporate behavior.

Another key characteristic of Japanese management often assumed to be true is that Japanese management focuses on the long run. It may be impossible to validate this claim dispositively. Many are skeptical, with justification, that there are biological or philosophical factors that may be at the root of perceived differences. It is very easy, however, to see that the institutional environment the Japanese manager is embedded in may explain the phenomenon at issue. Possible reasons, all of which could be more deeply researched, include:

1. In their application, if not in their conception, capital-budgeting and investment-selection techniques in the United States may value early payoffs higher than Japanese approaches do (see "The Japanese Financial System" below).
2. Lifetime employment for managers gives them incentives to pay attention to the long-term payouts of projects; promotion is certainly not based on early payoffs from projects in which particular managers are involved (Rumelt 1987).
3. Japanese firms enjoy lower costs of capital than do U.S. firms, future returns will be discounted at a lower rate.

The Japanese Financial System.   Over the last decade, there have been a number of useful studies that have explored the differences in employment and personnel management practices between the

United States and Japan (for example, Ouchi 1983). There has been a relative dearth, however, of research on differences between the United States and Japan with respect to investment and financial practices and on the implications for corporate marketplace behavior.

Particularly when compared with U.S. firms, there are some striking differences. Many have noted the large amount of debt, on average, in the capital structures of Japanese firms (Hodder 1986).[21] This heavy dependence grew out of an institutional environment where practices of securities firms forced virtually all new stock offerings until the early 1970s to occur at par. In addition, investors held an expectation that firms would pay an annual dividend equal to 10 percent of the par value of stock. Hence, Japanese equity had many features of U.S. debt obligations, and vice versa. To the Japanese corporation, debt (which was a tax-deductible expense) was much cheaper than equity, which was not tax-deductible.

The major source of external funding for Japanese companies has been the banks, led in each case by a "main bank." The main bank has the power to replace key executives as well as to direct major strategic decisions—and possibly some operating ones as well. The main banks' commanding position is not unlike that of a large stockholder in a closely held U.S. corporation.

An interesting research question is the extent to which the Japanese main bank relationship solves the kind of agency problems that some believe confront U.S. corporations. Relatedly, the main bank relationship may enable Japanese firms to deal with insolvency problems in ways superior to those permitted under U.S. bankruptcy laws.[22] A systematic comparative study is needed of American and Japanese instruments of corporate control, with an eye towards understanding the comparative performance aspects of each. This could provide the foundation for legislative and managerial changes to improve the performance of U.S. institutions. Alternatives to expensive takeover fights—what some have called "casino capitalism," or "paper entrepreneurship'—could be explored, using comparative analysis. In addition, awareness of important institutional differences ought to help American firms to anticipate the business strategies of Japanese firms inasmuch as these strategies are conditioned by the institutional environment of the Japanese economy.

The Japanese also do not have American-style venture capitalism; however, they have an elaborate private-public apparatus that channels resources to promising new companies and technologies. The Japan

Development Bank plays a critical role. What are the comparative implications for new-enterprise development in Japan and the United States?

A critical area for research is the relationship between the capital markets of the United States and Japan and long-term corporate strategy, particularly in making investments in R&D and in aggressively bringing innovations to market. That Japanese firms are relatively removed, for whatever reason, from the demands of short-term earnings performance has allowed them to be able to make the kind of long-term investments in R&D, capital, and human resources that U.S. firms have not. The next step is to explore ways in which U.S. firms might begin to structure their own environments in order to make similar commitments.

Differences in investment evaluation procedures also warrant further investigation. Hodder (1986) has suggested that the U.S. approach—where detailed project analysis is done by a small team or perhaps by one person and then presented by the analysts' boss to top management—causes top management to be unfamiliar with the assumptions embedded in the analysis.

In the Japanese firm, such a "black box" approach would be intolerable. Managers have to understand the analytic details (not just the results) in order to satisfactorily participate in the consensus formation process. There is almost a necessity for verbal analysis with simple ("back-of-the-envelope") calculations that everyone can follow (Hodder 1986). Such procedures expose underlying assumptions to careful scrutiny, and those who will ultimately manage the project are aware of key sensitivities.

These observations about decisionmaking are especially interesting when laid against Rumelt's (1987) rational theory of myopic decisionmaking. It could be that the detailed, "scientific" methods of project evaluation used in the United States require an organizational context different from what currently exists. In any event, a program of research that explores the implementation requirements for key analytic techniques is suggested by the emerging comparative literature in this area. Such a program would search for systematic biases resulting from the use of standard techniques in hierarchial environments.

Keiretsu Versus Conglomerates.   Japan has a distinctive set of institutions in its so-called industrial groups, known in prewar Japan as *zaibatsu* (financial cliques) and in postwar Japan as *keiretsu* (lineages) or *kigyo shudan* (enterprise groups). The well-known ones include Mitsubishi, Mitsui, Sumimoto, Hitachi, and Yasuda. Chalmers Johnson (1985:12) has remarked that they are perhaps most accurately called "developmental conglomerates." Contrary to the image in the West of corporate Japan, the *keiretsu* often engage in cutthroat competition and use cash flows from mature businesses to fund developing ones. We need to explore the nature and degree of competitive challenge that they represent.

Management Training and Skills in the United States and Japan. The United States has built a managerial apparatus in which corporate strategy has come to be defined more in financial than in technological terms. The popularity of the Boston Consulting Group's product-portfolio approach signalled the extent to which the corporate planning apparatus in America could divorce itself from notions of skill accumulation and development, and from hands-on management. In Japan, by contrast, management and the firm are committed to the concept that relationships and experience are closely linked to the industry one works in. As a result, neither managers nor firms diversify into unrelated businesses. The implications of this for the comparative performance of U.S. and Japanese firms need to be explored.

The Japanese Deliberation Councils.   Foreigners who try to understand Japanese legislative processes in terms of their own are likely to be misled. The *shingikai* ("deliberation councils") are official forums through which bureaucrats, businessmen, experts, journalists, and representatives of the people consider and decide on virtually all public policies. In the United States, similar legislative deliberations go on in Congress and are subject to the full range of lobbying pressures. By contrast, "in Japan they are conducted in private, shielded from interest groups or the press and under the control of Japan's elite bureaucracy. By the time a proposed Japanese law gets to the Diet, it has already been thoroughly debated or a decision has been reached" (Johnson 1985:15).

Cooperative and Competitive Research in Japan.   It is common to characterize research in Japan as highly cooperative and that in the United States as highly competitive.[23] Such generalizations appear on closer examination, however, to be wide of the mark. For instance, Matsushita and Sony maintained highly independent and competitive research programs for their respective VCR efforts, while in the United States collaborative research efforts appear to be on the rise. Witness the Microelectronics and Computer Corporation (MCC) in Austin, Texas.

Yet differences in the organization of collaborative research in Japan and in the United States are not at all well understood. While basic research is largely cooperative and nonproprietary in the United States—inasmuch as it is performed mainly in the universities—it is not clear whether Japanese basic research is mainly proprietary or public, cooperative or competitive. Neither is it clear whether generic research—of the kind conducted by MCC—is competitive or collaborative in Japan. In short, there is very little literature available in English on the organization and functioning of the research establishment in Japan.

Because the U.S. model does not represent the only way in which research can be organized, it behooves us to know something about how our principal competitors organize. The issues are not just academic, as the manner in which research is organizedis critical to its subsequent commercialization.

Developing a deeper understanding of international differences in the institutions of capitalism should be sought not so much with an eye toward imitation as with an eye towards evaluating the behavior and strategy of foreign firms as they compete in world markets. There is no question that the corporate strategy of firms of any nationality is conditioned by the institutional and policy environment prevailing in their domestic markets. This is as true for Japanese, Korean, Taiwanese, and West German firms as it is for American firms. It is rather pathetic, however, how little U.S. firms and business school professors know about the policy environment prevailing in several of our key competitors' economies. A program of comparative institutional research would yield important insights that would be valuable to corporate decisionmakers, policy analysts, and educators. One cannot compete effectively in any endeavor without knowing the strengths and weaknesses of one's competitors.

The Semantics and Politics of Industrial Competitiveness

Many American economists choose to argue that the Japanese challenge is not really a challenge. Superior Japanese performance stems not from industrial policies or planning, but from better macroeconomic management and, in particular, from a higher rate of savings and investment. As Robert Kuttner (1985:82) has suggested, there is a kind of intellectual bias in the dogma of professional economics, which "knows only that Japanese economic planning didn't help, because it couldn't have, a priori."

This same intellectual framework also attempts to suffocate the notion that there is an economic problem in the United States beyond excessive government spending and too much regulation. It is true that the United States has created millions of new jobs in the last decade while Europe has created none, and that the United States is currently in a moderate and hopefully sustained period of economic recovery. But as President Reagan's Commission on Industrial Competitiveness (1985:1) reported in 1985, during the recovery, "America's ability to compete internationally faces unprecedented challenges from abroad. Our world leadership is at stake and so is our ability to provide for our people the standard of living and opportunities to which they aspire."

Early attempts to address competitiveness issues often favored a massive increase in government involvement. In 1982, Robert Reich advocated such policy initiatives as employment vouchers, human-capital tax credits, regional development banks, and a national industrial board. An unfortunate consequence of these recommendations is that competitiveness issues become tarred with interventionalist notions of how to improve economic performance.

If more government intervention was going to be the cure for lackluster performance, then, many reasoned, perhaps subliminally, we were probably better off denying that a problem existed if the solution involved regressing toward New Deal-type programs. As Michael Porter (1986:258) has noted, "The Administration also seems to believe that the mere acknowledgement of a problem is a first step to greater government intervention in the economy, something it vehemently opposes. It seems convinced that even a discussion of the issue will open the door to an avalanche of wrong-headed policies." It seems clear to many analysts, however, that the United States already has a de facto, if piecemeal, industrial policy, through tax, DOD procurement, regulatory, antitrust, and protectionist policies that impact certain industrial sectors very differently from others. The deep intellectual question is whether the United States can monitor, coordinate, and improve upon the de facto industrial policies it already has while *reducing* and not increasing the role of government.

The report of the President's Commission is in no sense an interventionalist document. It did not call for more government, but for different government. Its chairman, John Young (1985:14), clearly believes that private initiatives are more important than governmental ones, noting that "the foresight of our strategies, our responsiveness to customers, the cost and quality of our products, and the commitment to developing our work force all affect our performance far more than anything government can do for us."

Given the confusion and fear that discussions of competitiveness have engendered in several quarters, it will be instructive to examine how best to make the intellectual separation between problem diagnosis and remedy prescription. It also is important to indicate that by embracing competitiveness causes, one is not eschewing the market and market-based solutions to American problems. Indeed, one is likely to be embracing the market with policies that reinforce rather than supplant market processes.

One can recognize at least two schools of thought on industrial policy: the so-called "preservationalists" and "modernists." According to Norton (1986:34), the preservationalists, of which Felix Rohatyn and some unions would be exemplars, argue that market forces are destroying our basic industries and should be resisted. Some preservationalists find themselves in sympathy with certain protectionist policies. Modernists, on the other hand, favor the development and rapid introduction of new technology, relying predominantly on market forces to bring this about.

This dichotomy is obviously too simple, but it does suggest that there is merit in mapping the intellectual terrain. An intellectual map would help identify the politics of competitiveness so that an action plan for the implementation of a national program to enhance competitiveness could be constructed. Its formulation, however, would require progress on many of the issues advanced above.

NOTES

1. There are many exceptions at the divisional level, partly because there are many divisions.
2. Whereas Japanese electronics firms are able to purchase from U.S. equipment vendors, U.S. firms are closed to Japanese equipment vendors, as they are mainly in-house (Hayes and Wheelwright 1984:368). In the United States, Von Hippel (1977) has pointed out that equipment suppliers commonly work closely with end users in designing and improving manufacturing equipment, but in most cases the new equipment is available to competitors through the vendor.
3. This section is based in part on notes supplied to us by Charles O'Reilly.
4. O'Reilly and Flatt (1986) have shown that the homogeneity—in terms of date of entry into the organization—of top-management teams is positively associated with organizational innovation.

5. The early development of managerial accounting as we know it can be traced to the American railroads, such as the Pennsylvania, in the nineteenth century.

6. That is, a self-seeking behavior by managers.

7. The high turnover rate of semiconductor engineers in the United States is well documented (Weinstein et al. 1984:61: Tilton 1971:77–81).

8. This section is based on notes supplied to us by Laura Tyson.

9. For a similar view, see Boskin 1985. For conflicting views, see Feldstein and Horioka 1980.

10. This section is based on notes supplied to us by Robert G. Harris.

11. "Dynamic competition" refers to competitive processes where changing technology and organization are the driving forces. Recent research in economics has begun to deal with models in which learning and innovation are dominant forces. Literature that explores the effects of learning-by-doing on competition includes Nelson and Winter 1982, Spence 1981, Lieberman 1984, Fudenberg and Tirole 1983 and 1985, and Smiley and Ravid 1983.

12. For an excellent discussion and survey of three different views on mergers, see Harris and Sullivan 1986. We indicate here that additional paradigms may well need to be crafted to account for dynamic competition.

13. For an excellent summary of the mainstream arguments, see Ordover and Shapiro 1985.

14. See, for example, Williamson 1986.

15. For a brief survey, see Miller and Davis 1983.

16. This section is based on notes supplied to us by Baruch Lev.

17. Such disclosure is arguably required under the materiality provisions of the 1933 and 1934 SEC Acts. Given the importance of international competition to many industries, it is hard to believe that performance data of an operating kind is not material to the investors' assessment of a public company's performance.

18. "Filing Chapter 11" means that all company obligations are frozen, including stock dividends and bank debt. No payments are required until a reorganization plan is agreed to by creditors and approved by the judge. Virtually any contract can be discarded.

19. A unitary state tax, such as that which is in effect in California, taxes a corporation based on its worldwide profits, according to a schedule that purports to measure the firm's activity level in a particular state. The idea is to block the unfavorable revenue effects of transfer pricing, as well as to charge for state-provided, social overhead capital based on a firm's activities rather than on its earnings derived in that state.

20. This kind of analysis is noticeably lacking in many popular treatments of the "virtues" of Japanese management.

21. For all nonfinancial companies listed on the Tokyo Stock Exchange in 1983, the average debt-equity ratio (3.55) was approximately 3.5 times that for U.S. manufacturers. Note, however, that there are Japanese companies, such as Matsushita and Toyota, that have relatively little debt (Hodder 1986).

22. Close ties between bank and firm in Japan help provide banks with the kind of information necessary to limit agency and monitoring costs. This helps produce a lower cost of capital.

23. See the section entitled, "Collaborative Agreements and U.S. Competitiveness," for the identification of related issues.

REFERENCES

Abegglen, J., and G. Stalk. 1985. *Kaisha: The Japanese Corporation*. New York: Basic Books.

Abramovitz, M. 1981. "Welfare Quandries and Productivity Concerns." *American Economic Review* 71 no. 1 (March): 1–17.

Ando, A., and A. Auerbach. 1985. "The Corporate Cost of Capital in Japan and the U.S.: A Comparison." Working Paper No. 1762. National Bureau of Economic Research (NBER) (October).

Aoki, M. 1985. "The Japanese Firm in Transition." Working Paper No. 39. Stanford Calif.: Center for Economic Policy Research, Stanford University (January).

Boskin, M. "Theoretical and Empirical Issues in the Measurement, Evaluation, and Interpretation of Post-War U.S. Savings." Working paper No. 52. Stanford, Calif.: Center for Economic Policy Research, Stanford University (July).

Brealey, R., and S. Myers. 1984. *Principles of Corporate Finance*. New York: McGraw-Hill.

Burstein, D. 1986. "When the Yen Leaves the Sky It May Capture the Earth." *New York Times* (September 3).

Clark, K. 1987. "Investment in New Technology and Competitive Advantage." In *The Competitive Challenge: Strategy and Organization for Industrial Innovation and Renewal*, edited by D. Teece. Cambridge, Mass.: Ballinger Publishing Company.

Cohen, S., and J. Zysman. 1987. *Manufacturing Matters: The Myth of the Post Industrial Economy*. New York: Basic Books.

Cole, R. 1979. *Work, Mobility and Participation: A Comparative Study of American and Japanese Industry*. Berkeley: University of California Press.

Coleman, S., and R. Samuels. 1986. "Applied Japanese Studies for Science and Engineering at American Universities." *Engineering Education* (January).

Committee for Economic Development. 1984. *Strategy for U.S. Industrial Competitiveness*. Washington, D.C.: Government Printing Office.

Dosi, G., and L. Soete. 1985. "Technology Gaps and Cost-Based Adjustment: Some Explorations on the Determinants of International Competitiveness." *Metroeconomica* 30, no. 3 (October):197–222.

Feldstein, M.S., and C. Horioka. 1980. "Domestic Savings and International Capital Flows." *The Economic Journal* (June).

"Five Small Japanese Imports." 1984. *Consumer Reports* (June).

Flaherty, M.T., and H. Itami. 1984. "Finance." In *Competitive Edge: The Semiconductor Industry in the U.S. and Japan*, edited by D. Okimoto, T. Sugano, and F.B. Weinstein. Stanford, Calif.: Stanford University Press.

Fudenberg, D., and J. Tirole. 1983. "Learning by Doing and Market Performance." *Bell Journal of Economics* 14, no. 2 (Autumn):522–530.

Harris, R.G., and L.A. Sullivan. 1986. "Horizontal Merger Policy: Promoting Competition and American Competitiveness." *Antitrust Bulletin* 31, no. 4 (Winter):871–933.

Hatsopoulos. G.N. 1983. "High Cost of Capital: Handicap of American Industry." Study jointly sponsored by the American Business Conference and Thermo Electron Corporation.

Hayes, R., and S.C. Wheelwright. 1984. *Restoring Our Competitive Edge: Competing Through Manufacturing*. New York: John Wiley & Sons.

Hirschman, A.O. 1958. *The Strategy of Economic Development*. New Haven, Conn.: Yale University Press.

Hodder, J. 1986. "Evaluation of Manufacturing Investments: A Comparison of U.S. and Japanese Practices." *Financial Management* (Spring).

Horwitch, M. 1982. *Clipped Wings: The American SST Conflict*. Cambridge, Mass.: MIT Press.

Johnson, C. 1985. "The Japanese Economy: A Different Kind of Capitalism." Unpublished manuscript, University of California, Berkeley.

Katz, M. 1986. "An Analysis of Cooperative Research and Development." *Rand Journal of Economics* 17, no. 4 (Winter):527–543.

Keys, J., and T. Miller. 1984. "The Japanese Management Theory Jungle." *Academy of Management Review* 9, no. 2 (April):342–353.

Kindleberger, C.P. 1973. Letter to the editor of the *New York Times* (March 1).

Kotler, P.; L. Fahey; and S. Jatuscripitak. 1985. *The New Competition*. Englewood Cliffs, N.J.: Prentice-Hall.

Kuttner, R. 1985. "The Poverty of Economics." *Atlantic Monthly* (February).

Landau, R., and E. Hatsopoulos. 1986. "Capital Formation in the United States and Japan." In *The Positive Sum Strategy*, edited by N. Rosenberg and R. Landau. Washington, D.C.: National Academy of Sciences.

Lawrence, R.Z. 1984. *Can America Compete?* Washington, D.C.: The Brookings Institution.

———. 1986. "Perspectives on Technology and Industrial Competitiveness." Edited transcript of a National Academy of Engineering Roundtable. Washington, D.C.: NAE (August).

Lieberman, M.B. 1984. "The Learning Curve and Pricing in the Chemical Processing Industries." *Rand Journal of Economics* 15, no. 2 (Summer):213–228.

Lipsey, R.E., and I.B. Kravis. 1985. "The Competitive Position of U.S. Manufacturing Firms." Unpublished manuscript, National Bureau of Economic Research.

Mansfield, E.; A. Romeo; M. Schwartz; D. Teece; S. Wagner; and P. Brach. 1982. *Technology Transfer, Productivity, and Economic Policy.* New York: W.W. Norton.

Miller, A., and M. Davis. 1983. *Intellectual Property: Patents, Trademarks, and Copyright.* St. Paul, Minn.: West Publishing.

National Science Foundation. 1985. *Science Indicators.* Washington, D.C.: National Science Board.

NEC Corporation. 1984. *NEC Corporation: The First 80 Years.* Tokyo: NEC Corporation.

Nelson, R., ed. 1982. *Government and Technical Progress: A Cross Industry Analysis.* New York: Pergamon Press.

———. and S.G. Winter. 1982. *An Evolutionary Theory of Economic Change.* Cambridge, Mass.: Harvard University Press.

Norton, R.D. 1986. "Industrial Policy and American Renewal." *Journal of Economic Literature* 24, no. 1 (March).

Ordover, J., and C. Shapiro. 1985. "The General Motors–Toyota Joint Venture: An Economic Assessment." *Wayne Law Review* 31, no. 4 (Summer).

O'Reilly, C. 1983. "Corporations, Cults, and Organizational Culture: Social Influences on Motivation and Control." Paper presented at the Annual Meeting of the Academy of Management, Dallas, Texas (August 14–17).

Ouchi, W. 1983. *Theory Z.* Reading, Mass.: Addison-Wesley.

———. 1984. *The M-Form Society.* New York: Avon Books.

———. and M. Bolton. Forthcoming. "The Logic of Joint Research and Development." *California Management Review.* University of California at Berkeley.

Pascale, R. 1985. "The Paradox of Corporate Culture: Reconciling Ourselves to Socialization." *California Management Review* (Winter):27.

Porter, Michael. 1986. "Why U.S. Business is Falling Behind." *Fortune* (April 28).

President's Commission on Industrial Competitiveness. 1985. *Global Competition: The New Reality.* Washington, D.C.: Government Printing Office.

Reich, R. 1982. "Industrial Policy: Ten Concrete Practical Steps to Building a Dynamic, Growing and Fair American Economy." *New Republic* (March 31):28–31.

———. and E. Mankin. 1986. "Joint Ventures With Japan Give Away Our Future." *Harvard Business Review,* (March–April):78–86.

Rosenberg, N., and Landau, R., eds. 1986. *The Positive Sum Strategy.* Washington, D.C.: National Academy of Sciences.

Rumelt, R. 1987. "Theory, Strategy, and Entrepreneurship." In *The Competitive Challenge: Strategy and Organization for Industrial Innovation and Renewal*, edited by D. Teece. Cambridge, Mass.: Ballinger Publishing Company.

Russo, M., and D. Teece. 1987. "The California Natural Gas Industry." In *Development in Energy Regulation: An Economic Analysis With Lessons from California.*, edited by R. Gilbert. Berkeley: University of California Press.

Saporito, Bill. 1986. "The Revolt Against 'Working Smarter.' " *Fortune* (July 21).

Schumpeter, J. 1942. *Capitalism, Socialism, and Democracy.* New York: Harper & Row.

Sethi, P. 1985. *The False Promise of the Japanese Miracle.* Marshfield, Mass.: Pitman.

Smiley, R.H., and S.A. Ravid. 1983. "The Importance of Being First: Learning Price and Strategy." *Quarterly Journal of Economics* (May):355–362.

Spence, M. 1982. "The Learning Curve and Competition." *Bell Journal of Economics* 12, no. 1:49–70.

Summers, L. 1983. Commentary. Symposium on Industrial and Public Policy, *Federal Reserve Bank of Kansas City*, (August 24–26) 79–83.

Teece, D.J. 1977. "Technology Transfer by International Firms: The Resource Cost of International Technology Transfer." *Economic Journal* (June).

———. 1981. "The Market for Knowhow and the Efficient International Transfer of Technology." *Annals of the Academy of Political and Social Science* (November).

———. 1984. "Economic Analysis and Strategic Management." *California Management Review* (Spring).

———. 1986. "Profiting from Technological Innovation." *Research Policy* 15, no. 6 (December).

———. 1987. *The Competitive Challenge: Strategy and Organization for Industrial Innovation and Renewal.* Cambridge, Mass.: Ballinger Publishing Company.

Tilton, J.E. 1971. *International Diffusion of Technology: The Case of Semiconductors.* Washington, D.C.: The Brookings Institution.

Tyson, L. 1986. "Creating Advantage: An Industrial Policy Perspective." Unpublished manuscript, Berkeley Roundtable on the International Economy, University of California (October).

Vernon, R. 1986. "Coping With Technological Change: U.S. Problems and Prospects." Paper presented at a symposium on world technologies and national sovereignty, National Academy of Engineering, Washington, D.C., February 13–14.

Vogel, E. 1985. *Comeback.* New York: Simon and Schuster.

Von Hippel, E. 1977. "The Dominant Role of the User in Semiconductor and Electronic Subassembly Process Innovation." *IEEE Transactions on Engineering Management*, EM-24:60–71.

Weinstein, F.B.; M. Uenohara; and J.G. Linvell. 1984. "Technical Resources." In *Competitive Edge: The Semiconductor Industry in U.S. and Japan*, edited by D. Okimoto, T. Suganio, and F. Weinstein. Stanford, Calif.: Stanford University Press.

Williamson, O.E. 1985. *The Economic Institutions of Capitalism*. New York: Free Press.

―――. 1968. "Economics as an Antitrust Defense: The Welfare Tradeoff." *American Economic Review* (March):18–35.

Yoshino, M.Y., and T.B. Lifson. 1986. *The Invisible Link: Japan's Sogo Shosha and the Organization of Trade*. Cambridge, Mass.: MIT Press.

Young, J. 1985. "Meeting Global Competition." *High Technology* (July).

Zysman, J., and L. Tyson, ed. 1984. *American Industry in International Competition*. Ithaca, N.Y.: Cornell University Press.

INDEX

ABOUT THE EDITOR

Antonio Furino is professor of economics and director of the Center for Studies in Health Economics at The University of Texas Health Science Center at San Antonio (UTHSCSA), on leave from The University of Texas at San Antonio (UTSA), where he teaches courses in economic policy, business issues, human resource development, and economic theory.

At The University of Texas Health Science Center at San Antonio, he is developing a program of studies and research in the economic and entrepreneurial aspects of the health professions and is an evaluator for the National Science Foundation in the NSF University/Industry Cooperative Research Program. He is also a senior research fellow at the IC^2 Institute of The University of Texas at Austin, where he is engaged in studies of technology transfer and business competition.

Dr. Furino is a consultant to business, government, and the non-profit sector on strategic planning and economic development. He has directed large research projects funded by the public and private sectors to promote human resource development, industry/university cooperation, business innovation, and technology transfer. His publications are interdisciplinary, with a focus on public- and private-sector interaction and on business problems and their implications for national economic policy.

LIST OF CONTRIBUTORS

Herminio Blanco
Senior Advisor
Committee of Economic Advisors to the President of Mexico
Mexico City, Mexico

Erich Bloch
Director
National Science Foundation
Washington, D.C.

W. W. Carpenter
Vice President—Technology Applications
Martin Marietta Energy Systems, Inc.
Oak Ridge, Tennessee

Henry G. Cisneros
Mayor
The City of San Antonio, Texas

349

Donald L. Cromer
Major General, USAF, and
Commander, Space and Missile Test Organization
Vandenberg Air Force Base, California

Somshankar Das
Strategic Programs Manager
VLSI Technology, Inc.
San Jose, California

Joseph D. Duffey
Chancellor
University of Massachusetts at Amherst

Robert D. Hisrich
Bovaird Chair Professor of Entrepreneurial Studies
College of Business Administration
University of Tulsa
Tulsa, Oklahoma

Peter T. Jones
Adjunct Professor of Business Administration, and
Director, Program on Competitiveness and Cooperation in the U.S.
and Global Economies
University of California at Berkeley

George Kozmetsky
Director, IC^2 Institute, and
J. Marion West Chair Professor
The University of Texas at Austin

Douglas McCormick
Editor
Bio/Technology Magazine
New York, New York

Edward A. McCreary
Director
Signal Projects Company
New York, New York

Kenneth McLennan
President
Machinery and Allied Products Institute
Washington, D.C.

H. Postma
Director
Oak Ridge National Laboratory
Oak Ridge, Tennessee

Walt W. Rostow
Professor of Political Economy
The University of Texas at Austin

John W. Rouse
President and Chief Executive Officer
Southern Research Institute
Birmingham, Alabama

E. J. Soderstrom
Director—Technology Applications
Oak Ridge National Laboratory
Oak Ridge, Tennessee

Alfred J. Stein
Chairman and Chief Executive Officer
VLSI Technology, Inc.
San Jose, California

David J. Teece
Professor of Business Administration, and
Director, Center for Research in Management
University of California at Berkeley

Laura D'Andrea Tyson
Associate Professor of Economics
University of California at Berkeley

Ezra F. Vogel
Professor of Sociology, and
Director, Program on U.S.-Japan Relations
Harvard University
Cambridge, Massachusetts

William P. Weber
Executive Vice President
Texas Instruments, Inc.
Dallas, Texas